CW01021399

CONTENTS

Foreword

Chapters   1 -25

SPIRITUALHART – A psychic healing journey

Foreword

I always wanted to write a book from about the age of 14, but this kind of book wasn't quite what I had in mind. As a 12 year old on holiday with my parents in Italy I befriended a boy named Karl of the same age from Newcastle. We shared similar interests and in particular our love of the greatest game on Earth, football, at least I thought it was back then. We would play football and swim all day, but every time we took a break he immediately picked up a book that he was reading, even if only to read a page at a time. I have to admit I thought this was a bit nerdy really, but I found myself sat beside him after a while reading over his shoulder to ease my curiosity at his intrigue. The book in question was Fluke by James Herbert and I immediately became hooked reading with my new friend every time that he did. Unfortunately for me though he also read before he went to bed, so I became very frustrated at missing out on several pages each day as he read them without me.

I was determined to read this book such had it gripped me and on returning home to England I went straight out and bought it. Well actually I didn't buy it, I had been lucky enough to win sportsman of the year at my junior school and had received a book voucher worth £2.00 for WH Smiths, so I spent it on the book. The book was about a man who wakes up to find he has been reincarnated into a dog and is desperate to find his way back to his family. It's quite a humorous but also a very sad tale, and as I was to find out, not a typical James Herbert novel at all. James Herbert is actually a horror novelist and a very good one too. I went on to read all of his published books at the time and his new work after, plus many books by other authors of the same genre, as I became hooked on horror and my personal library started to expand.

Not exactly what you'd expect coming from someone who does the spiritual and psychic work of a healer is it? But that's how my love of books began, not just with horror and fiction either, I love knowledge and learning facts too, which is something I realised my school days didn't bring me enough of. Don't get me wrong, teachers have their part to play in our lives, but most teachers I found only taught what they had been told to and didn't encourage young questioning minds. This used to frustrate me a lot and stopped me having an opinion when I got to senior school, as most teachers didn't want to debate a topic, just dictate it, so I drifted away my studies and school in general quite a lot.

Luckily as I mentioned my love of reading became not only my pleasure but my self education too, as once I left school there was nobody to make me conform to their curriculum and I immersed myself in many things of interest to me, particularly the work I do. I have no wish to discredit any one particular teacher at my senior school, after all, they were just doing their job, but when they pulled David Lister Senior High School down in 2012 it was of no loss to me.

So, that's why I decided to write this book about my life so far. How I got where I am, and what I'm doing to help and educate others about it. Well, that's half the truth, my spirit guides and my psychic friends have been pushing me to do it for a few years now and I finally felt it was time I appeased them all. I have taken the liberty of not adding dates or full names to any of the cases discussed out of courtesy and confidentiality, to those involved. Confidentiality is something I promise and keep to.

I hope you enjoy this journey with me.

Dean Kingett

<u>1</u>

I was born on the 29th November, 1972 to parents Maureen and Trevor Kingett and it was a close call whether I was actually supposed to be. My birth was not an easy one as I couldn't breathe, and I was whisked away immediately to be placed in an incubator in the hope that I would survive. My parents anguished over the days not knowing if I would live or die, and they were not even able to hold me, which they tell me was the hardest part. Knowing your child may die and never have been able to hold him. However, it would seem now that the spirit world had far too much work in store for me, and the powers above saw me recover rapidly to start me on my physical and spiritual paths.

My Dad was working at Spiller's mill on Cleveland Street, Hull when I was born, and my first home was to be number 3 Woodhall St. It's not a place I remember with any memories as such as I was only a baby, and soon after my arrival we moved to Escourt St, living down a terrace called Ilkley Villas. Number 3 again as it happens, a number which has played such a significant part in my life and work, and continues to do so. The three of us, (see, that number again already), lived there until I was 5 years old. My Mam was working in a big fashion store in Hull City centre called C&A back then. It's been gone a long time now but she worked there nearly 30 years until it finally closed down.

My Mam's sister Judy lived only two streets away with her husband and my two cousins and we all spent a lot of time together as we grew up, not just as children but through my teenage years and young adult life too. I say all but to be honest I don't recall her husband doing anything with us really, so I guess it was just the three of them and the three of us, but we did have some great times together. Paul was the oldest of my cousins, though most people knew him as Tommy, as his surname is Thomas, and kids changing things to suit themselves as kids do. Michelle was the youngest and I spent more time with her in my childhood years as she was only two and a half years older than me. I have fond memories of Escourt St and in particular one of our neighbours, the Houghton's. Irene and Charlie lived at the back of our house with their son Charles and daughter Sue, and I loved them all. Irene became my Auntie Irene and Sue my first best friend, despite being a few years older then me, but then again, if I look at my life that's always the way it's been, I've always had older friends. Not that I disliked people my own age or younger, it's just I see now I craved others awareness and their knowledge of things I was yet to discover. I loved learning, I guess, even back then. I also tired easily of kids my own age quite quickly too, of course I liked playing like all children, but their conversation was something that didn't fulfil me much or for long.

People who think they knew me in the past would probably say I was just like any other child, teenager or adult growing up. What they didn't know though was the thoughts I was having about lots of different things. Even my parents to this day don't know all about me and how I think. That's not a bad thing.

They are fantastic people, always have been, but I understand now and did long ago that we are on very different levels upon this Earth plane. So much so that I kept a lot to myself until I could figure it out. I still do now to be honest, although at least I have a lot of like minded friends that I have met through the years who understand most of it and who I can share information with. Some things in life people just can't help you with because they're living their own, usually conformed, lives of how it's supposed to be, and a lot of my thoughts and thinking didn't and still doesn't fit into this category of "normal society."

At the age of 5 we moved again to 53 Mersey St, and I attended Mersey Street primary and junior school until I was 13. Primary school was a fun time and I made a best friend, Paul Garrigan, immediately and our friendship was to last through our primary and junior school years, but not so much our senior. My passion at the time was dedicated to rugby league and in particular Hull Kingston Rovers. My Dad would follow them with my Grandad and when I said I wanted to go one day my Dad obliged me and I was instantly hooked. Every Sunday they played at home I couldn't wait to go, adorning myself in the red and white regalia with scarves, rosettes, badges and such, I loved it. I guess rugby league really started my passion for physical sport at that young age.

We spent 3 years down Mersey Street eventually moving to a brand new house not too far away at 1 Middleham Close. We watched it being built from scratch, which didn't hold too much attention for me at that age but it was a huge moment in my parent's life. It was a nice two bedroom semi-detached house, and I stayed there until I eventually bought my own home at 18 and moved out. We were not a rich family by any means but I have to say I was brought up well and most things I wanted I had. It must have been hard at times though as my parents also took care of my Auntie Judy and her two children, plus my Nanna and Auntie Jackie as both families were going through the turmoil of divorce at that time.

Growing up in the 1970's brought the punk rock era to me, and I was hooked on the speedy guitar riffs and fast lyrics. It was violent music, a rage against society that I didn't understand anything about at that age, but I loved the passion with which it was delivered from the various artists. Lyrics also didn't mean a lot to me at that age, not like they do today, it was all just about the beat and the noise back then. What I realise now though through my work as a healer, is it is all about the sound vibration, that electrifying feeling that certain sounds create through your body of pure energy, as sound healing is something I use from time to time in some of my healing sessions. My favourite creators of this awesome noise at that time were the stand out punk band the Sex Pistols. It wasn't until I was 35 years old that I finally got to see them play live at Manchester, but if they ever invent time travel while I'm still on this Earth plane I'm definitely going back to see them in their prime. Seventies punk is still very much my music passion today, and I love to catch up with the bands from back then when they are on tour whenever I can. It's amazing that some of these bands singers are in their 50's and 60's now, yet they still deliver to the crowd that passion they had in their prime, which is always great to see.

Charlie Palmer, lead vocals of the U.K. Subs is an absolute legend. Born in 1944 he is still rocking the punk scene as I write this, and I had the pleasure of seeing him and the band perform in Cleethorpes. I was even lucky enough to buy him a pint after the gig, which he duly poured into his can of XXXX, stating he didn't like glasses. I couldn't believe my luck that we were sat chatting with the band after they had just finished the show. Now that was a night to remember. My other favourite punk bands of the seventies that I still enjoy listening to today are the Anti-nowhere League, Exploited, Ruts, Crass, The Damned, Dead Kennedys, Iggy Pop, The Clash, 999, Joy Division, Siouxsie & the Banshees, The Ramones and Stiff Little Fingers to name a few.

When I was about 9 years old my parents bought a static caravan at a local seaside resort on the East coast, called Withernsea which was a hugely popular place at the time. We stayed there most weekends through the open season in our little four berth, joined by my Auntie Judy, Paul, Michelle, my Nanna and my Auntie Jackie. Cramped was an understatement as eight people in a four birth caravan really doesn't fit that well, but we certainly had some fun times. We had other family and friends on the camp site too, in particular my Uncle Eddie, Auntie Hilda and my cousins Darren, Sean and Kerry. The two boys got me interested in fresh water fishing and we spent many of our days at a fishing pond in Halsham seeing who could catch the most. Darren was brilliant. How he never turned professional I'll never know, he was always the winner by a country mile. He did win many trophies as he got older but it was always just a hobby and leisure time to him. My Dad also around this time had become a local bus driver, which he did for over 20 years until a series of heart attacks forced early retirement upon him at the age of 57.

I found another real passion at that time too, playing football, joining Greatfield Y.C. under 10's after passing a couple of trials. I'd not given up watching rugby but school was more football orientated and I found I had quite a natural ability with a ball at my feet rather than in my hands. As I was still in primary school they didn't have a team so I found myself in the Sunday morning local league and loved it. We were brilliant for our age and I gained a great reputation as someone you just couldn't get past in the centre of defence position I occupied. Seeing everything from the back line and being able to read the game I know now was a good learning curve for me. It helped me see things from a different perspective and analyse the game, something I have incorporated into the way I live my life, thinking things through and assessing the outcomes. We won many cups and trophies through my years there including the league, and many summer five a side competitions.

My time there got me recognised as a reliable centre half, and as I moved into Mersey junior high school I started playing for them too. I also found myself entering trials for my home town club Hull City boys. My Mam and Dad were very excited when I was selected to represent Hull City at schoolboy level as was I. There were some great players there who I had played with and against in the Sunday league and we all pretty much got on despite the Sunday league rivalry. Travelling to away matches was a real buzz too, especially by coach. We all felt we were on our way to the big time even though it was only a small step, and at that time Hull City were still in the lowly fourth division. Some of the players did go on to play professionally though, Nicky Barmby rising to the very top and even playing for England. I must admit he stood out a mile at that young age. I don't think there was ever a doubt in any of our minds that Nicky wouldn't make it. He had a great career in football playing for some of the top clubs around the country, before finishing his playing days back where it all started at Hull City, helping them to promotion to the premiership for the first time in 104 years of their history, what a moment that must have been for the home town boy.

It was about this time too that I was disillusioned at some of the things I was being taught at school, in particular religious education, it just wasn't sitting right with me. This ended up with me putting my Dad very much on the spot one evening, and I'm so glad I did as he seriously opened up my eyes and mind. He introduced me to the acknowledgement of the spirit world and I remember it quite clearly to be honest, the date escapes me but I know for a fact it was a Tuesday evening. My Mam used to play darts on a Tuesday night for Victoria Dock Tavern, a public house, on Great Union Street in Hull. These nights were when Dad and I would chew the fat with each other about various (as I thought grown up), topics and I was allowed to share a can of beer and lemonade (a shandy) with him, very grown up indeed. I grew to enjoy the chats and as I got older I appreciated what he was actually doing and teaching me. Sometimes the topics could be a bit mundane (I thought), but he was really just educating me about life and some of its lessons that I would need to know and confront.

I can't remember how he actually broached the subject of spirit to me, but I know he found it a little awkward. I don't think he really knew if I would accept it at my age or whether I would just laugh at him, but what he got was an intrigued child, and this was a lot more interesting then the religious lessons I were having to endure at school. Talking about death is not an ideal conversation at any time. Talking about a spirit world and an afterlife to a 12 year old is now something I know was very hard for him, but I so appreciate him taking the time to do so and not fobbing me off with my questions. My Dad at that time was not practising spiritually as such, but was merely passing on a knowledge he'd had passed on to him from his own Father, my Grandfather, Charlie Kingett. I listened and I questioned him and I believed every word he told me. Like any child, who was I to doubt my Fathers words? Time passed by and if I'm really honest the subject very rarely came up in conversation again. Death is not exactly everyone's favourite topic is it? However two years later death was very much in my thoughts and unfortunately it concerned the very man who had spent the time to teach me all about it, my Dad, but we'll get to that time soon.

My start with Hull City schoolboys, though an achievement, didn't entertain me as much as it maybe should have? We did make it to the semi-final of the cup that year and I was invited to play for them the following season, but I turned it down (it wasn't for me). It was a big surprise and shock to everyone. I don't think people could understand my decision, but I didn't like the way things were being run at the club and I am not one to do what I don't want to do, and this was so even as a child. It wasn't that I couldn't get my starting place in the team I had virtually no competition for the centre half spot and was always one of the first eleven players on the team sheet. I was never substituted either, they knew what they had and what they got from me but it was such a phoney set up, and so I left. Some would say a big mistake throwing an opportunity away like that, but as I look back, I know I would never have been a professional footballer and I don't regret the decision to leave. Far too much has happened in my life to get me on my true path which I walk today as a psychic healer. I needed the experiences life threw at me even if I didn't realise it at the time, and I am more than happy with how it all turned out.

I continued playing Sunday league though and I still had Judo, Ju Jitsu and Kobudo which I had also taken up to keep me occupied. Martial arts, a spiritual healer of love and light doing martial arts, why on earth would I want to fight and be aggressive you may ask? The truth is I didn't want to be a fighter I disliked then and still do now any violence towards another. It was the discipline, the actual art of it, the way your body could move with training, the respect amongst opponents, win or lose. It also taught me how to fall or roll over without injuring myself, a trait I had taken on to the football field and I never suffered any real long term injuries whilst playing. Unlike football though, I was never into the competition side of martial arts. To be honest I liked it to be a bit of a secret, and it quite amused me when, from time to time, particularly older or so called tougher kids would try to pick on me and my friends. They found out soon enough that I could hold my own though, usually to their embarrassment, and even if they eventually did get me to the floor, it wasn't without a lot of effort and they didn't really bother me again. It was easier for them to go and pick on somebody else.

I only ever entered one Judo competition and that was only because it was at my Do'jo (judo school), and my teacher wanted me to. I was good for my age and weight category, but I frustrated him and the other teachers because I was still just a white belt. I wasn't interested in going for belt grading's to get a different colour and rise up the ranks, I liked just being a white belt. I looked like a beginner and I liked beating those who wore higher belt grades, that was enough for me, but I did agree to this one competition. I did well too, easing through the early rounds and getting into the semi-final, but this is where the fighting stakes were raised. I had to fight an experienced orange belt that was very good and he was odds on favourite with everyone against me, a lowly white belt, apart from my Mam and Dad obviously.

Now, a typical Judo bout lasts about 3 minutes if it runs to its full time, then a decision is made by the judges to decide the winner, which is usually the one who has attacked more. After our 3 minutes though, the two judges couldn't decide, so they asked us to continue fighting and put 90 seconds back on the clock, and so we did. Still there was no decision though and the judges asked us to fight on for another 90 seconds, and I finally got the points and the decision, pinning him down and winning my place in the final. A lot of people weren't happy though. The lad I had beaten was popular and a regular tournament participant, and this was my first tournament, plus me only being a white belt didn't go down well at all. I couldn't worry about that though, I had only 15 minutes to recover and fight for a gold medal in the final.

My opponent in the final was someone I knew well and he was a green belt, even higher up the Judo ranks than my semi-final foe. Not surprisingly I was the underdog again but I gave it my all and after about 60 seconds I finally got him to the ground, not with a quality throw admittedly, but he was down and I desperately tried to gain a headlock to stop him getting up again. We thrashed around on the mat for a while, but I couldn't get the full lock on and eventually he wriggled free as we started back on foot. My exertions in the semi-final and my frantic start to the final took there toll on me then. I ran out of steam and he wore me down and onto the mat, eventually getting a headlock on me that I just didn't have the strength left to squirm out of.

So a silver medal for me in my first ever and only Judo competition, presented by the women's Olympic Judo champion Karen Brady. My parents and my teachers were very impressed, but I never entered another and remained a white belt much to their frustrations, until I finally left when the school changed its location. Football had taken priority, especially as I was playing for Hull City schoolboys at the time, but as I mentioned, I soon grew disheartened with that set up.

I didn't miss playing for Hull City boys, but not long after leaving there, my Sunday league team also started falling apart. I don't remember a lot of it but there seemed to be unrest between manager, coach and parents alike, resulting in players leaving and diminishing our once great squad. I too had had enough and left at the end of that season. Other clubs wanted me to start training and playing for them but I'd lost interest. I had started playing with older lads and men and enjoyed this tougher test, playing against kids my own age had started to wear off. I started playing in a men's Sunday league team. They weren't a great team, but that didn't matter to me. I was playing harder football against men and getting the better of them, and that's all that mattered, but again I soon got bored of that too and left.

My Dad at this time was 39 years old and an experienced long distance runner. Not a professional, it was just a hobby that he and my Mam had taken up to keep fit. They had been running for a fair few years and Dad had run a number of marathons, but it was the London marathon in 1988 that would prove to be his biggest test. He was carrying an injury and was struggling with his knee after only three miles. He told his best friend Darrell to run on ahead as he didn't want to hinder his finishing time, and also to inform my Mam and me of what had happened and to expect Dad to finish a lot later than his estimated time.

Darrell protested though as he wanted them to cross the line together, but Dad insisted he must go on and warn us. Reluctantly Darrell ran ahead and finished the race in the time expected and sadly told us about Dad's knee. We were all upset for him as it was his dream race but we knew we would see him when he eventually finished. It was to be a very long time later that we saw Dad though and it wasn't at the finish line. Dad unfortunately had a heart attack about two hundred yards from the finish line. We didn't actually see it happen and for that, I am extremely thankful.

He was given CPR and rushed to Westminster hospital where he was placed in the intensive care unit under 24 hour observation as he still wasn't able to breathe for himself. It was nine hours after the start of the London marathon when a policeman told us Dad had been taken to hospital and that he was going to escort us there. He never told us what had happened, just that Dad was in the hospital, so we really weren't prepared when we entered the room and saw all the tubes and machines attached to Dad's body. We honestly thought it would be something to do with his knee, definitely not this.

My Mam totally broke down in tears, but for me it was a bit weird. I was 14 years old witnessing my Dad in a state where the nurses had already told us he had died, but a St Johns ambulance volunteer had resuscitated him and brought him back to life. I never shed a tear, not once. I was a rock for my Mam and I made the phone calls for her sister to come down to London to help us. I never took the sleeping pills the nurses recommended us to take in order to rest as I felt in full control. It was four days before my dad opened his eyes to acknowledge the world again and it was my Mam's birthday of all days too. I popped off to the nearest newsagent bought a birthday card and got my Dad to scrawl across it. It wasn't even legible but it broke my Mam's heart to receive it.

It was a torturous ten days stuck down in London and its effect on my Mam was huge, but why not me? I looked up to, and respected this man. He'd been my best mate and Father for fourteen years, why couldn't I let the tears flow? I know now why. He'd told me so much about the spirit world and the afterlife that I knew if he had to leave us he'd be fine and that some day I'd see him again. Strange thoughts for a 14 year old I agree but that's exactly how I felt. I couldn't lose tears over a dead man when it was my Mam, the living who would need me. I am so glad that Dad lived through his ordeal, and he understands and was quite proud how well I handled the situation at such a young age. It was my first taste of death and luckily this one came back to us, but a few months later the next one wouldn't be coming back at all.

It was my Nanna on my Mam's side who was to be the first close relative I lost to death, or rather make her transition to spirit. I was very close to her, and, as I mentioned earlier, we spent a lot of time in each other's company due to our caravanning weekends, and I still enjoyed staying over at her house on weekends too. She'd had some problems with her kidneys and was admitted to the Hull Royal Infirmary for a number of weeks. She needed an operation and it was possibly going to mean she would have to live the rest of her life using a dialysis machine, but unfortunately she never made it out of the hospital as that's where she passed away.

I remember my Dad coming home one afternoon just as I was about to leave for my friends house. We were in the kitchen and he said he needed to talk to me. I didn't give him chance though, "Nanna's dead isn't she?" I said first, just like that. He said yes and asked me if I was okay about it. My reply again for one so young was not exactly to be expected. "I'll see her when I see her I guess. How is my Mam taking it?" I know my reply caught my Dad a little off guard but I think I'd made it a whole lot easier for him. We chatted briefly about it and Dad was glad I understood. My Mam, however was distraught, and it took her a lot of years to get over it. She cried frequently and couldn't sleep and she spent a lot of time grieving with her two sisters.

My Dad and my Uncle Trevor did most of the running around to sort the funeral arrangements out, but me, I just carried on with life and school. As far as I was concerned it was out of my hands, what was done was done. I was confident I'd see her again some day, however long or short that time would be, again, was out of my hands. I know reading this you could be inclined to think what a strange, callous unloving boy, but it just wasn't like that. I remember looking at photographs of her and willing myself to cry, but the tears just wouldn't come. All I could think of were the good times we'd spent together and they kept making me smile. I loved her and knew I'd miss her but I believed whole heartedly in the spirit world and that made everything easier for me to accept the situation, it was just how life goes.

Weeks and months went by and my Mam still couldn't handle the loss of her Mother, so she finally agreed to my Dad taking her to a spiritualist church in the hope of receiving a message or proof of some kind that her Mother was fine and well in the spirit world. This proved to be, however a little bit of a problem. My Dad was acknowledged immediately by the mediums as they visited the spiritualist church, even though he had never set foot in one before. He had been working with spirit in his own little way for years, and because his Father had been psychic Dad had often prayed and sent out healing for those in need. The mediums picked up on this through various spirit guides and told my Dad that he would become a healer, and for that very spiritual church, the Temple of Truth.

As they attended each week Dad started to heal people in the Temple which was a truly great thing, but my Mam became ever more disheartened at the lack of a confirmation that her Mother was safe in the spirit world, and eventually she stopped attending with him. My Dad though pushed on and eventually got himself invited to sit in a circle and through his development and my interest in the spirit world we began to meditate together at home. It was a nice thing we shared but my Mam began to resent it so it wasn't something we talked about much around her. She was missing her Mother deeply but her own lack of faith and understanding had turned her away from what could have helped her immensely.

Looking back I think it was other people laughing and cracking jokes at what my Dad did that made my Mam give it up back then to be honest. Pure peer pressure and people's derision caused her a lot more years of upset and tears, but Dad went from strength to strength with his healing, earning his healer's licence and getting insured to practice in the spiritualist church which he did whenever he could. Over a number of years he became quite in demand, healing at the Hull Royal Infirmary, churches and people's homes. He had some great results and was revered by many people. On the down side he also helped a lot of people pass over which often took its toll on him emotionally, but he never refused to be there for people if they requested him to be by their death bed. So that was pretty much how the spiritual path started for me. I attended my Dad's spiritual church infrequently with him and we meditated together at home, just a peaceful hobby or so I thought back then.

School, as with most kids, I was not a huge fan of. Mersey primary and junior high I have fond memories of, but senior school, age 13 to 16 at David Lister I would say is best left forgotten. Students and teachers alike did nothing to allow me to enjoy a lot of my time there that much, despite being a popular lad. I did find a huge interest in girls there though. Even a teacher wrote on one of my school reports, "Seems to prefer the company of the opposite sex." This was actually for good reason as the people I hung around with I wasn't exactly that tight with. My stimulation always came through older people and for obvious reasons girls. I was losing my interest in school friends and I could see myself pulling away from them, as they were unwilling to do anything different than hang about the streets, which was starting to bore me.

I had started working part time at a fruit and vegetable warehouse when I was 15 years old on a Saturday morning and during the school holidays, so I had money and wanted to do things, but none of my friends did. They weren't bad times by any means. I had some great laughs still, but I wanted a lot more than was on offer and would most nights go home early after seeing friends, only really staying out if a girl was involved. Hence, once I started work, it was goodbye to all my school friends, as there was a world out there waiting to be explored.

I left David Lister Senior High school in April 1989 a couple of months before everyone else left, as I had passed my examination and interview with the Royal Mail. I was employed as a Postal Cadet and I loved it. I felt like I was a millionaire on £77.00 a week at sixteen years old, as opposed to the youth training schemes of the time that only paid £27.50 a week for the first two years employment, if you were lucky enough to get on one. The cadet scheme was brilliant. Part of it was to do a little college work which was a bit of a bore, but they also put us through our computer exams, first aid courses, driving lessons and test, and even sent me and the other cadets on an outward bounds course in the Lake District for a week. We were paid to go on holiday, brilliant!

Although I wasn't a fan of going to the Thomas Danby College in Leeds as part of my cadetship, at least it was only for four weeks. It did, however, give me one of the most memorable days of my life spending a day working with people with down syndrome, though I'm ashamed to say back then I really didn't want to do it. In my ignorance, at 17 years old, when I was told about the day the College had planned for us in Shiptonthorpe, I was horrified at the thought of having to spend time with these people, especially as we were to take them out in public. I remember as our mini-bus pulled up outside the building and they all ran out, about forty of them, banging on our windows, smiling and pointing at us, picking us to be their friend for the day. It was quite scary, this was a whole new experience for me. They had no fear of us, yet here was I feeling very insecure and unsure of what to do. They soon enough boarded their own coach though and we followed them down to a playing park where a treasure hunt had been set up for us all to take part in.

I was feeling even more uncomfortable now that I'd seen them and I was very quiet on the short journey down to the park. When we got there the carers split us all up into about six or seven groups, then they gave me a map and some crayons and said I was to be my group's leader to help them find the treasure (sweets) that had been hidden around the park for them. I was seriously not impressed with this interaction that had been forced upon me. I had been hoping to just lag behind and not get involved and there was no chance of that happening now. As we set off on the hunt though, something remarkable happened that changed my thoughts, fear and anxiety. I felt someone take hold of my hand and as I looked down, a 40 year old man looked up at me grinning with pure excitement. It's such a long time ago now I regret to say I can't remember his name, but this gentleman changed a whole lot for me that day and forever more.

This man, with Down syndrome, completely put me at ease when he said, "Don't worry, I'll look after you, I've been before". I thought I was hearing things and started to laugh, as did he. He pretty much held my hand all the way around the park, my mood changed completely as we chatted away whilst the others found the treasure. He had a Leeds United football shirt on so I told him I supported Tottenham Hotspur and that was it, we talked non-stop football, he knew everything about his club, all the players, history, statistics, you name it. He also cracked a lot of jokes, corny ones granted, but he kept me smiling all day.

By lunch-time my attitude had totally changed, I was enjoying myself and having a lot of fun with my new friend and our little group. I was also getting a little bit annoyed too as I could see people with their children steering clear of us or giving us a wide berth as we passed them in the park, some even screwing their faces up at us as if we were diseased. It really started to get my back up, but then I realised only a few hours ago my ignorance had got the better of me too. I, only a short while ago, was no better in my thoughts than they were, and that made me feel very stupid. Yes these people were different, but not that different. They may have had a child's mental age in an adult body, but that didn't mean they weren't allowed to have fun and enjoy themselves like everyone else. It certainly didn't mean they had to be kept hidden and out of public places. They were part of the public and had every right to be in that park or anywhere else. I have since encountered peoples naivety many times over the years and that's exactly what it is, naivety, people should not condemn what they don't understand. I'm glad I learnt the error of my own thinking that day, it was a lovely wake up call for me and something I needed at that time.

At the Royal Mail I was a workaholic, and have never stopped being one to be honest. I loved the job and so if there was overtime on offer, I was always available. This working overtime was not a greed thing though, I genuinely liked being at work. It was fun and there were some great characters there. I enjoyed working and learning from them, not just about the Royal Mail, but about life. I was in the real world now, no boring school and its mundane drivel being pushed at me anymore, this was almost paid entertainment. As well as earning the money though, I liked to spend it too. I was out living it up in the pubs and clubs more or less every night, despite my 6.00 a.m. starts as a cadet, and 5.20 a.m. starts as a full time postman. Who needed sleep? Not me at that age. I was too frightened I'd miss out on something if I slept, so I did very little of it.

This earning a lot of money and blowing it all in pubs and clubs although fun prompted a more sensible side of me too. As I found out more about the world we live in, I had no intention of being a slave for the government and working until retirement age. My plan was to knock at least ten or fifteen years off it (probably unrealistic, but a goal worth setting in my mind), and hopefully retire at 50 or 55 if possible. I worked hard, I partied hard and I played hard, but I saved hard too through the years. That's why at 18 years of age I decided to get my foot on the property ladder, buying my first house down Rosmead St for £30,000, figuring by the time I turned 43 I would at least be mortgage free, if not sooner. Naive thinking perhaps in some ways, but very good thinking in others.

That house, when I eventually sold it, and after I invested the money for a few years enabled me to build my own home with Susan which we now live in and I work from. We built the healing and teaching sanctuary next door to the main house. Back then though I had no idea of what life had in store for me down the line, I was merely planning ahead the best I could, determined to make life work for me, not the other way around. My Dad told me that my Mam found it hard to take that I'd left home not so long after leaving school, and that I had grown up far too fast for her. I didn't move far away though and I was still round at their house a lot and they were often at mine, but the new found freedom of having your own place was a real buzz for me.

I'm nothing if not honest, so I will not lie to you, I was not a saintly young adult. Partying and drinking was an enormous way of life for me, and added to that were women. I had far too many one night stands and four 'living together' relationships before I met my partner Susan. And as much as I got on in the living together relationships they were never enough for me and far too constricting with the conformity of what they wanted from me, marriage and children. This terrified me and I had visions of being trapped and unhappy with a wife and child and that was not how I wanted my life to be. Not that growing up with my parents had been bad, it was a great childhood, and I'm not knocking it, or anyone who does it, it just wasn't for me.

I worked hard, earned good money and I had no intention of raising a family and letting life pass me by. I was here to enjoy my journey as much as I could, so getting engaged was as close as I ever came to conforming. Never for long though, I always left sooner or later. I needed my freedom and I hated the petty nit picking living together brought, it grew tiresome so the end inevitably always came. I'm a big believer in if you're not happy change things, so I do and it's probably why I have changed jobs so often too. I knew what I wanted and paternal I wasn't, family life and I didn't go together. I was too young for any of that in my late teens and twenties.

Unfortunately for me as much as I loved working for the Royal Mail, just as things were going so well, a kidney operation was needed when I was just 21 years old. An abscess had grown inside one of my kidneys causing much pain and it had to be removed. This incident coupled with terrible back pain which I had been suffering with since I was 15 eventually lost me my job with the Royal Mail. I was pensioned off due to health reasons, and I never found another job I liked as much, until I started healing and teaching, and that became my passion, and still is to this day. It has truly changed the course of my life, and continues to do so in the most amazing ways.

After leaving the Royal Mail and taking some much needed time out to recover, my cousin Paul (aka Tommy), got me an interview where he worked at Autoglass. I was not to be employed as a fitter, just a general assistant and cleaner, but it was a good place to work and the lads there took their time to teach me the trade and how to do things. This was noticed by the manager who was suitably impressed with my willingness to learn, and he started to put forward a plan to make me a trainee fitter at the Scunthorpe depot, as there wasn't a full-time place at the Hull branch. I was over the moon with this but it was short lived as about three weeks later I was made redundant due to company cut backs, I was, as you can imagine, a bit shocked and dismayed.

I didn't end up out of work though, as the references from my supervisors and manager got me a job straight away with a local car glass fitting firm. It was not what I expected though, the manager (also the owner) was horrible and although he knew I wasn't a qualified fitter and had only been learning for about two months, he did not have the patience or time to teach me. He was also very derogatory towards me and started to get my back up. I only lasted four weeks, I couldn't stand the man anymore and I didn't like the feelings of anger he built up in me. I remember sitting outside the work place waiting for him to turn up and open the workshop one Monday morning, and a voice in my head said, "Its time to leave, if you go in there today there's going to be trouble". I didn't take much persuading. I had not enjoyed my four weeks so far and so I started my car and drove off home. This wasn't the first time I'd listened to my intuition, I'd had it a lot over the years but I must admit it was about this time in my life when it really started to get stronger.

At home I had a quick scan through the local newspaper to find another job, but there was not much doing in there, so I ventured off to the job centre to see if there was anything available. As it turned out there was a vacancy for a butcher/porter/driver at a place called Weddel Swift driving a 7.5 tonne wagon and I ended up with an interview there that very afternoon. I dashed home, put on my suit and went for the interview hoping I would get it despite not knowing a thing about the meat industry. I was in luck and I was given the job on the spot and started the very next day, so no joining the dole queue for me. The gamble to simply walk away from my last job had paid off. It wasn't really a gamble at all though, I know it was my spirit guides working through my intuition, and they took me straight to another job. However, this proved to be just another stepping stone in jobs for me too, I lasted just eight weeks. Due to the heavy work load lifting animal carcasses up to 350lb, my severe back problem just couldn't take all the daily lifting and I had to leave, but again I fell quite lucky.

As I mentioned earlier, my Dad was a bus driver and he had asked me many times to join him on the buses. I never fancied it though, sure I loved driving, but I just didn't fancy it. But needs must and I ended up applying, getting my PCV licence and starting work for Stagecoach all within a month. To my surprise I enjoyed it as most of the two hundred plus drivers were a good laugh and I made some good friends on there. I was well liked by the inspectors and management and only just missed out on a promotion after only six months of being there. The reason given for me not getting the role was that the other applicant had more years' service than me. I was a bit disgruntled at that but they made it up to me, giving me a fantastic job doing a weeks tour for the morning television programme GMTV. What a week that was, hardly any sleep, but mixing with all the stars they had on the show each day and staying in posh hotels with them every night was a proper eye opener to how the stars live and the glamour of the TV world. As the driver I didn't expect them to pay any attention to me but I was wrong. The GMTV crew let me get involved with a few things like following the cameraman and feeding him cable so he could move around filming. I would also sit in with the sound technicians too, just watching it happen each day was a real buzz to be a part of it all.

Most of the presenters and stars on the show were nice too, though some as you would maybe imagine thought they were far too important to talk to riff raff like me. Lorraine Kelly couldn't have been nicer though, she even spoke to my Mam on the coach telephone, telling her I was doing a good job looking after her and the cast. I remember having a chat with Peter Andre, the singer, over a glass of champagne in the green room one morning too. He was very quiet back then and very polite. It was a great adventure and I met and chatted with most of the star guests through the week. It certainly didn't feel like work that week that's for sure, it was far too entertaining.

After two years on Stagecoach I moved on to a different bus company, then with a girlfriend at the time I got into the pub trade. She had passed her exams to become a Landlady and I became her unofficial manager of the old Shire Horse public house (also known as Mr Q's, now at the time of writing this Propaganda) on Ferensway, Hull. All was good and well until the brewery sold the pub to a small outfit who ruined it all for us. Everything we wanted to do in the pub they wouldn't agree too, they even stopped us serving food which lost us a lot of day time customers. We weren't happy either when they purchased a second pub on Anne St which they named Buzz Bar and asked us to run that instead, sharing the accommodation with another Landlord who we did not get along with. I quit the pub trade after about three months and started working with my mate Andy as his labourer, tiling bathrooms and kitchens. Boy we had some laughs. The work was hard for me, what with my back problems, but we had some hilarious times working around the local areas. I'm truly thankful to him for taking me on and keeping me in work at that time, but my back, ever the problem eventually forced me to move on again.

My next job was back driving a 7.5 tonne wagon again, for Johnsons Apparelmaster, delivering around the Hull and Grimsby areas. It wasn't ideal work for my back but I liked my colleagues, my supervisor and I liked my immediate boss. But after only three months I had an accident which really caused me severe back pain and also hindered my walking. I needed to find something else as I was getting older, still only 28 years old at this time but taking care of my back was something I seriously needed to do.

Over the years I had been to the Doctors and hospitals numerous times. I have a problem with my spine with the discs in my lumber region, particularly L1 and L5. They have no jelly coating around them which basically means I have no cushioning when I walk or move, hence the constant pain. Also the pain at this time had been increasing and it had become so severe at times I had started to collapse. The pain in my spine would become so intense that I would lose the feelings in my legs. It was like being paralysed as I just had to lay wherever I was until the pain subsided and the feelings returned so I could get up again. The medication the Doctors kept prescribing me was no help either. It was not touching the pain, nor were the spinal injections I had been for at the hospital.

So, as I recovered a little, I gave some serious thinking as to what I was going to do next. I was limited with my options now. Whatever I was going to be, it had to have as little effect on my back as possible. I decided I was probably best sticking to a driving job, so I ended up working for a local coach firm. It was a bit daunting at first as although I'd been driving double decker buses in the past. They had always been around Hull, coach driving was a whole different ball game and a lot wider area to cover and know your way around. My fellow drivers were helpful though and one of them I had known from my time on the buses before, and we struck up a great friendship during my time there.

It was during my time coach driving that I met my current partner Susan. I was sent to cover a job for one of the other drivers who was on sick leave, and she was sent to collect the money for the trip I would be doing, also covering for a colleague on sick leave. A chance meeting, where she thought I was someone else and I thought she was someone else, turned out to be a big attraction for us both. Suffice to say after a few texts messages we eventually went out together and have at the time of writing been together eleven years.

I had to be quite open about my involvement with the spirit world to Susan one evening as Lauren, her daughter who was 6 years old at the time had really bad earache. Susan had given her Calpol and a hot water bottle wrapped in a towel to try and ease the pain throughout the day but she just wouldn't stop crying. I had come to see Susan on the night after work, but she was sat on the bed upstairs with Lauren trying to soothe her in the hope that she would go to sleep, all to no avail. She did eventually come downstairs, exhausted and decided she should call the doctor out, but I asked her to wait a minute and disappeared upstairs. Susan waited anxiously for about ten minutes or so and then she realized she couldn't hear Lauren crying anymore, and so she crept back up. She looked in Lauren's room and saw me with my hand over her ear and she was sound asleep. She was relieved and surprised as she whispered to me, "What have you done?"

I explained as we sat downstairs that I had simply given her spiritual healing to help ease the pain and that it was very relaxing. Susan was quite intrigued and pressed for more information of how exactly this healing worked. So I explained that I had asked the healing guides and angels to help Lauren's pain and hopefully take it away. I also told her that the heat from my hands had a relaxing, calming effect on her daughter and she had simply drifted off to sleep. I didn't really explain at the time that this 'process' involved spirit being present in her house as this might have really freaked her out. We hadn't been going out that long and what I'd done can seem quite weird to some people. She was really quite amazed though and so I told her more and more including some remarkable stories about my Grandad, my Father and myself and the connection we all had with the spirit world. I was so relieved that she took it all on board back then. I guess witnessing something special helped, and seeing is believing as the saying goes. Susan is my biggest supporter in what I do now and pretty much runs the whole administration side of Spiritualhart. I'm pleased to say she has also developed her own psychic and healing gifts with my guidance and tuition over the years too.

It was nice being a coach driver and travelling around the country as I enjoyed the motorway driving, but sitting for such long periods of time was, again, not helping my back much. Then one morning, I had an accident whilst driving my coach doing an early school run. The brakes failed and I hit a parked car at about 30 mph. I couldn't avoid it as there was traffic coming the other way and I was on a country village road. As I hit the car I was flung forwards out of my seat and then jolted back into it. Luckily it was at the beginning of my route and I had only picked up five children who were sat right at the back of the coach and so they didn't feel the effect of the crash. The boss brought another coach out to me and I finished the run. I was in shock to be honest, but as I headed back to the coach yard my neck and my back really started to hurt me. I was in a lot of pain and so I went to the hospital where they put a collar on my neck as I waited for x-rays. Luckily it was just whip lash to my neck and the pain in my back I was well used to, but it had flared it up with a vengeance. I spent a few weeks on sick recovering and, to be honest a lack of contact and co-operation from the boss made me consider my options regarding work, so I handed in my notice and left.

My partner Susan helped me decide to take a part-time job with the local authority, driving their coaches, picking up and dropping off disabled children and the elderly at various centres and their homes. It was all local work so I wouldn't be sat for too long at a time and no heavy lifting which I hoped would be better for my back. This was a great job. I really enjoyed it, I had not enjoyed a job so much since my days at the Royal Mail, and after a few months I started getting full time hours too. This job was even better for someone like me who knew of their spiritual gifts. As I was pushing people around in their wheelchairs or interacting with them, I would send them healing energy and no one else would know except me and perhaps sometimes them. So finally I'd found a job again that I was very happy in, but like the others, it soon went wrong for me again.

I do and always have given the best of my abilities in every job I have ever had. I have always gone that extra bit further to help people or benefit my employer. This is not because I am a goody two shoes, but because I have always liked to help people and I find a certain satisfaction in a job well done. This aspect of me was duly noted as I worked for the local authority and it opened many different doors for me with regards to my work, my hours and my overtime. It was nice when a regular driver would be on holiday or sick leave and their centre managers would request me to cover for them. It wasn't just the managers and the staff from these centres that were happy for me to work with them, but the clients too. They never seemed to forget me, even if I didn't go back for months.

But as I said, all this eventually went sadly wrong for me as I was sexually harassed, bullied and victimised in the work place. What started out as funny to me and my fellow colleagues got out of hand, as two women, one being my charge hand, one doing my duty allocations took offence to their embarrassing mistreatment of me being common knowledge and so colluded to keep trying to get me into trouble and in their hopes dismissed. They started sending me wrong information about where I should be or what I should be doing, and they started to stop giving me work and cut down my hours, presumably to force me to seek employment elsewhere. It wasn't a nice time for me and despite me eventually having to report all of what had happened and what was continuing to happen to higher management, they didn't want to know. It felt to me that because it was two women harassing a man they just wanted to sweep it under the carpet, and also because it was the local authority, they didn't want the attention.

This was a terrible time for me, I was suffering through no fault of my own and nobody in management wanted to help. Even some of my fellow workers couldn't believe nothing was being done about it and that the two women were getting away with it. The final straw came when my charge hand actually reported me for being drunk at work at 12pm in the afternoon, bearing in mind I'd been at work since 7am that morning. One of the bosses said I had to go up to the head office to discuss it with him, but this would have meant an immediate suspension of my duties until the matter was resolved. I wasn't stupid (neither was my partner who told me to go home instead), so I left work, went to my GP and told him what was happening. He signed me off sick and I tried in vain to get things sorted out whilst I was off work, alas to no avail. I could drag you through the details but I won't, suffice to say it is a memory long gone and I am far better off for going through it, as it really pushed me onto my healing and spiritual path more, and doing what I now love the most. The two women involved I have no hatred for, though they did anger me at the time with their collusion and lies. What they tried to do and put me through is something they will have to live with, and as you can imagine, I am a big believer in karma.

Though life hasn't been easy through the years with various troubles, jobs and the persistent back pain, I can, and do, look back at how it has all got me where I am today. I guess I was never meant to be anything other than what I am now but I just couldn't see it back then. If I'd have paid more attention to my intuition then perhaps it would have happened sooner, but then again probably not, and certainly I wouldn't have learned and understood the things I do now to help people. So, while the local authority dragged things out and I spent the time on sick leave, my intuition told me I needed some me time, some guidance and inspiration, and I found myself back in a place I knew I was finally ready for again, the Temple of Truth Spiritualist Church.

2

The Temple of Truth has moved on from where it used to be when I first attended aged 15. A far bigger and better venue opens its doors to those who seek help and wish to learn more now so I'm told. But when I returned after many years away for my own help and guidance, it was still just a downstairs shabby Labour party meeting room. The furniture was sparse, the chairs were uncomfortable, the nets were ill fitting and ripped, in fact most things had seen better days. I don't think I ever saw more than twenty people attend a meeting, and sometimes as few as five. It was a nice place to be though and people found their answers, guidance and wisdom from the various mediums who donated their time to channel spirit messages to the congregation.

As I was going through a tough time with the situation at work, I decided it was time to go and find some answers for myself. My intuition and guidance had served me well through the years and had definitely got stronger from the age of 25, but I was feeling blocked, lost and frustrated with what was going on and I needed some clarity. I had a knack of knowing the things that were best for myself and others through the years, but right then I was well and truly stuck with the local authority's reluctance to do anything about my plight.

It had been a long time since I'd been in the Temple of Truth and I didn't recognise anyone as I found a seat at the back, trying to make myself invisible. I was aware of everyone looking at me and whispering as they took in my younger age and probably the fact that I was alone. As much as I enjoyed my time and guidance at the Temple for a while, I also found it unfortunately a den of gossip for a lot of the regulars in attendance. Luckily all eyes soon returned to the front as the service began with the introduction of the guest medium of the day. I can't remember her name but after the initial hymn and prayers she came straight to me with a message from spirit. I was so embarrassed. Here I was the stranger who had just walked in and was the first to get a message. She (the medium), said to me, "It's about time you got yourself back here". I'd never seen this woman in my life, so she couldn't know I'd been before. I knew it wasn't her saying it though, she was just relaying spirits words to me, and how right they were. Spirit spoke through her to me for only four or five minutes, but that was enough. They knew everything that was going on in my life and why I'd found myself back at the Temple, but that wasn't all. She also said that I was to be a very good healer and that it was my life purpose to do so. I took this on board but I wasn't convinced as I didn't have the time or inclination to be a full-time healer, I needed to work to pay the bills etc, anyway.

So that was my first time back in the Temple for years and I didn't, even at that point, know if I would be going back again. I did though, every week for almost a year, and the messages from the different mediums all kept telling me the same thing, that I was to be a healer. I became a familiar face over the weeks and months, and I took it upon myself to write down other people's messages as they received them, so they could remember what they had been told. The guidance given from a medium is often hard to remember, also it puts people on the spot and they can feel a bit embarrassed or self conscious and forget things. Writing it down for them meant they could take it home with them and go over what had been said to them in their own time, taking what they needed from it.

I was continually guided with my own situation and life in general which was very helpful through my own messages, but then one day a guest medium told me Harry Edwards (spirit), was standing next to me and was one of my healing guides who would help me on my path with my spiritual work. This raised some eyebrows in the Temple and drew me some odd looks, but I at that time had no idea why or who he was. I left and spoke to my Dad about the message and he was suitably impressed with this spirit guide's appearance. He told me that he was one of the greatest healers of modern times, so I decided to use Google on the internet and find out what I could about him. When I did I found out about the legend that is Harry Edwards, who had helped thousands of people throughout his life time right up until his transition to spirit in 1976.

In 1893 Harry was born, one of nine children, in London, were he lived in Balham. His father was a printer and his mother was originally a dressmaker. After completing an apprenticeship in printing himself in 1914, Harry enlisted in the Royal Sussex Regiment in order to serve his country in World War I. He was eventually promoted to Captain and was posted to Persia (Iraq), where he took charge of local labourers recruited to build a link between the Baghdad and Mosul railway. Poor conditions saw many of these locals come to Harry with their various injuries and illnesses. Unfortunately, Harry had only limited essentials to treat them with but never the less he had a gift for healing people and the recovery rate was quite phenomenal, and news soon spread of his amazing healing powers.

When Harry returned home in 1921 he married Phyllis whom he had met years earlier as both families lived in Balham. They opened a stationers shop and printing works together and his long standing interest in politics led him to stand for Parliamentary and Council seats on several different occasions.

Harry Edwards was actually very skeptical of spiritual beliefs until he attended an open circle in 1936 which caused him not only to change his mind but to become a medium himself. Other mediums he met at these circle sittings convinced him that he was in fact a healer, and he was asked to help someone dying of tuberculosis. Harry obliged and the patient made an amazing recovery. His next ill fated patient was suffering from terminal cancer but following Harry's spiritual healing they soon became well and even made a return to work. Many patients came after these two and with the great healing successes came an increase in media interest. Just who was this Harry Edwards? His reputation and spiritual healing in general was becoming widespread throughout the land. Spiritual healing now started to take over Harry's life in such a big way that it threatened his availability to run his printing business. He healed on evenings and at weekends as the queues grew ever larger outside his home and requests and progress reports kept arriving by mail.

As World War II broke out Harry joined the home guard providing healing to the service men and even to his own son. He continued to heal even through the unfortunate bombing of his own home where he lost all of his distant healing records. After the war was over, Harry moved to Stoneleigh were he used the front room as a healing sanctuary. News soon spread about this new location and soon enough his lost distant healing patients contacted him again, having benefitted from the healings before, they wanted to reacquaint themselves. Spiritual healing finally took over his life completely in 1946 when his brother took over his printing business, allowing Harry and one of his sisters and her husband to purchase Burrows Lea in Shere, Surrey. Burrows Lea is set in several acres of beautiful gardens and woodland giving out the feeling of peace and tranquility, a place I myself have visited.

Harry lived here with his wife and children, one sister and her husband. The ground floor featured offices in part and the billiard room was extended to become his healing sanctuary. Not long after moving in it became quite clear they needed to employ many typists in order to keep up with and respond to the thousands of letters requesting distant healing. Also the local people came to help with the healing, administration, managing the estate and driving Harry around the country to and from his many appointments. Harry was now receiving around ten thousand letters per week and in 1948 he gave a spiritual healing demonstration in Manchester in which six thousand people attended, such had his name become known. This was just one of many demonstrations given as Harry, with both his humor and humility, rolled up his sleeves to heal all people of all ages and backgrounds. In fact even celebrities received Harry's spiritual healing and publicly acclaimed his gift.

In September 1951 Harry gave one of his most famous appearances at the Royal Festival Hall in London, where he demonstrated spiritual healing to a packed auditorium. The medical profession and the churches were by now publicly disapproving of this spiritual healing, even despite the fact that many of them were healers and were willing to accept the evidence and results of spiritual healing practiced by Harry and many others. In 1953 an Archbishop's Commission on divine healing was created to investigate the whole subject, and in 1954 Harry spoke to and showed them documented evidence of a number of cases (with the patient's permission), for the Commission to examine. Whilst they deliberated with the medical profession, Harry held a public demonstration to six thousand people (including several members of the Commission), at the Albert Hall to launch the 10 o'clock healing minute. This healing minute is still observed around the world and taken part in daily.

The Commission's eventual report stated that the church and the medical profession would not admit that any other agency could achieve successful healings. The huge amount of evidence contrary to this view was ignored by the report which explained away these miraculous healings as "being outside the scope of the investigation". Unbelievably Harry Edwards was never sent a copy of the medical assessments for the cases he had submitted. Despite this apparent set back Harry's reputation for spiritual healing grew and grew, and to this day thousands of people from all points of the globe contact the sanctuary he founded at Burrows Lea to benefit from the healing help given.

Burrows Lea is a registered charity which carries on Harry Edward's incredible legacy, bringing hope and spiritual healing to all. It is a huge Victorian house set in thirty acres of countryside in Surrey, England. People benefit there not just from the spiritual healing but also from just sitting quietly in their prayers or meditation. What an unbelievable man and healing guide I was to have working through me. I was back then and still am now truly honored to carry on his work helping others, and I hope I can keep reaching many more through the years with his guidance.

I was, I admit, a little embarrassed at not knowing of this great man and his miraculous work, so I offered my humble apologies in a meditation. To my pleasure I could sense him all around me as his energy vibration came close giving me my confirmation that he was with me. I am not the most visual person when it comes to working with spirit, but I do sense and feel their presence at times. My intuition also lets me know they are with or around me.

After only about four months of attending the Temple I was invited to sit in the Thursday night psychic development circle. This was a closed circle that you had to be invited to, and as I had been getting so many spirit messages of what I was to become, I think this definitely prompted the committee members to ask me to attend. I found it hard to develop though. I was not very visual with the meditations and the tarot reading work was never really explained properly to me. I know my intuition had served me well through the years but here, trying to give someone a psychic reading just didn't seem to be happening for me. We would pick out cards and swap them with a person to give them some psychic guidance, but I very much felt like the weakest link at this, and I was always apologising to whoever got lumbered with me as a partner.

One day though I was paired with a woman who was about my age and who had just started attending the Temple after leaving a spiritualist Church from across the City. I told her I was useless at the tarot work and not to expect much, but she took the time to explain things to me on how to do it. I laughed when she explained its simplicity, it seemed too easy, but I tried it anyway, and abruptly the laughing ceased as I told her things about her life I couldn't possibly know. It wasn't anything mind blowing, but it was a start of things to come and it certainly amazed me. I'd been struggling and trying too hard in the hope for psychic messages or images to come to me in the past, but she had now shown me a much easier way, a way in which I hardly had to concentrate. I had found my way to connect with spirit and use my intuitive thoughts. It also dawned on me then that a few weeks earlier a medium had given me the same first name as this woman to watch out for in a message which I couldn't place at the time. Coincidence? I don't think so.

I will kid you not, psychic work takes a lot of time to perfect for most of us. It is still not my strongest spiritual gift, although I have improved and I have given much guidance, wisdom and direction to people and patients alike through the years to help them. I started to develop my psychic reading work back then very slowly, but over the weeks and months, one word answers turned into sentences and soon enough I was writing a page or more. I felt I was really getting somewhere and my healing work was coming through stronger too. I had even started healing in the Temple after services so my practice and confidence was growing. People started commenting on my healing abilities as they were relieved of minor aches, pains and headaches. They could feel the stress and tension disappearing from them too with the healing energy, bringing them a sense of calm, relaxation and peace.

Soon through my time back at the Temple I was given a chance to further develop my meditation, healing and psychic work by one of the committee members and resident mediums (MB). I was invited to her house on Friday mornings to meditate, do some tarot work and send out distant healing. I enjoyed these private sessions between us and started to feel and sense more as my awareness grew with my knowledge, which I was also expanding through reading and studying more than I ever had before. I'd always loved reading, studying and learning but this was more fascinating to me than anything else. There were no boundaries or limits to it and it covered the physical world we live in, not just the spiritual one as some might think.

Everything I was learning I could incorporate into mine and others lives to help and enhance us all. I couldn't understand why all this beautiful knowledge and better way of living wasn't taught to us in schools. Why would people not want to know this stuff and save themselves a lot of pain, anguish and grief? I had known about the spirit world and worked minimally in my own way with them through the years, but the more I learned and understood, the more I wanted to share it with others, as so many people were blind to it, disbelieving or in fear of it.

Further learning and studying has taught me exactly why this knowledge is not readily available, but that is not an avenue I wish to take you down in this book. Only to say that if you knew all about it, you would live differently and not conform as much to the oppressive ways that we are governed, and that is something the powers that be fear most, losing their control over us.

After a few months a man (GL), who also attended the Temple of Truth occasionally joined our Friday morning sessions, or sometimes we would go to his house to practice. He was also a medium and he not only heard spirit but saw them quite clearly too, so through our meditations and studies we helped each other with guidance upon our physical and spiritual paths.

I had also at this time started to create energy balls in my hands while channeling healing energy. Each week they seemed to get bigger and bigger, and colder too, eventually taking my arms out to full stretch, which felt like I had a huge snowball in my hands. This is not an uncommon thing for healers to do as they work with energy it was just new and fascinating to me back then. One Thursday night in the psychic development circle I remember the group all sending out distant healing together, and as we did, the energy ball started to grow between my hands as usual. It was, as always, a pleasant feeling but when the group finished channeling the healing energy I couldn't stop, it was like I was in some kind of trance. I was aware that they had all finished but I just couldn't, nor did I want to. It felt too good as the energy vibrations coursed through my body. The group watched me for a while but then they became concerned as I started shaking with the energy and unbeknown to me, my nose and lips had started to turn blue with the coldness of it. They started to talk me back into the physical world and back to room awareness then, but it took a while, as I was well and truly in another zone.

When I finally opened my eyes and had a grip on reality again I was shivering and my teeth were chattering. They piled their jackets on top of me to warm me up and were about to call an ambulance as they thought I might have got hypothermia due to the blueness in my face. I told them not to though as I felt fine, in fact I felt fantastic, just cold, and within a couple of minutes, I was back to my normal self, the blue lips and nose having vanished. It was certainly a conversation point and one I'm glad they all witnessed, and I know now it was some kind of spiritual attunement raising my vibration, as a week or so later exactly the same thing happened at one of my Friday morning sessions. This time though it wasn't a vibration lift for me it was for my medium friend MB. We had done our meditation and Tarot work for the morning and as usual we were finishing off our session by sending out distant healing. The energy ball started to grow in my hands again and as I rolled it between my palms I could feel the pressure between them as it gradually expanded more and more. It was very cold again, though not as cold as my previous experience with it, but another unexpected thing did happen.

My spirit guides told me to place the energy ball over MB's head, so slowly and carefully I rose up from my seat and carried the energy ball over to her. My movement had prompted her to open her eyes, and I told her that this energy ball was now for her. She smiled and nodded her confirmation to me before closing her eyes again, awaiting the gift. I placed it over the top of her head and then guided my hands all the way down her body until I reached her feet and the floor. I slowly stepped away from her then and took my seat again, keeping my palms facing towards her, continuously sending her energy. I think it took between five and ten minutes for her to accept the energy and she described some wonderful feelings, sensations and visions when we talked about it afterwards.

We continued learning together each week and decided that in order to help people more with these spiritual gifts we had to venture outside the Temple of Truth. Susan, my partner, set up some small psychic demonstrations for us to do, mainly in community centres as we tried to bring awareness and an understanding of the spirit world to people. This also enabled us to raise some much needed funds for the centres that we worked in. I remember the first one we did. I was useless and completely froze in front of the small audience of thirty three people, I didn't say a word throughout the full two hours. Luckily GL and MB were used to standing in front of a few people at our spiritualist church and their mediumship did not let them down as they relayed messages to everyone who came.

They were applauded and thanked after the demonstration and then we asked if anyone wanted to stay behind for some healing. To our joy about a half a dozen people did and I was able to contribute something worthwhile to the day's demonstration. As a trio we had been working with the healing energy in a triangle formation. This was a shape that I had received in a meditation, though I had no real understanding of its meaning or its power at the time. We stood around each person and healed them in our triangle for about ten minutes, relieving headaches and a few minor pains, and bringing a sense of peace and calm to them all, much to their amazement.

It was a very successful day and on leaving I did apologise to GL and MB for my lack of input. I told them I would not let them down again and that I would do an opening introduction at the next event. I was true to my word and I introduced every event after that with them, I still do today with the various people I work with. I am still incredibly nervous when doing demonstrations, even after doing so many now, as being everyone's focus point can be a little bit daunting. However, I have adapted as best I can, and, I know that my spirit guides never let me down when I ask them to give me the strength and the courage to face audiences. They also help to open the minds of those who are sceptical about the spirit world with messages and the healing energies.

As well as doing local demonstrations we also decided to set up a website for people to contact us through, and this was how Spiritualhart came to be. MB didn't have a computer so it was down to GL and myself to set this up, and, to be fair, back then I had little computer experience myself. I remember sitting at GL's house one day as we tried to come up with a name. We wanted spirit something or something spirit but wasn't sure what. Then I came up with Spiritualheart which we both liked, but on checking the internet there was already a website hosting that name. With that my intuition kicked in and said, "Lose the e, Spiritualhart?", we checked the internet and the name was available, we were very happy, but it wasn't till a few weeks later that I found out exactly why spirit had guided me to that name.

My main spirit guide is Ben Black Elk of the Native American Sioux tribe and he pretty much runs my life, constantly guiding and directing me. I'm sure this is the reason Susan and myself got together too as her spirit guide is Lucy Looks Twice, Ben's Sioux sister. Their father was the famous Nicholas Black Elk, an amazing man of his time and of his people, and I would definitely recommend the book "Black Elk speaks" by John Neihardt, which Ben Black Elk interpreted, about his life and his spiritual teachings. Though his father stands out in Native American folklore, Ben himself achieved much in his lifetime continuing his Father's work and ensuring the Indian culture would not be lost and forgotten.

As the white man took over most of the plains in the late 1800's through many unnecessary massacres, the American Indian numbers dwindled and they were forced to become more civilized (in the white mans eyes). Schools brought education about the white mans world and way of living and if not for the likes of the Black Elks and others, this beautiful culture could have been eradicated forever. Many uneducated people view these Indian tribes as savages, but they are very ill informed. They were people of honor and respect and although they had their bloodbath wars with the white man, these wars were not by their choice, as their land was taken from them by force or they were conned out of it by deals that were reneged on.

We would do well to take note of the simple way the Native American Indians lived back then. They roamed the land and followed the Buffalo in order to survive which is a fact well documented. Hundreds and thousands of Indians living together out in the open land, and unlike us, in harmony. They looked after one another back then as they understood that we are all brothers and sisters on this Earth "Mitaku oy sin" ("We are all related") is their way and everyone helped for the good of the tribe. They did not go on killing sprees and hunt down more than they needed, for they knew the Buffalo was sacred to their survival. Not only did it feed them, it clothed them and kept them warm. Bones were made into tools to work with to construct tepees and furrow the land. Nothing was wasted and everything was respected. When these tribes moved on from one place to another as the seasons changed to follow the Buffalo, you could hardly tell they had been there. No fires were left and no rubbish was left as the land was left to grow again so that they could once again return. Mother Earth had their respect. They took only from her to survive and made sure they replenished her with the care she needed to help her to grow.

Like many people do now, the Native American Indians meditated for higher learning and understanding and for a better use of their world. They also watched the animals that were sick to see what they would eat to make them well again, and these remedies they took back to their villages. The Earth was given to us to live off and they knew this. An abundance of energy flows through the plants and fruits of the trees, yet in this day and age we constantly ply ourselves with junk food. Water was given as the only purity our bodies needed but now typical diets include fizzy soft drinks and caffeine.

Ben Black Elk took all his knowledge of the Native American Indian ways and made it not just available to the white man, but to all colours and creeds. He was the long standing tribesman and medicine man teaching simplicity to life and the traditions of the old ways for the good of Mother Earth. I respect this man, my spirit guide, with all my heart and I am honored to have him with me. When help and direction is needed, Ben is always there for me. A true and very, very trusted friend.

And so the reason behind using the word Hart instead of Heart became obvious to me. When I looked into Deers and Elks I found that they are known as Harts. No wonder my intuition had prompted me to change it that way. The Spiritualhart logo apart from having Elks on it also has a heart representing love and the triangle shown represents a powerful healing shape which I often work in with others or with some of my spirit guides. The triangle is full of the colours of the chakras, the main energy centres of our body. Once the name and logo had been decided the website soon followed.

Through this time I had started to self heal to help me with my ongoing back pain. I had decided to give up the prescribed medication as the strong doses were making me lethargic and not actually helping to ease the pain. This coincided with myself and a friend taking our Reiki level I attunements, with a wonderful and very knowledgeable Reiki Master called Samantha. I must admit I didn't know a great deal about Reiki or attunements at the time, only that they could enhance your spiritual gifts and my intuition was guiding me to do it. During my attunement Samantha also taught me the history and teachings of Reiki which I will briefly share with you.

Reiki most recently was discovered by Dr Mikao Usui in the late 19th century where he was the Principal of a Christian school in Kyoto, Japan. One day whilst teaching his class the miracles that Jesus had performed, and in particular healing, a student asked him "Why, if Jesus said we could, didn't anyone have the ability to heal anymore, like his disciples in the Bible?" Dr Usui was ashamed that he could not answer the question as his teaching position was a great honor in Japan, and so he resigned from his post to begin a very long quest to find out just exactly how Jesus had healed, and why indeed nobody could do it anymore.

His studies took him over to America where he attended the University of Chicago for seven years. After gaining a degree in theology he still felt none the wiser about how to heal so returned back home to Kyoto, Japan. Dr Usui then discovered there was a man named Buddha who had healed the sick in a similar way to how Jesus had. He began to search through ancient texts, learning first Chinese before moving on to Sanskrit (an ancient Indian language), in order to read the original texts rather than translations which he felt may have overlooked or misinterpreted the originals. Through these studies Dr Usui is said to have finally found a way to contact a higher power for healing in the Indian Sutras. He wasn't sure what to do with his new found knowledge though until he arrived at a Zen monastery and became friends with the Abbot who was also interested in healing. It is said that this Abbot suggested that Dr Usui meditate on the information he had found, so he decided to go to a mountain outside Kyoto, sacred to the monks called Kori-yama.

As he walked up the mountain he apparently collected twenty one stones and put them in a pile next to where he sat to meditate and fast for three weeks. Every morning as the sun rose Dr Usui tossed a stone away to count the days, but nothing else happened. As the time passed by one can only imagine his desperation. After all the years he had spent searching, learning languages and reading ancient texts, he knew he had a connection to a higher power but didn't know what to do with it. Early morning on the last day as he sat in the darkness before dawn he prayed that something would come to him, and as he looked ahead he saw a light heading towards him. The light was extremely bright as it sped towards him and Dr Usui realized it was going to hit him if he didn't move. He was in fear but was determined enough to stay put, after all the years of study he was now prepared to die rather than avoid the experience coming at him.

They say the light suddenly struck him on the forehead and he lost consciousness. When he came to the sun was already high in the sky so he knew he had been unconscious for hours, but luckily he could remember everything. After the light had struck him he was aware of many beautiful colours. This was followed by an intense white light with large transparent bubbles forming before his very eyes. Each of these bubbles contained one of the symbols he had seen in the Sanskrit writings he had studied. As each bubble passed Dr Usui was given just enough time to memorise the symbol and understand its use before the next one appeared. He realised now that he had been given the secrets of the ancient healing art and that this was universal life energy which he named Reiki. Dr Usui was so excited that he now knew how to heal that he couldn't wait to return to Kyoto. When he finally got back to the monastery he found that the Abbot was in bed suffering from his arthritis. So he gave the Abbot a demonstration of his new found gift and relieved his pain. Then the two men discussed in depth what Dr Usui should do with this new found gift, and they decided he should go to the slums of Kyoto and try to help the beggars there.

Dr Usui spent many years working the slums helping the people to become well in order that they could go out and seek work for themselves. After a few years though he started to see familiar faces coming back so he began questioning them and realised that although he could heal physical pain there had to be more to this healing. He wanted to give them some spiritual guidance so that they would take responsibility for themselves so he taught them about the five spiritual principles he had developed. He also realised that to give Reiki freely was not getting the gratitude it deserved. People were still not helping themselves so he vowed never again to give Reiki to anybody who did not appreciate its full value. Instead he began teaching them Reiki using the symbols he had been given on Mount Kori-yama so that they could treat themselves and others, and he also started to train men as Reiki masters.

Now, I'd been healing regularly at the Temple of Truth and our demonstrations, but I could never really feel the energy flowing through me whilst I did it like those could who were receiving it. I could when I was creating energy balls or sending distant healing, but not when doing hands on healing. This struck me as odd, as people would tell me how good it felt after a healing session and that certain aches and pains had disappeared, that they could feel the energy as tingling sensations or vibrations running through their body. However, once I had been attuned to Reiki we were asked to use the energy immediately to heal each other. I put my hands over my friend's body to heal her and I couldn't believe the sensations I felt flowing from the palms of my hands. It was an amazing feeling as I went through the hand positions I had been taught, and I could feel the warm or cold energy as I moved my hands over her. This truly felt like a step up the spiritual ladder and I was not short of people wanting to receive this healing energy from me.

As anyone who has been through the Reiki levels will know, once attuned, there is a twenty one day self healing process to integrate the energy into your system and start the detoxifying of your own body. This was perfect for me as not only would it raise my energy, vibration level and detoxify me, it would also help with my back problems. Twenty one days passed and I just kept going, in fact I still do. There's rarely a day goes by when I don't self heal. This is not just to help my own physical problem though this is also about keeping myself, as a channel for spirit to work through, as pure as I possibly can. The better I am, the purer I am, and the better people can receive spirit's help through me.

I was living with Susan at this time and she helped me set up a small healing room in the spare back bedroom of her house where we lived on Northolme Road, Hessle. Sure enough people started to visit for treatments. I was not a practitioner at this time but I wanted to help people and the more I learned through my studies and meditations the more spirit seemed to give me and push me on. I was absolutely buzzing at this time, everything was coming so fast, the love, the energy, and the pure white light around me was beautiful. I was healing people regularly and I was getting more in tune with spirit but then I realised lessons had to be learned and quickly! Unfortunately, there is a negative and dark side to this spiritual work and it was something my spirit guides wanted me to learn, understand and work with.

3

I had heard stories about the negative and darker side of the spirit world through the years, more so at the Temple of Truth, but I hadn't given it much of my attention. It was not something I had an interest in or wanted to attract to me, I was a light worker, I worked from the heart and purity and positivity was all I needed in my life. My spirit guides, however, had other ideas. They knew my path upon this Earth plane and certainly woke me abruptly up to it.

It was one Sunday that I learned a very valuable lesson whilst sitting in a healing circle of all places. I attended my Reiki Master and friend Samantha's house for a day of meditation and healing with ten other like minded guests. We were told of the day's proceedings and when our breaks would be before being led upstairs to the meditation room. Some of the guests began to lie down to relax and prepare themselves, but I myself was quite happy to sit on a chair. I was not that experienced with meditation and I didn't want to run the risk of falling asleep and missing things. Not that it mattered I lasted for about sixty seconds of the first meditation, before I had to dash out the room to the toilet, where I promptly vomited and emptied the contents of my stomach. I was so embarrassed, but I couldn't stop retching and the pain in my head was like a vice squeezing it.

Samantha after talking through the first meditation to the group briefly left them to take in the healing energies and spirit guidance. Then she tapped lightly on the toilet door I was in and asked if I was alright. As I opened the door she helped me to my feet and I apologised profusely to her. I told her I would leave but to my surprise she said, "You will do no such thing" and led me into another room to sit down and recover. She surprised me even further when she said, "Why was that aimed at you?" Luckily for me she had seen everything that had happened. I told her I was looking forward to the meditation but shortly after I closed my eyes I felt a drunken feeling come over me. My head started spinning and my stomach started to do somersaults and I thought at first that maybe the healing energy was too strong for me. I knew within seconds though that this wasn't the healing energy, it felt nasty and like it was attacking me, so I struggled to my feet and left the meditation circle as I thought I was being psychically attacked. She confirmed my beliefs and said she saw a dark negative energy cross the room to me and she knew who it had come from. I knew too "Why would they do that?" she asked.

I knew exactly why it was sent to me but I will not inflate their ego by saying so here. Samantha knows now too. She also asked me why I was so unprotected when doing spirit work and my poor naive excuse was, "I'm with you I thought everything would be fine today." She again told me I would not be leaving and she did a quick grounding and protection meditation with me before returning back to the group and bringing them out of their first meditation. She did not discuss with the group what had happened to me, only to say I was very sensitive to energy and would be rejoining them soon which I did. I felt better and calmer now and I was welcomed back into the group, and as it turned out I stayed and enjoyed the full day and it was the perpetrator who eventually had to leave early.

A very valuable lesson was learnt that day and I have never, and will not ever fully ground and protect myself when working with spirit or other people again. There are some fantastic light workers among us doing fantastic work and I am lucky and honoured to know some of them, but there are also those who wield their spiritual gifts and like to exert the power. These people you would think should know better, but that's hubris for you and human error, and they eventually will have to face their own karma which you'd think they would know wouldn't you?

So, I'd had a taste of negative energy. I wasn't impressed and I didn't like it, but there was worse to come in my salad days as they say, and some I'll get to later. The first I wish to tell you about though and which took my healing work in a new direction was on a 65 year old lady suffering with chronic face pain. This lady had been all over the country and even to European hospitals to see certain specialists in the hope of help for her condition, all to no avail. She had suffered with this pain since she was 40 years old and to be honest (and I'm not surprised), she was very cranky and not a believer in energy healing at all. I was, as they say, a last resort that her daughter had talked her into trying, and I told her and her family that given the time scale she had suffered one healing session was not going to cure her. They agreed to have six weekly sessions with me in the hope of some respite, if not a cure, and I knew my spirit guides would do all they could for her. After three healing sessions though there was no change and I was a bit concerned by this. I had not had anyone yet who hadn't seen some sort of change or gained some sense of calmness before, and usually in just the first session.

Whilst meditating before the fourth session with her though, spirit told me that she was carrying negativity. This didn't mean a lot to me back then until they said, "You are trying to heal negativity. This is not the way, it needs to be removed". Removing stuff was not something I had done before, sure I'd heard of it. Psychic surgeons removing foreign bodies and performing operations which was way out of my league (or so I thought), but removing negative energy from a person, that was definitely a new one on me! Anyway, to cut a long story short my spirit guides told me through meditations and day dream's that part of my path on this Earth was to help rid negative energies and entities from people and places. This did not go down well with me and I flatly refused. I did not want to go anywhere near the negative and dark side of things. I was a light worker and I planned on staying in and with the light to do my work.

My refusal of course was my prerogative, but my spirit guides answer was far wiser and painted a very bigger picture out to me. They told me that I came down to this Earth plane to be a light worker, that much was true, but I wasn't at this time understanding the full meaning of the term. I had also chosen to come to Earth to help the light grow and help vanquish the darkness and negativity that plagued people and the universe. If I didn't do it, my healing work wouldn't develop. That was a bit of a shock to find out, I didn't think I was ready for this sort of thing and I knew very little about it because I wanted no part of it, but now I was being told it was a path I must walk. I procrastinated a while but there was no way of getting out of it. I found myself in a bit of a catch twenty two situation. I could dig my heels in and refuse, but I would not progress and grow doing the work I loved so much.

I'm glad to say I conceded to my spirit guides' wisdom and knowledge as I trusted in them to keep me safe and show me how to do things. I was both excited and apprehensive with the new learning to come and the direction I was moving in, and I was very concerned at what I would be coming up against. This was probably when, as I look back now when I made a not too good decision regarding my work, I asked my spirit guides to close my third eye down. I told them if I was to walk this new path with them then I did not want to see what I was up against. Sensing and feeling was one thing but seeing negativity and grotesque entities I did not want imprinting in my mind, certainly not at that early stage anyway.

As for the lady with the chronic face pain, in my next session with her we removed the negativity before healing her. Unfortunately she stopped coming after this fourth session but luckily her daughter got in touch with us and said she had calmed down a lot and her attitude had changed for the better. This is the frustrating part of my work when people benefit but stop coming, but it is their choice and I have to accept that.

So a safety error on my part and a big learning curve in my work, all in the space of a couple of months. I was moving on and learning fast, but there was a lot more to come from both the healing side and the negative side. I'm glad to say I got better equipped for it all as I studied further and my knowledge grew.

It was also about this same time that I was asked to sit on the Temple of Truth's Committee. The work I'd been doing and my commitment wasn't going unnoticed and I felt quite honoured to be asked actually. My Dad, years before me, had been a Committee member too, it seemed like I was going down a similar road to him when I accepted the offer, but my spirit guides had other ideas much to my embarrassment.

One Monday afternoon I was called to attend a Committee meeting at the Temple of Truth. The Church President and all the other Committee members were there and others like myself who were about to be sworn onto the Committee. The meeting didn't get off to a good start though, there was lots of shouting and arguing and to this day I have no idea what it was all about. The other new members and I were asked to go outside and wait in the back while they discussed things. It didn't seem like a pleasant discussion was taking place by what we could overhear.

We waited outside for over an hour, so I'm glad it was a warm and sunny September day. During this time though, I changed my mind about accepting the Committee's offer and position. I don't like confrontations, never have, and what was going on inside the Church didn't look very appealing to me. Then my spirit guides confirmed my thoughts and told me to get out and leave. They told me that this would be my last day at the Church as they had far too much work ahead for me. I was a bit thrown by this, as I knew I didn't want to be part of an argumentative Committee if that was how things were run, but I wasn't planning on leaving altogether, only now my spirit guides were saying I had to. This was going to be awkward to say the least. Two weeks ago I had happily said yes to a place on the Committee, saying "no" now was something I wasn't looking forward to doing.

We were all eventually called back into the Church but the atmosphere and energy wasn't good. I remember feeling it's heaviness despite the President and Committee members smiling at us, it was a very false façade. I felt very uneasy as we all sat there and the order of events were read out to us. I wasn't looking forward to turning their offer down now after saying provisionally I would accept it, and wondered how they would respond, given the negative atmosphere they'd created. I was not the only one to be sworn in that day, there were others before and after me, so as the proceedings started I began channelling positive energy into the room in an attempt to lift and raise the energy and vibration. I didn't have long though as they swore in the first two quite quickly, and then it was my turn and I was asked to take the position as a Church Committee member. I declined and all eyes zoomed in on me because that was not the expected answer I was supposed to be giving. As I waited for their reaction I actually felt relief at saying no, though I thought I would be put on the spot now and asked about my decision. Instead they more or less moved on to the next person, as I relaxed and took my reprieve. I think they were a bit flummoxed actually and continuing without comment seemed their best way forward. It also stopped any conversations about my decision, and left the Committee still in control of things.

As the meeting came to a close I just wanted to get out of there as quickly as possible. I had a lot of thoughts going on in my head that I needed to sort out, like what was I going to do now and where was I going to learn etc. The last thing I wanted right now was any hassle about turning the position down, but as I made my way to the car park I heard footsteps catching me up and they belonged to the Church Vice-President. I cringed and bit my lower lip and thought, "Here we go" like a despondent child. She spoke first and to my surprise said, "I'm really proud of you today Dean", which really caught me off guard, and with a confused reply I asked, "Why?"

She said, "I could see how uncomfortable you were with everything today, you really didn't like all that arguing did you?" I apologised and told her arguing was not my thing I couldn't accept a Committee position that would involve so much confrontation with people I classed as my friends. She agreed and said it was not all love and light on the Church Committee, they often clashed and decisions were never made easily. She walked me to my car and before leaving said with a smile, "Well done, see you on Thursday". I thanked her but didn't answer the question as I knew I wouldn't be there on Thursday for the development group circle as my spirit guides had already told me, my time with the Temple of Truth was done. I had a lot of things to fathom out now, no Church meant less healing and meditation time. Sure I still had Friday mornings, but where did I go from there? I needed more answers and fast, and my spirit guides didn't let me down, giving me plenty of guidance and direction over the next few weeks and months. They had quite a lot in store for me that I didn't actually think I was capable of, but I vowed to give it my best shot, and things certainly started to change and progress for me.

4

Free from the Temple of Truth and its limited educational levels, I found myself and my knowledge expanding quickly without the confines of religious indoctrination. I am not against any religion in anyway and understand that some people take great solace in it, but it had never sat right with me, not even as a child. It was far too political as far as I was concerned, it felt more like a controlling manual and if you went against it you would surely perish? I have read and studied the Bible and other religions too in my quest to advance physically and spiritually and although there are some nice stories I cannot take things written thousands of years ago as the whole truth, that to me would be very naïve. Ever heard of Chinese whispers and how a story can change as it's passed on, if you have you'll know what I mean?

Having said that I do believe in a lot of the characters from the Bible and also from Buddhist, Hindu and other religions too as they work with me through my healings and meditations on a daily basis. I do not wish to challenge anyone's faith here, what works for each person is fine with me. What I will say though is Jesus and his disciples, Mother Mary, John the Baptist, Buddha, Krishna, Ganesha, Lakshmi, Shiva and many more that I work with each day, week and month have no interest whatsoever in religion, only in helping to heal us and guide us upon our physical paths. Yes, they may be portrayed in religious texts and worshipped as Gods but that is just our human self adhering to what we've been taught from an early age. They do not fight wars over which is the best religion in the spiritual realms. Why? Because they are highly evolved beings and know better, which is why they try to help us understand life here. But unfortunately man, in its infinite wisdom, decided long ago that greed and gain, hatred and killing was the way to educate the masses (more like control), or at least those in charge back then did and the politicians nowadays try to have most of us learn and think exactly the same.

However, this is not a book to preach to you, I have no interest in doing that. It is a book about my own personal journey, no one else's, so take from it as you wish. People learn things in their own time and we are all at different levels and stages in our lives, this is why our thought processes can be so different from one another. What I am trying to convey is just my understanding and knowledge at the time of writing. There is no right or wrong, just my experiences at my own personal level and evolvement that I am choosing to share with you.

This greater freedom of thinking and knowledge that I had now started to develop with the help of my spirit guides also got me to finally get to grips with technology. I am not a fan of gadgets and computers held very little interest for me, but the internet holds a lot of accessible information that most libraries don't, so I increased my study time massively. I had always been an avid reader of fiction and even through fiction you can learn a lot. But what I was learning now though was more addictive than anything I'd ever been interested in before. This was reality, confusing and frustrating as it was at times, and still can be, but I was waking up more and more, as my spirit guides pushed me more and more to what I needed to know, and to what was real and what was not. Much had been hidden from me for far too long and I began to soak it all up and take it all in. My understanding and awareness got better and my universe got bigger, and the more I studied (and still do), the more new spirit guides surrounded me to help me, constantly pushing me on with my work.

My own spirit guide Ben Black Elk, as mentioned earlier, is always with me, as is Dr Usui whenever I do Reiki treatments, but I had also acquired a guide from the ancient City of Atlantis called Senistoom. Through my studies I had read a lot about Atlantis and I felt a connection to it, so when this guide came through and revealed themselves I wasn't too surprised. Nor was I when I found out that I had lived in Atlantis in one of my past incarnations. There were many other spirit guides that started to surround me and work with me too, but not being a very visual person I had to rely on other psychic friends to inform me about most of them or describe them to me. All this was very good to know as I was growing spiritually and raising my vibration, but it was also a little frustrating that I rarely got to see any of them. I started to realise then that I had probably made a big mistake in asking my spirit guides to close my psychic eye down when I agreed to do the negative work.

Slowly adapting myself to technology and the benefits of the internet, I gave in to people's advice and finally set up a Facebook account. Though I didn't initially like all its negative statements and comments, I did find it useful in connecting with some like minded people as we helped each other with our shared spiritual experiences. I met some incredibly genuine and knowledgeable people who gave me a lot of their time and helped me understand a lot more about the things I was constantly learning. This helped me open my mind even further by not just sticking with my own point of view, which at times could be narrow, and I soon started to see a bigger picture in all aspects of life.

I started to understand more about universal balance in life and I eventually took my level II Reiki to become a practitioner. This enabled me to get my insurance to practice as a healer. I had grown in confidence quickly whilst healing mainly family and friends, but spirit kept telling me there were many more people to reach and help. I wasn't one to argue with them, they guided me well, and the healing energy they put through me and the results were evidence enough that we were really starting to make a difference for people. I was working with sacrosanct symbols now and not just the ones given to me through my Reiki attunements and teachings. Some of these ancient symbols carried so much power to help not just with healing but also with protection on both the physical and the spiritual playgrounds. These symbols were a big help to me and also helped speed up a lot of my work, especially now I had really started to work on getting rid of the negative energies and entities from people and properties where protection was essential.

I also received my first of many testimonials about this time, some of which I'll share with you throughout this book. I share them as an honour to the amazing spirit guides that work with me and through me, and also to help those who maybe a little sceptical about what I do to understand the help that's available to them if they wish.

Testimony

Last week I visited Dean Kingett's wonderful healing sanctuary. The energy there was amazing, a place which is cleansed all the time. Now firstly I must admit I have not been the biggest fan of Reiki healing. My mind has now been changed by the healing gift of Dean, in my mind a truly great healer in his own right. The experience began with a chat about what was going to happen, which was calming and very informative.

Dean decided to work on the chakras first as he placed crystals on various points of my body and as soon as he placed the gem on my 3rd eye the connection took place.

When Dean worked his way down to my stomach I have a lump just under my belly button which is a hernia and he placed his hands either side of it. Now I have been lucky to work with spirit doctors but this was unreal. Inside my belly I felt the problem being pulled back down into the muscle. Yes that's right, it was a bit uncomfortable but not painful as it was pulled back into place with love and care. Other things happened too which are personal to me but I take my hat off to Dean and his spirit guides Dr Usui and Harry Edwards, or angel Harry as Dean likes to call him.

A truly eye opening experience, so much so I will say Reiki does work and I am very, very sorry for disrespecting this form of healing for so long. So if you are reading this and you feel the same as I did, the only words I can say are don't let ignorance deny you this wonderful healer and healing.

One of my most spiritual experiences to date.

GL, Hull, England

Through Facebook my spirit guides also guided me to start doing worldwide distant healings. I started setting up the odd healing nights where I would set a time, usually 7pm to send out distant healing to all who wished to take part. These started to get quite popular and the feedback from people, from various countries around the world was wonderful. All they had to do was sit or lie down and relax at the agreed time and they would receive a free thirty minute healing from me. It didn't matter where they were in the world they could feel it as I sent the energy out to all of them at once. This may sound quite an amazing feat to those who don't know much about energy, but really it's quite simple, it's all about setting your intent with spirit and letting them do the work through you.

This was just another way my spirit guides were pushing me again to think outside the box, expanding my awareness of what we as human beings were actually capable of doing and how far we could reach. It was also bringing me more trust in them and myself, and I was starting to understand just how powerful energy could be. Not everyone around the globe could make the scheduled time though and were left a little disappointed, but not for long. My spirit guides soon helped me to understand that as well as sending the distant healing at the allocated time for those to receive it then, I could also allow the others who couldn't make it receive it later at their convenience. This kept everyone wanting it happy and meant nobody had to miss the opportunity.

As I progressed more and more I started itching to do my level III Reiki and become a Master/Teacher. This was not something I had envisaged before as I had never taught, nor had I ever wanted to, but again, my spirit guides had other ideas. My own Reiki Master who had taken me through the first two levels though had unfortunately become unavailable due to her own work commitments. I couldn't wait for her though as there was an urgency to do it from my spirit guides, but I'm glad I also listened to their guidance again, as they found me a new teacher who became a very good friend. I had been in contact with a lovely female soul from Scarborough through the internet for a few months, but I had no idea she was a Reiki Master, amongst other things. I was telling her I had booked in to do my level III Reiki, but two days before I was supposed to do it they had turned me down on the grounds I wasn't experienced enough. This was a shock and I was a bit disappointed at first, but, everything happens for a reason as they say.

I had a lot more experience spiritually than they did but they were conforming to rule, and in their opinion, I was two months short of their timescale to move up from level II to level III. I must admit I found this a bit pedantic considering they attended the Temple of Truth and so knew me and of my work and reputation there. Naivety and conforming lets people down in this life, a fact I have learnt more and more as I have grown up. I cannot say I have always thought differently about things, that would be a lie, but I can say I have done things in my life a lot differently to most. Not because I like to shock people or go against the norm, but because I don't like to be restricted. I am perfectly capable in knowing the difference between what is right and wrong. I am a free spirit experiencing life. I simply think about things then make my choice, I have a brain and I like to exercise my right to choice.

All was promptly put right though as I relayed my quandary and disappointment to my friend Raine Hilton. She told me she was a Reiki Master and Teacher and would happily attune me to level III Reiki in a couple of day's time if I wished. This was brilliant news to me and I told her so. Scarborough was only about an hour's drive away from me and I was willing to travel up to her for the attunement. Travelling though, she informed me, would not be a problem, as she would visit me via the astral plane to do it, we just had to set up a mutual time. Now this impressed me. I'd done distant healings but this was going to be a distant attunement, and the fact she was going to be with me through the astral plane to do it intrigued me.

My intuition told me that this was the way forward for me and I would learn much, as indeed I have and still do. Raine and her husband Phillip opened my eyes and mind a lot. They are both true advocates for all spiritual work and a better way of living on this Earth plane. Raine not only sent me the Reiki level III information manual but the level I and II manuals as well. This was all extra knowledge for me to take on board and study and over the years we have traded lots of information, e-books and music with each other as we share our love of this work and continue to grow with it.

Taking an attunement either in person or distantly is pretty much the same as having a healing session. It's just about relaxing the body, slowing the breathing and the heart rate down and working with the energy vibrations and sensations as you are attuned. Anything that you feel, sense or see even with your eyes closed is all part of the attunement process, as it raises your energy vibration to enhance you as a channel to heal yourself and others. Not all attunements are just about healing though there are many others for protection, abundance and much more.

As Raine attuned me to level III Reiki I again felt a raise in my energy and also in my capabilities as a healer. I spent a long time writing my own Reiki manuals as now that I had gained the Master/Teacher level my spirit guides wanted me to spread the word to many. I am not a writer so putting them together didn't come easy, but I was happy with them when they were finished. I wanted them to be easy for people to understand as I had learnt there really isn't anything hard about the spirit world, it's just a case of opening your mind, and stepping outside the boundaries that most of us have been brought up to accept.

5

As I had been contemplating teaching not just Reiki but psychic development in general, I obviously needed a place to do it. I had been told a year or so earlier by a medium that I would be moving from Northolme Road, Hessle, but at the time I had no real plans to. Susan and I were quite happy there. We began looking at properties though but nothing was really grabbing our attention. Especially as another medium had said for me to watch out for the white house? The property we eventually settled on though wasn't white at all, it was a bungalow not a house and to be honest it was a ramshackle collection of "add ons" to a very small property. I really wasn't interested when Susan took me to view it but she was convinced it was a perfect project to take on. That "project" word frightened me, I was useless when it came to D.I.Y. and was ridiculed, albeit good naturedly for my efforts.

Susan was determined though and she talked me into it, so we bought the property named Sunrise and set about transforming it. This was a greater task than anticipated. We knew it needed a lot doing to it and we knew how we wanted to extend it when we bought it, but it became pretty apparent soon enough that it was in a worse state than we thought as we started work upon it. To cut a long story short, there are now only three walls left of the original Sunrise building as the more we uncovered, the more we had to pull down or the more that simply fell down. This probably sounds like a catastrophe and it certainly felt so at the time for a while, but luckily it all worked out to our advantage. Our builder was brilliant, he just laughed as Sunrise fell apart, and assured us everything could be re-built as we wanted it.

As I mentioned D.I.Y. is not my thing, but I learnt a lot over the next eighteen months rebuilding Sunrise and the Spiritualhart sanctuary which I now work from. The construction of it all was obviously left to Dave the builder, but Susan's father Eric was hands on with most of the internal work and I worked with him a lot, as much as my back pain would allow anyway. He knew I was useless with my hands though and didn't give me a lot to do at first, but then, over time as I picked things up, I started to help him more and more, even fitting the roof on the sanctuary, which hasn't leaked yet, touch wood! It was frustrating at times with the different trades and the lack of detailed drawings. It wasn't fully finished inside when we had to move in as we had sold the house at Northolme Road, but at least we had nice flat walls and ceilings instead of just bare brick. I would never ever do it again though. It was far too much hassle and far too big a project. But I must admit when we finished it, it really was the house of our dreams and the sanctuary to work from is just perfect.

Just as we purchased Sunrise I was contacted by a friend of mine about her daughter and asked if I could help her. Her daughter (CS) had been through IVF treatment to have a baby but unfortunately with no success. She had been offered the chance to try again and wondered if my healing work would give her a better chance. I explained that a one off healing session was not going to be enough to put everything she needed back in working order, so she agreed to see me weekly in the hope that we could change things within her body to help her. The reason she and her partner had chosen to go down the IVF route was because she had polycystic ovaries which where causing problems with ovulation. They desperately wanted a child but the biological clock was also ticking and they wanted to try anything to enhance their chances of conceiving.

I told CS that I would only heal her up to the time the doctors placed the eggs back into her body after they had fertilised them, then it was all down to nature to run its course. I have no problem healing pregnant women, babies, people with pace makers etc, but unfortunately we live in a corrupt and a "no win, no fee" world. Spirit will not ever do anything wrong to anybody through any form of healing work because it's done through love, but if things are not to be they are not to be, so as a healer I have to unfortunately safeguard myself against peoples' blame or disappointment. My own Father has a heart mechanism fitted and has regular healing with me which causes no problem at all when healing him. The healing energy is intelligent as are the spirit guides that help us, which is why nothing can go wrong, but a lot of people don't understand this.

I worked on CS weekly for about eight weeks preparing her body and some amazing things occurred during our time together. One in particular that even astounded her doctors, especially as they didn't know she was having the healing treatments with me. I, myself, am not a Doctor, and in truth I know very little about the physical anatomy or how most of it works. I don't have to, spirit know exactly what they are doing, I just provide a channel for them to work through and do as they direct me from time to time. So when follicles had started to grow back where there had been none on previous x-rays before, her doctors had no explanation as to why. CS knew though, so did I, and it gave us both a lot of hope that spirit were repairing her, in fact actually reconstructing her in preparation for what lay ahead. But would it work and had we allowed enough time for them to get it all ready?

The IVF technique involves removing (or harvesting) eggs from a woman's body, fertilising them in a laboratory and then placing them back inside the womb. So when they doctors removed the eggs CS still came to see me for treatment to make sure everything was as perfect as it could be for their return. Only once they were placed back inside her did we cease our sessions together and leave the rest to Mother Nature keeping our fingers crossed. It had been a pleasant journey working with CS over those weeks but only time would tell now if our work was to be a success. It was also nice that all we had gone through had left its spiritual imprint on her too and I received a lovely letter from her shortly after our time together was done.

Testimony

Thank you so much for healing me over the past weeks. Every session has been invigorating and everything you have picked up on has been so true. It has been a very uplifting journey for myself. My life is more balanced, I am calmer, stronger mentally and physically and no longer negative.

It would be cruel to not tell you the outcome of CS's journey so I will continue. Her first attempt with IVF had been so unsuccessful that on assessment of her eggs, none of them had given her any chance of becoming pregnant much to her disappointment. However this time round with my spirit guides assistance it was a different story altogether, as on assessment she now had a staggering thirteen chances of becoming pregnant. I'm pleased to say she did too, and nine months later she gave birth to a beautiful and healthy baby girl who she named Annabel. It was lovely to finally meet Annabel a few months later, and I was very happy when CS and her mum brought her to see me. She is CS's miracle baby, loved and adored and a happy ending for the time CS put her faith in the spirit world to help her.

Some people do class this as a miracle that took place but I don't really see it that way. It's amazing, as is all that spirit can do through us or with us but when you work with spirit guides, angels and more like I do, what most people term as miracles are in fact just reality taking place. Not to get into religion but even the Bible quotes Jesus telling the masses that:

"Truly, truly, I say to you, he who believes in me, the works that I do, he will do also, and greater works than these he will do" (John 14:12). Which is all I or any other healer is trying to do, because he told us we can. Granted, we are not anywhere near as good as Jesus was at healing but that's because we don't vibrate at a high enough frequency like he did. The fact that some of us have trust and faith like he did though, means we are able to do some quite amazing things at our own individual levels.

The air that we breathe today is polluted by many things like gasses and smoke that we inhale into our bodies daily. Most of the food that we eat is either grown by force or sprayed with chemicals, and if that's not bad enough there are all the preservatives and such that are added to it for us to consume. Fluoride is put into our drinking water and aspartame is put into our soft drinks, and there is much more besides these that hinder us on both a physical and spiritual level. They are all damaging to our health but still allowed to be used because they make money, millions and billions of it.

Again I do not wish to take this book off track or too much down a political road, but the reason I mention the above is because they all lower our vibration and frequency, which hinders or even shuts down people's ability to access their spiritual gifts. Let's face it, if everyone knew how to heal themselves and others the pharmaceutical companies would lose a fortune, and that in turn would lose the politicians a fortune, as that's where a lot of their money comes from. Ever wonder why we are still not allowed the cure for cancer yet? I leave that for you to research yourself if you wish.

As a healer I learnt that the way for me to improve my healing work and myself as a channel for spirit to work through, was to improve what went into my body. I gave up things like fast food and fizzy drinks and changed to a healthier diet eating more fruit, vegetables and salads. I had never liked hot drink's so these were never a hindrance but my alcohol intake was, so again I changed this accordingly and water became my daily fluid. Now, as I mentioned our food and drink is not as good for us as we think it is, so I started changing how this entered my body by energising it first. This meant I started to heal my food. Sounds a bit strange I know, but I did, after all, healing people is just using energy to make them well, so I just started making my food and drink better for me before consuming it. This not only benefitted my body but benefitted my taste buds too as there was a significant difference when energising my food and drink, an experiment I have done with many of my students in various classes and workshops.

This doesn't mean I became all saintly and boring, it simply means that with my spirit guides help and guidance I could benefit myself and others more. It also made sense as why had I been putting such bad foods in my body through the years? It didn't take a genius to realise now that when I had been run down and lethargic a lot was through my own doing. This is how most of us grow up though, not that well educated on diet and not surprising given all the fast food advertisements that are constantly thrust upon us. If you do your homework you'll find out who owns most of the big fast food and drinks companies though, which is exactly why they can get away with what they put in them, mostly designed to make us ill. Not immediately mind you, but long term, the more you consume of them. It's a knock on effect, eat the food and you make the powers that be money, become ill and need medication, and once again you make the powers that be more money, it's a vicious circle, and I really do mean vicious. I am glad that more and more people are starting to realise this though and there are lots of petitions and lobbying to make changes, and I do hope they are successful.

I was evolving spiritually and mentally the more I worked with spirit and a lot of my attitudes started to change about things too. I was starting to see the bigger picture, not just around me but particularly with what was going on in the world. I had always thought a little differently from others but the more my spirit guides told me and the more I learned, the more I wanted to know and change things however I could. I was looking forward to the sanctuary being built and ready to teach, but I knew I wasn't going to do things like I had been taught back in the Temple of Truth. As much as I had enjoyed my time in the spiritual Church back then there was no real education to be gained from the weekly circles. I wanted people to not just know about the spirit world and their help and guidance, but to know how to use it all in many different ways. With this in mind, I started putting things together over the next few months in preparation for when the Spiritualhart sanctuary would finally be ready.

As summer approached a lady from the South of England contacted me and we struck up an online friendship. She was a medium and I enjoyed swapping stories with her and after a few weeks she told me she was deaf, and had been since she was born. My spirit guides gave me a kindly nudge when she divulged this information and she asked me if I could maybe help her, so I offered her some healing sessions to see if we could make a difference. The lady agreed to six healing sessions with me, one a week for an hour which was to be done through distant healing, due to the two hundred miles or so between us. I explained exactly what she had to do which was just to lay still for the duration of the healing, and only to move when it was over on the time we had mutually agreed. I had done many distant healings in the past but this one went a lot differently to normal and it was not what I was expecting, although it was fun.

As we started the first healing session the lady's spirit body presented itself on my healing table, and I was guided to start reaching inside her ears to remove the blockages there. I would be lying if I said I could see her body on my table because I couldn't. I am not a very visual person psychically and it's not often that I see things clearly. However, I do feel and sense energy which is why I knew she was with me, and obviously my spirit guides were directing my hand movements to remove whatever needed clearing. This happened over our first four sessions together and she was so impressed with what she had experienced and the results, she asked if she could write a short testimony for me.

Testimony

I have been having some wonderful absent healing from Dean and his spirit guides in the past couple of weeks, and I have got two more treatments to come in the next two weeks. I am a 34 year old lady who was born profoundly deaf and I asked Dean if he and his spirit guides could help me to hear, or give me a little improvement, as I don't expect miracles to happen to every individual on this planet, but it does happen on rare occasions.

I always believe in things as I was born gifted as a spiritual person and medium, and have been working with the spirit world since childhood. I love to help my friends and family and even strangers if they need me for a spiritual reading and some guidance. I would say it's powerful and very energetic when you're connected with the spirit world.

Since I have been having the treatments from Dean I have been amazed. When I woke up after the first hour of my treatment, my ears felt mentholated and scooped out, and my ears were buzzing with an amazing feeling to them. I put my hearing aids on and I had to turn the volume down as it was much too noisy. Every treatment since has shown a different improvement. My hearing aids have made it clearer for me and I am hearing things better all around me.

On several absent healing treatments I had a lot of different lights and effects, and I saw Dean's spirit guides bending over towards me. I felt my body was poked and prodded and it amazed me how he does it with his spirit guides? I would say Dean has got the most amazing gift in the world that I've ever experienced.

I really don't know what to say, unbelievable! He deserves an O.B.E seriously.

I thank you and your spirit guides so much Dean.

Love and Light

JH, Hastings, England

As JH rightly says it was quite an amazing few weeks we had treating her and working mainly on her hearing. What made these healing sessions even more special though was that we finished the six treatments just before Christmas, and it was the first time in her life that she had been able to hear her children's voices and their obvious excitement. Now that's what I call a Happy Christmas!

6

As we moved into a new year my spirit guides had told me I would be renewing a lot of old friendships and acquaintances, particularly from my school days. These mostly came through the internet and Facebook and although some of them couldn't understand what I was doing for a living, a lot of them did and they came to seek my help and see what I could possibly do for them. In January, a former senior school class mate (JL) contacted me asking if I could possibly help her. She confessed to not knowing anything about what I did but wanted to know if it could help her with her anxiety and panic attacks. She had suffered with them for many years and they were a huge hindrance to her life as they stopped her from attending social functions. Even going out for a meal with her family was too much of an ordeal.

I explained what I could try to do in detail and assured her there was nothing to fear, but not to expect too much in just one session as there was a lot of deep set issues that needed to be worked on. She agreed to have six sessions with me, one a week, to see where it took her. She was determined to rid herself of these episodes and wanted control of her life again.

I'd not seen JL for nearly twenty years and she had now become JH since her marriage. It was interesting getting to know her again as we shared what we had been doing since we last saw each other. She told me a lot about her attacks and I sympathised at how awkward her life had been and still was. It was a shame that many years had gone by and she'd had to miss out on a lot of things most people would take for granted, and I desperately wanted to change that for her. Our first session although good was not, as I had explained, going to rectify everything. But she enjoyed it and it helped her to be more relaxed for the next one. Over the weeks the improvements came and she even sent me a message on my mobile phone one week telling me she had gone out for a family meal with no panic or anxiety attacks. This was a massive achievement for her and I thanked my spirit guides for their help. A new way of living had started to take place for her and she, her husband and children started making Friday nights a family outing for their tea.

I had also given her a lot of advice through our weekly sessions including the use and benefits of crystals. She took all of what I said on board and started to utilise what I had taught and told her in her daily life going from strength to strength over the following weeks and months. So much so that when I eventually got the Spiritualhart sanctuary built and open, she began sitting in my psychic development classes, further enhancing her physical life with what she learnt each week, opening her eyes and mind as she became more and more spiritually awake.

Testimony

I knew Dean from school and had lost touch, as you do, however we were reacquainted 12 months ago. I didn't really understand what Dean did, but had checked out his website and was pleased life seemed to be working out for him. A few months later I was drawn back to his website and took another look and realised he might be able to help me. I have been a sufferer of panic and anxiety attacks for around 15 years. I have had counselling but had come to accept that they were a part of my life and I just had to live with them. After reading Dean's website I began to wonder if Reiki would be something that could work for me.

I am not a spiritual person per se, it intrigues me but I didn't know anything about it or understand it so I was very sceptical. However knowing Dean I felt I could trust him and after talking to him believed he could help me, and if not rid me completely of panic attacks then could make my life easier. I was very nervous and put my 100% trust in him and I have to say he never let me down.

I have to be honest the effect was not immediate for me, but still trusting Dean I persisted. I found the sessions really relaxing from the start. Dean is nothing but professional and explained exactly what would take place in detail, which made the whole experience less daunting. From the first session I could see the calming colours and swirls during the Reiki, and at the third session I experienced a blinding white light. Despite my eyes being closed I felt I should be wearing sunglasses it was that bright, it wasn't uncomfortable though quite the opposite. That happened a second time too and it was really comforting! Sounds bizarre I'm sure but it wasn't at the time. At times I could sense cobweb like feelings around my face, hot and cold sensations, and tingling throughout my body during the sessions, all of which were comforting too. It even felt like other hands were working on me too sometimes?

Slowly as the weeks passed I began to see small improvements and was able to face situations that would normally trigger attacks. I was less anxious in these situations, making them a more pleasant experience for me and my family, because unfortunately the attacks could impact on them too. When I did feel attacks coming on Dean taught me how to ease them using crystals and these have been a big help to me as well as the Reiki.

Accepting Reiki from Dean has certainly improved my life, I haven't had a panic attack for some time now and whilst I can still get anxious I have the tools, if you like, to help ease the symptoms. I am so grateful and thankful to Dean, his spirit guides and my spirit guides for helping me. I really had thought panic attacks were just a way of life for me but not anymore and long may it last. I wouldn't hesitate in recommending Dean's help to anyone, he and Susan are very welcoming into their home and sanctuary. In fact as soon as you walk into their home or sanctuary there is an air of calm that is relaxing, even before the Reiki begins.

Thank you again Dean.

JH, Hull, England

I started to take more attunements in order to help raise my energy and vibration further. These had also brought in a lot of new spirit guides for me to work with especially animal guides. Not just for healing people with but for my own protection too as I was doing more and more negative clearances of people and properties. I really loved all aspects of the work but I wasn't happy with some of the effects I was feeling when dealing with negative energy and in particular strong dark entities. I knew how to ground and protect myself to a degree, but I was still feeling the attacks from negativity. I was becoming more aware of negativity everywhere I went, and I never left my home without my Tiger and Bear spirit animal guides beside me. It was brilliant having these animal guides around me, not just to protect me or help me with my healing work, but also to talk to. Who as a child hadn't wished their dog or cat could talk? When I first met these spirit animal guides I must admit I was a bit apprehensive because my physical brain kicked in and I knew how powerful some were on our Earth and how they could harm me. These were spiritual animal guides though and meant only to keep me safe in my work.

I remember the first time I met my Bear spirit guide in a meditation. He was huge but gave off such a lovely energy to welcome me and put me at ease. I asked what I should call him and I laughed when he said, "Baloo". He knew that the Jungle Book was one of my all-time favourite films, so he made our meeting simple and friendly by using the name of the bear from the film, which was a funny and lovable character. I learnt also through meeting various spirit guides that they really aren't bothered if you know their names or not, they just want to help us. As humans we like to label things or give them titles, but in the spirit world this all seems quite irrelevant. Simplicity seems more their way and they don't over complicate things for us. Being of the physical nature though I and many others sometimes make it hard for ourselves.

This is why I say to my students when they come to the sanctuary to learn with me, "Leave your physical brain outside, it's useless in here". In order to achieve more when trying to work with the spirit world, you must move away from physical logical thinking or it will stifle you and your progression. We have to remember that our spirit guides are on a completely different vibration to us and can do a lot more things than we can ever imagine, and that these things on a physical level to us would seem impossible. However, nothing seems impossible in the spirit world which is why it constantly astounds me, and by learning with my spirit guides I think a lot differently to how I used to. This enables me to keep opening my mind and do the things I do. It has also helped me to know I can do more in the physical world too, as the knowledge that has been hidden from most of us as we conform to a learned, rigidly ruled life, is shared with us by the spirit world to make our lives better and easier.

If you think the governments and intelligence agencies around the world don't know about the spirit world you would be wrong. They have their own special branches or departments dealing with the paranormal, astral travel, remote viewing, telepathy and much more. Their purpose, unfortunately though, is not to use these wonderful gifts to help the world, only to help themselves. Power and greed is all they want to use this knowledge for. Spying and manipulation, and, of course "dumbing down" the population, so we don't know and learn about it all for a better way of living, that's paramount. This is not a book about politics though, so I won't take you any further down that road. Suffice to say that there is enough information out there particularly on the internet if you want to educate yourself and wake up to a more enlightened lifestyle.

As well as working with spirit animal guides I was also drawn into the ancient world of Atlantis. I had always been interested in this ancient lost City and when my Atlantis guide Senistoom made himself known to me, it started to make sense that Atlantis was a lost reality, and not a myth. Apparently I also had a past life link with Atlantis, and so this prompted me to take the Atlantean & Gaia trilogy attunements to strengthen my connection both on a communicative level and a healing level. The Atlanteans were very much into their healing using crystals, so this also struck a chord with me as I used them a lot in my own healing work.

Crystals carry amazing energy and can be used for lots of different problems and ailments, whether mental, emotional or physical. Unfortunately though, in our ignorance, we mine the Earth for them, blowing the crystal caves and caverns up, traumatising them and weakening their energy, which in turn actually weakens the planet if you think about it. This is usually to make jewellery and money and most people have no idea of the importance of the crystals they may be wearing. Some crystals though do make it to shops and can be bought as healing aids which can be helpful, but it's not exactly the best way to utilise their energies.

Crystals grow in the ground for a reason, because they are meant to be there. They heal our planet and help it to grow so by constantly removing them from Mother Earth we make it tougher for her. Science has proved that Earth is living, breathing and functioning in a similar way to how we do, so by destroying her from the inside and taking away some of her essential needs, it's like taking away some of her vital organs. It would not make sense would it, if we removed vital organs from a human body as they would surely die the more you removed. You don't have to be a rocket scientist to do the math here do you, just think about it?

Crystal caves and caverns can and should be used in the right way, by going down into them to receive the healing energies, not by blowing them up for tiny coin size trinkets. I suppose this would not make anyone rich though would it? Imagine how nice it would be though to travel down into a beautiful crystal cave hospital, where the walls, ceiling and floor permanently healed you and aided recovery freely, naturally and quickly. This is not to say that doctors and nurses would not be needed, that would be a foolish suggestion. But patients would benefit so much more through the natural healing process with crystal energy if we only used them properly. Yes I do know some of the crystal energies in the Earth would be far too strong for us to go near for long, but given the scientific technology today, we could get near enough to be healed sufficiently.

So too would the doctors and nurses working there benefit as the environment would be a lot more positive, lowering stress and emotional levels for them. Most if not all viruses, diseases, aches and pains could be quickly dealt with in the various crystal rooms we could make available, and broken limbs would heal a lot faster.

Crystals are a natural resource not only to help the Earth but to help us, but we are not utilising their benefits properly. Instead we are just trying to profit from them, missing the bigger picture while the damage we are causing the planet gets neglected. Understanding this I decided I needed to bury my crystals and give them back to Mother Earth. I had enjoyed working with them but there had to be another way to enhance my healings and help people. Consulting with my spirit guides I started to work on some new ideas, or rather they gave me them through my meditations and day dreams.

I started working with ordinary pebbles from the beach and my garden. Nice, natural and available stones. I cleaned them all thoroughly first then consecrated them, as I do with everything I work with for a higher, positive purpose. I then set about channelling energy into them using Reiki with the Cho Ku Rei (power), and Sei He Ki (mental/emotional) symbols. This felt to me just like a healing session, but my intention was different It was not to heal the stones, it was to create the stones as Reiki healing channels. I hadn't told anyone what I planned on doing so when I gave them out to a few friends to try they looked at me as if I was a bit odd, until they tried them.

I told them how to use the stones and asked them to experiment with them for me.

The Cho Ku Rei symbol I said could be used for meditation by simply placing the stone on either the crown or brow (Third eye) chakra, or just holding it in their hand allowing its energy to flow, bringing them a closer connection to the spirit world. It could also be used for healing by placing the stone on any area of pain they had and asking for its healing energies to bring relief. Placing the stone under their pillow may bring them a better night's sleep and they may find they wake up feeling more refreshed. They could also place the stone in their bath for a more relaxing soak as it healed their aches and pains.

The Sei He Ki stone I told them could be meditated on the same as the Cho Ku Rei stone, but it would concentrate more on emotional and mental issues. It could also be used to heal their emotions when stressed, depressed or suffering anxiety or panic attacks, just by holding the stone or focusing on it, imagining their woes flowing from them. Quizzical they were, but here's what three people said after using them.

Testimony

Staggering results from Dean's healing stones, absolutely awesome, I can't recommend this form of energy contact enough. I can say with my hand on my heart that I believe in the energy that Dean, with the help of his spirit guides, has infused into these stones.

After suffering a fractured spine and having to live with daily pain and painkillers, I have been pain free since my morning meditation with the stone. I'm assured by Dean that I can use the stone again when necessary at my will. Pain aside, I also took an astounding personal meditation journey and met with spirit guides who responded to a particular request of mine, which totally blew me away!

Thanks Dean for your thoughtfulness, and I hope you can reach out to many others who may benefit from the meditation and healing stones.

LB, Selsey, England

Testimony

Let's just say that the stones have blown me away, almost literally! I love them the energy is awesome, really powerful. I have been in a vortex of energy, all good and profound experiences have abounded. As I have mentioned to you my energy was everywhere and I felt the dreadful vertigo I had been experiencing recently was part of some major shift in Earth energies. I am used to the dizzy lightheaded feelings connected with my postural hypotension, but this was a whole new horrible feeling. It only started recently and was so bad that even turning over in bed caused the whole world to spin in huge slow circles.

When your Reiki stones arrived I welcomed them and sat with them in the afternoon. They had a gentle effervescent energy coming off them, yet a laser like beam of focused energy too. That night I slept with them and had the best nights sleep for months and months, this from a fully paid up member of the professional insomniacs club is something in itself.

I had become wary of getting up in the mornings due to the vertigo, so gingerly I raised my head a little, nothing happened, so I propped myself up on my elbow, again nothing happened, so I sat on the edge of the bed with my head as low as I could keep it, nothing? BETTER! No dizziness, then or since. I have also seen significant changes with my psychic and clairvoyant abilities and have now the chance to further them to help others. Thank you seems a little underwhelming but it is from the heart, brightest blessings.

Namaste Dean and thank you for being part of my healing journey xxx

KO, Perth, Scotland

Testimony

A few days ago I received a set of Reiki healing and meditation stones from Dean. I took them home and opened them and I was not ready for what happened. I have heard first hand stories about the power and energy of these stones but these were from people who are far more aware of energies and the spirit world than I. Although I have been attuned to Reiki and I see shapes and colours and sometimes feel a presence during healing sessions, I expect nothing and I am thankful for everything.

I opened the stones and as I stood there with the one with the power symbol on in my hand I felt what can only be described as a rush. It was as if a gust of wind had shot down the corridor and into my body, and the temperature dropped dramatically all around me. The only way I can put this is it is like when people say someone has stepped over their grave, only a lot more intense. It was awesome to think someone like me could feel this wonderful energy surge through them, truly magical.

I decided to do a self healing and placed the stones around me. I laid there taking deep breaths and did my grounding, then called upon my Angels and spirit guides to assist and protect me during the healing. Then respectfully, I asked for the energy to flow and straight away I felt someone stroking my feet and felt a presence surrounding me. I asked if my spirit guide could come up to my shoulder as I always imagine them at my feet, I don't know why, it's always been that way. I felt someone put their arm under my pillow and gently lift my head as though to make it more comfortable. I just laid there eyes closed saying thank you, thank you, as I went on to see some pleasing images, then when the healing was over I was so relaxed you could have poured me through a tea strainer.

I just want to thank a special person for bringing Reiki into my life, they know who they are, and I want to thank Dean for getting my head in a far better place than it was six months ago. I have always said I have only ever respected two men in my life, my father and grandfather, now there is a third and that's Dean Kingett. I respect his total dedication to what he believes in and I respect his desire to spread the goodness of Reiki as far as he possibly can. You have my respect and friendship for as long as I am here Dean.

TB, Hull, England

The Reiki stones proved a great success and I started creating more and more of them with lots of various spirit guides. This was to give people more of a choice of energy that they could relate to, and also to further open their minds. I am not a religious person, it's not for me, but neither do I knock anyone who is. So when I created the Jesus, Buddha, Ganesh and Angel stones, they were accepted by followers of different faiths which meant I could reach and help them all.

As well as creating all of the new healing and meditation stones, I found I could also channel any crystal energy into a stone. This really impressed me as there was now no need for me to purchase crystals that had been mined from and disturbed Mother Earth. I could just create my own to help people and so I did, lots of them, and I still do. I also found that the crystal stones I created are better than the ones that had come out of the Earth. This is because they are ethereal and untainted, and they don't need to be cleansed or charged either, which is another bonus to them as they will not take on negative energy.

All of these new stone creations I would take to the various psychic fairs, mind, body & spirit events or markets that we had started to attend. They got a lot of funny looks at first but when I put them in people's hands to try they were quite surprised at what they could sense and see in their minds eye with them. I could even create them there and then for people if I didn't have a crystal stone ready made for their particular symptom, helping people on a wider, yet more personal scale. I loved the learning and knowledge my spirit guides kept presenting me. It was and still is addictive learning as my vibration level continues to rise and I continue to expand my mind.

7

One of the questions I get asked the most is how can you do what you do and not advocate religion? The simple answer is because my spirit guides and helpers are from many different religious backgrounds as we know them on this Earth, but they are only interested in helping everyone, no matter what race or religion they are, through love. I feel exactly the same way as these spiritual guides and helpers do, which is why I try my best to help everyone I can. I would never turn anyone away from my sanctuary because of their religious beliefs or race, I just want to help them all.

Religion for me is far too hand in glove with politics and it seems more about greed and gain than helping people today because it is big business. To single one out you only have to look at the Vatican and all the billions it has to understand this fact. Why is it that the donated money is not all being put to good use? After all, isn't that what it's supposed to be for? A lot of that money donated freely by people from all over the world is not being used to help others as it should be. It is just making more money for the Church in the name of religion as they invest it in various banks and businesses, a fact that is well documented but allowed to continue.

You only have to look through history to see the problems religion has caused throughout the years as has politics, forcing people to fight and kill in the name of God. Isn't God a creator? At least that's what religion has us believe in their text books, so why would the Divine want us to kill each other? The Divine doesn't, but religion and politics do. It makes them bigger, and it makes them richer, and that and unfortunately not our lives are what are most important to those who head them. Religion and history has constantly been changed in order to make us feel some sort of allegiance and patriotism worth fighting for. It's despicable, but our indoctrination from childhood and throughout our lives makes most people conform to the untruths they are taught to think. Forcing many innocent people to kill in the world wars horrifies me, and the wars that are happening today do too. People don't want these wars, greedy politicians and the elite families and money men who pull the political and religious strings do.

Unfortunately we are taught that a certain way of living is right and most people accept and conform to it without questioning, even if they know or feel it is wrong, because they fear being different or ridiculed. I questioned religion when I was twelve years old because what I was being taught in school didn't sit right with me, so I quizzed my Dad who helped me to open my mind when he told me about the spirit world. My beliefs are reality to me, because I am witnessing all that I do on a daily basis, as are many others. I certainly don't know it all though. I don't think I ever will. But I do know a lot more than the powers that be want me too.

Not to knock anyone's belief system here but I find it quite odd that people can put their entire beliefs into events they have never seen or heard for themselves. The knowledge of religion has obviously been passed down through the years but it has also been amended and rewritten many times. It's been a bit like Chinese whispers. You started off with the truth then ten people down the line the story starts to change, maybe not much, but by the time you get to the hundredth person it's changed a lot, and so on as it goes down the years. So how can you be sure that what is preached today is the original story?

I have studied the Bible and Christianity and have read up on Buddhism, Hinduism, Judaism and many more through my life. I am honoured that a lot of the people written about in these books work with me on a spiritual level, which is also why I consider myself non-religious.

8

One day my good friend Nelly Moon contacted me about someone she was healing and trying to help, but unfortunately she didn't seem to be progressing much. Nelly is an amazing lady and some of her nightly journeys on the astral plane that she has shared with me are nothing less than totally mind blowing. She has a wonderful Navajo spirit guide she calls Grandfather and I'm pleased to say he likes me and what I try to do to help others. I found this out when Nelly was suffering from some pain and I offered to heal her to try to alleviate it. She told me Grandfather didn't permit others to heal her, she said he would just stand in front of her with his hand up stopping the healing energies coming through to her. I had not heard of this happening before so I asked if she would still like me to try and really hoped that she would. She agreed, but she wasn't expecting anything. To her surprise and my joy, Grandfather let my healing energies through bringing her the relief she needed. I still to this day don't know why Grandfather lets me heal Nelly but not others but I'm glad he does and I thanked him for doing so.

Anyway, the woman Nelly had been healing was suffering very badly from depression and had been for a number of years, this was also causing her to hate herself and her life in general. She was also very anxious and suffered headaches from all the confusion in her head and panic attacks too. She was agoraphobic and couldn't go out the house much and she had no interest at all in her family life, she was that low. Nelly was growing increasingly concerned for her welfare through their sessions together, and when she explained all the symptoms to me I told her that the woman was carrying too much negativity and that it was more than likely repelling the healing energy.

This brought up our usual debate about negativity which Nelly doesn't believe in, that's not just her human mind thinking either, Grandfather has told her it doesn't. I am not one to go against what our spirit guides tell us as they know far more than we do, but I'd been getting rid of negative energy and entities from people and places for quite a while, enough to know that it did indeed exist, and could be quite nasty to get rid of too. I offered my help to Nelly and told her that I would do a negative clearing session on the woman concerned to remove anything that was causing the problems. I also said that I would give her four healing sessions after to help her heal and hopefully get her life going in the right direction again. Nelly said she would inform her and try to convince her to have these sessions with me. She didn't believe in this negative part of my healing work but she knew I would try my best to help this woman's sorry plight.

I was happy when the lady agreed and made contact with me introducing herself as LC. I got some bad feelings when conversing with her but not about her, it was what was attached to her, the negativity that was causing her all the problems. I could sense the darkness around her and it wasn't very nice, as I explained what I wanted her to do, and what I was going to do to try and remove it to help her. Talking to her I realised just how down she was, she couldn't have been any lower, the negativity had taken its toll and she had given up. I hoped desperately that my spirit guides could remove it and help her, and I had every faith that they could. I can't remember how soon we did this after our conversation but we set up a mutual time and date to do it quickly, as I did not want the negativity to make her change her mind and pull out. I have found through my work that negativity is a kind of controller, so even if a person knows exactly what is best for them, they will more than likely do the opposite, making them suffer more in some way especially if they are trying to do something positive to help themselves.

That sounds quite bizarre but that's how negative energy works. It preys on our weaknesses like depression, fear, anger, worry and all the things that upset us the most, mentally and emotionally. It drains our life energy so we can't be bothered to do anything positive for ourselves, making us weak, lethargic and gullible, and that's exactly what it had been doing to LC for a long, long time.

I explained to her that she could have someone present with her during the clearing and the healing, that it wouldn't be a problem and I hoped it would help reassure her and make sure she went through with it. As I was doing this distantly it would make no difference to me. I was simply going to astral travel to her at the agreed time and do what I and my spirit guides needed to do, in the hope of removing all that was draining her and stopping her from moving on in life. I asked LC to drink plenty of water beforehand as part of the work I was going to do would start a detoxifying of her body, and plenty of water would help her to detoxify quicker after it was over.

On the agreed day I told her to lie down on her bed approximately fifteen minutes before the clearing was due to start, to enable her to slow her breathing down, relax and imagine she was in a safe place, somewhere she felt comfortable and secure. I asked her to tell whoever she may have with her that she may act in a strange manner throughout the clearing, and that she may feel as if she wanted to get up off the bed, but that she must not do so. It was very important that she stay on the bed until it was all over. I told her she may experience involuntary movements and want to leave the room too, but again she must refrain from doing so. Also that she may feel strange sensations within and around her body, which was perfectly normal and she should not worry about them. She may feel as if something or someone were touching her throughout the session too, and that this again was perfectly normal to sense or feel, it would just be me or my spirit guides working around her. Her main focus was at all times to try to keep thinking positive thoughts and ask her own spirit guides for the negative energy to be removed from her.

After the clearing was done I told her I would continue straight on with a full healing session, as the negative removal could often cause energy damage which would need repairing. This is because negativity doesn't want to leave a person's body, and it can knock the chakras out of balance and rip and tear a person's aura as it is removed. This cannot be felt as physical pain by the person, but if not repaired it can take them a long time to recover and leave them feeling a bit out of sorts with themselves, as well as leaving them a little vulnerable to any illnesses.

LC understood all I told her and to her credit despite how down she was, I genuinely knew she wanted this to work for her, and I was sure it would. I also said she was going to have to be strong, as this could be quite an emotional ride for her, but once it was removed and over, she would feel like a huge weight had been lifted. If she needed to cry throughout the session then I told her to just go for it and let them flow. Tears were not a sign of weakness, they were just a sign of release and she so needed one. If only men would learn to cry, they would learn to release so much of the anger, hatred and frustration that burdens them, instead of wanting to punch the living daylights of someone or something, which usually results in the further burden of regret or guilt. The feminine side is in all of us for a reason, as is the masculine, and women in general utilise tears well. So do some men, but not most. They really should learn to cry when needed.

So we were all set and ready to do it. LC knew what she had to do and so did I. I prepared myself on the day in my sanctuary, as usual, protecting myself fully with my spiritual armour and grounding myself. Some people think I'm really over the top when it comes to protecting and grounding myself but I'd rather be safe than sorry, so I take no chances. In my early days working against negative energy and entities I suffered some awful sensations, dizziness, headaches, stomach pains, nausea etc. They were not nice feelings I experienced but I had to learn, and I'm pleased to say I did. I feel little, if any, effect from anything negative nowadays and I don't mess about with it. I do the job, get rid of it as quick as I can and then heal the damage it has caused to a person or raise the energy and protect the property I'm working on.

As I sat in my sanctuary I could feel the warm and cool breezes of spirit energy building up around me, as I prepared to leave my physical body for a while and astral travel to LC's home. This sounds dramatic, but for me it isn't, it's just something that I've learned to do to help people. I arrived at LC's home in a second as there is no time or space when working with the spirit world and my physical body back in the sanctuary could feel the negativity as I arrived. It's a bit like when you walk into a room and you could cut the atmosphere with a knife, that's bad energy, that's negativity. We've all felt it at some point in our life. Just most people don't know what it is, but they do know they don't like the feel of it and usually want to vacate the room.

What I have learned through my work with the spirit world and listening to fellow light workers experiences of their work, is that we all have our own way of doing it, similar, but different. There is no right or wrong, there is just our own unique way and how we feel comfortable and are guided to do things. I am going to share how I do things with you here not as an absolute, but how it feels right to me and helps me focus, nothing more. I knew my spirit body was with LC but I was not really aware of what it was doing and as I have mentioned I am not a very visual person. Remote viewing is not a strength that I have. This is not a hindrance though as I have one hundred percent trust in my spirit guides and helpers to do whatever is required. So, as my spirit body or energy is away on the astral plane I use my physical body in the sanctuary to tune in to what's happening.

I work on my healing table as if the person is actually there with me placing my hands on various parts of their body to heal it or remove any blockages. As this was a negative clearance on LC I started at her feet first, filling her body with pure positive love, light and energy as it flowed through me and into her body. This helps to force the negativity out of a person though it does take time depending how strong it is. As her body filled up with this positive energy the negative energy started to move up her body to distance itself from me. Negativity does not want to leave the person's physical body and won't go without a fight, but as much as it was trying to move away from me, it was also determined to stay.

I started to work up her legs constantly filling her with positive energy and as I did I could feel the pressure in my head as the negativity tried to attack and thwart me. I had been in this position many times before though and as it attempted to cause me head pain, I knew I was well protected and it wouldn't succeed. My spirit guides were just letting me know it was there and that was all they would allow me to feel, just the energy presence until we had removed it all. I had got used to working this way with my spirit guides now. Just because I wasn't visual, didn't mean I couldn't sense and feel things and use my intuition.

In my experience of working with negativity within the physical body, it tends to cling to the seven major chakra areas, probably in an attempt to shut them down I suppose. Again my spirit guides made me aware on my body where the problems were on LC's as we continued to work up her body together. This is where using my ethereal hands comes in as I started to reach inside LC's spirit body on my healing table to remove the negativity bit by bit. I cannot do any damage to the physical body when I do this because we are just working with the energy of the person, but it is effective and negativity doesn't like me doing it one bit. The more negativity that was removed from various places, the weaker it became and fifty or so minutes later the pressure in my own head disappeared and I knew it was all gone from LC's body. This to me is a fantastic way of working without having to be with the person physically. It means just by focusing my intent and my desire of what I wish to do, it will be done, and I can sense the outcome as it happens with the help of my intuition and spirit guides.

The negativity was all gone but it had caused damage to the chakras and her aura which we had to now repair. We also had to work on her mind to help her out of her depressive decline. Negativity had no hold on her now which meant she could start to function properly again, but this can take time with a lot of people who have suffered depression for a long period, especially years, as they have unfortunately got used to the rut they have got into. I had promised four healing sessions to LC to give her a good chance to turn things around and get her life moving in the right direction again, and it started with this first one, straight after the negative removal.

Again my spirit energy left my physical body to be with LC and just like the clearing I worked around my healing table as if her actual body was with me. As I mentioned earlier my main spirit guide is Ben Black Elk and I like to use some of the old Indian tools out of respect in some of my healings, particularly my Shamanic rattle. I shook the rattle over her body and up and down it for several minutes as my spirit guides and helpers repaired LC's aura. They started filling it with beautiful colours and energy and this helped it to expand outwards around her to exactly where it needed to be. When that was done I placed ethereal crystals inside each one of her main chakra's to bring them back into balance and align her body, and I could feel the healing energy had started to flow through me as we spent the next fifty minutes doing everything we could to help repair, restore and reconstruct her.

After this first negative clearing and healing session the improvement in LC was quite astonishing, and over the next three weeks and three more healing sessions you would never have thought there had been anything wrong with her such was the change in personality. This agoraphobic lady was now going outside and taking the children to school each day. She had started exercising, swimming, playing with the kids and having fun again. No more were the days spent in her pyjamas wallowing in self pity at the deepest depths of depression. LC was back and full of life again. The speed of the change was amazing, even the daily headaches had disappeared. I was elated at what my spirit guides had done for her as it is, as always all their work, not mine. I am merely the channel for them to work through, and that is a joy to be. Here's what LC had to say about her experience.

<u>Testimony</u>

I want to say thank you for giving me back my life. For as long as I can remember I have been full of despair and hatred for myself. I was diagnosed with depression and social anxiety about eleven years ago and was put on medication and had the usual therapy, but this only treated the symptoms and didn't really deal with the cause at all.

My childhood was awful and I had huge issues with my father, this was affecting me so much that I was unable to let go of the past and lead a normal life. I became a virtual prisoner in my own home, trapped inside my own chaotic mind. This was affecting not only me but my husband and children too. To be honest I really thought that this was going to be how I would live the rest of my life and that was a very bleak prospect. I was saved though by a very kind man who could see something in me that I failed to see in myself, Dean.

The very first healing I received was amazing. I could feel all the negative energy being pulled from my temples and the weight lifted off my mind. Over the course of the four healings I received I continued to feel more like the person I knew was inside of me. The headaches that had been a constant daily battle were no more. I haven't had a stress headache now for weeks and I feel fantastic. Even when I was faced with a recent event meeting lots of new people I was able to maintain my panic, something that has eluded me for so many years.

At the start of my healing I admit to being very sceptical and doubted I would see any changes, but I cannot believe the difference I feel. I am able to move on from the past, I feel in control of my life and I am ready to give something back to the world. My life was saved by the most humble and generous man I have ever had the pleasure of knowing. I don't think I could ever find the words to thank Dean enough for what he has done for me.

LC, Nottingham, England

I have had many cases like LC's and it is amazing the change that can happen so fast with people once the negativity is removed from them or their environment. My good friend Nelly was obviously happy at the sudden turn around too, and as we discussed it I came to the conclusion that our spirit guides must just want us to learn and understand certain things, but not others.

Negativity is very real to me, but not to Nelly. That doesn't make either of us right or wrong though. It simply means that on our respective paths on this Earth plane we have different experiences to encounter and understand, and we are happy with that knowledge in our minds now although it did frustrate us for a while. This understanding has helped to open my mind more too as I do not dismiss out of hand what others in my profession tell me. They are all walking their own paths so what is common knowledge to some, doesn't always apply to others. I'm learning and growing all the time, always have been, so to disregard information as nonsense would be foolish. After all, some of the things I do now I would have found to be unbelievable ten, fifteen and twenty years ago, so who knows what's to come? It's why I love what I do. It changes all the time and it constantly fascinates me.

Something I definitely never thought would happen one day did, when I agreed to give a rescue dog a home. I am an animal lover, always have been and through the various charity donations Spiritualhart has made we have adopted many Tigers to help the species survive and we also regularly support the Hessle Dog Rescue Service. I never actually wanted a dog in the home though, as I felt it too unkind to leave a dog alone all day whilst everyone else was out at work and school. But as I was working from home now this wasn't an issue and I didn't need to feel guilty. Still, I shocked the family when I said we had to have Jade, a pure bred Bearded Collie. This wasn't just a physical wanting though, my intuition was playing its part, there was just something about this dog and I needed to give her a good home.

Jade was incredibly timid, the slightest unexpected noise and she would lay down cowering as if in trouble. She had been shaved completely which as a long haired Bearded Collie is not a good or natural look for them. Added to that she was eight kilograms underweight and shockingly you could see all her ribs along her body. The first three days we had her she hardly even slept, she was so wary of the environment which was to be her new home. We bought her lots of toys but she had no idea what to do with them other than a tennis ball, which soon became her favourite and I've lost count of how many she's gone through. We weren't sure how old she was when we got her but the vets decided she was probably between six and eight years old.

We soon got her weight up and her coat grew back as she transformed from the freakiest looking animal into an adorable best friend. Everybody loved her and fussed her and it was great to see Jade adapt to her new life so quickly. I've no idea what she'd been through in the past other than she was used to herd up horses instead of sheep, and this became quite relevant when taking her for walks as whenever we passed a field with horses in, she used to set herself down watching them waiting for a command to stalk and herd them up. It was quite funny to see how intensely she would watch them and I presume she must have been very good at it.

It was quite clear from the off to everyone that Jade was my dog as she was always near me and would follow me around the house more or less every time I moved. It was more than that though, animals are very perceptive and I knew she felt safe in my energy. It wasn't long either before I started noticing Jade's head following unseen things going across the room, and as I followed her gaze I would see spiritual energy or lights and know that someone was with us. This made me smile as the dog was probably more psychically aware than I was. My friend Nelly had also told me that Jade needed to find me, and that we would have a special connection. She wasn't kidding and I found that out in the most delightful way.

As we moved into our new home it was not quite ready but the internal work was nearing its end, and I was in on my own with one of the joiners one day who was laying the laminate flooring in the games room. He asked me to give him a hand moving the pool table and I really should have said no, due to my back problem, but the stupid, helpful side of me said yes instead, which wasn't to be a good idea. As we lifted the table together not only did my back go as I collapsed in a heap on the floor, because of the awkward way I'd tried to lift it to take the weight off my back, I'd also (I later found out at the doctors), pulled and ripped my chest muscles. I could hardly catch my breath and I couldn't expand my chest due to the pain so my breathing became very short and fast which very much worried the joiner. He helped me up though and slightly embarrassed I said I was alright and that I would just go and lie down for a bit. I slowly made my way upstairs and into the bedroom where luckily we have one of those electric beds, so I started to raise the bed with the remote so I could get on it, as I would never have been able to lie down flat. With that I heard Jade clambering up the stairs after me, no doubt wondering where I had gone to. I eased myself very delicately onto the bed and managed to get my legs up, and as I lay there rather pathetically still breathing short and fast and in a lot of pain, an incredible thing happened.

My left hand was down by my side at the edge of the bed and Jade started licking it. This was not unusual. We had discovered that Jade was affectionate to us all with her big happy licks, but I wasn't really in the mood for it then. I just wanted to be left alone so I could start self healing and hopefully reduce the pain in my chest. I was about to move my hand away from her when I suddenly felt strange yet familiar sensations moving through my hand and up my arm. I couldn't believe what I was feeling. Was this actually healing energy coming up my arm from Jade? It certainly was and not only was it coming up my arm, it started to spread across my chest. I was quite dumbstruck as I lay there feeling this energy so I let her continue despite my now wet and sloppy hand.

I cant remember quite how long she continued licking my hand for but at a rough guess I would say about seven or eight minutes, which is quite a lot of licking time. When she finally finished she did something else that amazed me. She turned away and started coughing and all the pain she had took from me came out of her mouth as bad energy, then she just sat looking at me wagging her tail as if awaiting approval. This was unbelievably brilliant. My own dog a healer like me, wow, how cool was that? No wonder Nelly had said we would have a special connection. Through all the licking I hadn't really noticed but my breathing had slowed down and returned to a normal rhythm. The pain had subsided too and although I couldn't take massive deep breathes yet, I could breathe deeper and I sat up without too much effort, thanking and fussing Jade.

Since then Jade comes with me everyday into the sanctuary as I set it up for the days healing and teaching work. She has a good look around upon entering as always and I know she can sense and see the spirit guides waiting to work with me, then she settles down and as I usually start my day sending out distant healing to all upon my free healing list, (which Jade is on too). She takes her own healing energy in, and promptly falls into a blissful slumber.

Jade hasn't just healed me though she has also done group healing sessions on some of my psychic development students. When I told them Jade would be healing them to start our classes instead of me, it drew some laughs at first as they thought I was joking. They were soon left amazed though by Jades ability as she healed both my Wednesday night and Thursday classes one week. When people come to visit our home Jade knows if they need healing or not. She doesn't fuss people or want stroking when visitors arrive, but if she senses they're not well in some way, either physically, emotionally or mentally she will go to them and as soon as they try to stroke her she goes straight into licking mode to heal them. As you can imagine, not everyone understands or likes this, but those who do get the healing she gives them. Sometimes she will do exactly the same as when she healed me, coughing up the bad stuff as she finishes healing them.

It was a big moment for me when the Spiritualhart sanctuary was finally ready and open, and it saw my first ever students start in my weekly Thursday psychic development class. It was an exciting time but I was very nervous as I had not ever envisioned myself as a teacher. In fact I still don't class myself as one, I just know stuff and I like to share it to help people. I had vowed though not to teach how I had been taught, not that I was taught wrongly, it's just I wanted to give my students more freedom to expand their minds and open their eyes, I also wanted to keep religion out of their thinking so it didn't restrict or prejudice them. These first students were from different areas of Hessle and Hull and their ages ranged from early twenties to late fifties. It was a nice mixed group and one that had taken a few months to put together. All the students had been hand picked and invited, but not by me by Ben Black Elk, my spirit guide, and it soon became apparent why.

Ben wanted me to bring the Sioux tribe back together. I didn't really understand what he meant at first by this but as the students developed in the weekly class, it soon came to light that they all had Native American Indian spirit guides. Even to this day Ben gives the nod to who can and who cannot sit in my development classes. This doesn't mean people are not good enough to sit in my classes, it usually just means they are not ready to accept my teaching yet, or they may have a different path to follow which they would be best finding or following elsewhere. Some people do get offended by this but I don't make the rules, it's just how it is and when they start complaining about it, it kind of proves a point of why Ben doesn't want them in the class. My classes are not just for those with Native American Indian spirit guides though as I have Pagan and Wiccan students too. As I said earlier, neither my spirit guide's or myself entertain prejudice or negativity, it's not welcome in my sanctuary.

Anger is negative too and that's not welcome in my sanctuary either. It can lower the vibration and one negative person in a group can affect all, and that's not something I wish to let happen. My students are not perfect, they all have their own issues and problems like everyone else, that's life, but in my classes they get to work through them positively, and that apparently is what Ben and my spirit guides want me to help them with and teach them. So why don't I help the others you may be thinking? I try to. I offer alternative workshops which some of them take part in, and usually when they've learnt a thing or two, Ben will give me the nod and they will be welcomed into a psychic development class to further help them move forward and develop their awareness and abilities. It's a bit of a process I suppose as people are at different levels and at different phases of their lives. Helping them in this way though helps not to hinder the regular class members, until they reach a similar understanding, enough to join them.

This first psychic development class was soon to be joined by a second one only two months later on Tuesday afternoons. The sanctuary was in full swing and we'd only just opened, but it was all happening just like my spirit guides had said it would and it was starting to draw people's attention.

10

I also at this time got chatting to an American lady called Angie Anderson via a mutual friend and she eventually asked me to do some distant healing work with her, which we set up a mutual date and time for to do it. Here she explain in her own words why. –

"I had already studied and utilised alternative healing modalities for many years when I met Dean on an online forum on healing. My interest in alternative therapies initially came from a desire to heal myself, due to chronic health issues, so when we met and I learned of what he was doing, I was immediately interested in giving it a go."

"I have to admit I was a bit nervous about long distance healing, but certainly willing to give it a try. We agreed to one session, to see how it went first, and then I would continue on if I found any encouraging results. Dean was very open about exactly what he does and why and what I may expect during the healing session. While the initial session wasn't Earth shattering, I felt significantly different the following couple of days, so I updated him with how I was feeling and asked to continue with further sessions. The next several sessions however were really quite remarkable."

"With each session I found I felt a stronger connection to Dean and the work he was doing. I felt strong visceral reactions to his work, which ranged from peaceful to euphoric. To this day I am not sure how exactly it works at such a long distance, but I absolutely now know that it does."

"We also had a session of intuitive training that really blew my mind. Dean quickly and easily guided me through some exercises to tap and explore my own intuitive capabilities via the internet and the results were really quite astounding."

This was great distance work done with my American friend, and not just the healing but teaching her too. Living across the Atlantic Ocean over five thousand miles away in California meant nothing as energy has no boundaries, and just my will, intent and my spirit guides help meant she could receive all that I sent her, seeing and feeling the results after each treatment.

This may sound a bit grandiose but its not. As most other healers will tell you, everyone has the capability to do it, they just don't know how or believe they can. I have done many different healings, negative removals, soul rescue's and teaching work through the internet in many different countries throughout the world, and it is really wonderful to hear the feedback and positive results that people experience. Angie was no exception to these experiences and after a few persuasive conversations she talked me into an interview on her internet radio show, as she explains here –

"I decided after my healing sessions and brief intuitive work with Dean that I would like to interview him for my internet radio show – Life improvement."

"Dean told me that he had declined radio interviews before, because he was uncomfortable with such blatant promotion. He prefers promotion of his work through doing the work, and he likes the credit to go to his many spirit guides for the results achieved, and not himself. As he says, he's just a channel for spirit to work through in order to heal and help people, nothing more, he's happy and honoured to be a part of that."

"I explained to him by doing the show he may reach more people who need help, so with this in mind, he finally agreed! I was excited to share his gift with our listeners, as I believe he works as a powerful conduit between this world and the world of spirit. My co-host, Cat and I hosted a fascinating hour long interview with Dean via Skype. Every conversation I have ever had with Dean, public or private, has always been fascinating, illuminating and inspiring.

"I've watched Dean through the years, as his ongoing research and experimentation has helped him refine his gift into a truly, as I see, fail proof healing system that helps folk on many levels, depending on their needs?"

"Dean has become a friend through the years, but most of all, someone I respect highly as an intuitive healer and an overall truly caring and honest man. He has old-fashioned values of integrity and an unrelenting passion for helping others."

The radio show was very nerve wracking for me, but I did enjoy it I must admit. To date though I have not done another one and I do not want to as yet, despite having a few offers. I still get stage fright when I do my psychic demonstrations and even though I couldn't see the radio show listeners, just knowing that people were out there at the end of the airwaves was enough to jangle the nerves. When I listened to the show after I didn't even think it sounded like me, and if you ever hear the live recording, you can tell in my voice just how nervous I was. All in all though I didn't think I did too bad, and true to her word Angie was not interviewing me to interrogate me, but to give me a chance to speak about some of the things I do, or at least some of the things I did back then, as I do even more now.

You can read the interview conversation at the end of this book (Appendix 1).

11

Around the same time of the radio interview I had a very profound spiritual experience that I'd like to share with you now. I couldn't sleep one night as I couldn't get comfortable because of my back pain, so after tossing and turning I decided to self heal. I called upon all my spirit guides and the Reiki energy started to flow through me for about thirty minutes, after which I thanked them as always. The pain had subsided which was a good thing but I found myself wide awake now, so I decided to ask the Angels for some help.

I called upon Archangel Michael, Gabriel, Zadkiel and Purah to help me to sleep, bring me peace and calm, visit me in my dream state and help me to remember it all (I have a very poor memory). I must have dropped off but awoke abruptly as a wave of energy ran over and through my body. I was quite startled having been awoken like this and my heart was racing and I felt a bit anxious, so I quickly called upon my spirit guide Ben Black Elk to be with me. I never saw Ben wholly but an Indian head dress came into view and I was calmed immediately. I thanked him and as I did another spirit guide, Dr Usui stood right before me and I could see him as clear as I would see anyone. Again I wasn't expecting this and it made me jump, and with that he promptly disappeared. I apologised to him for appearing startled and told him I was not afraid, just in awe at the clarity, but there was nothing forthcoming, so I thanked him again for his healing and his brief appearance.

I lay there pondering this for a while before I tried to settle down again to go back to sleep, again asking for the Archangels help and that's when this spiritual experience took place.

I awoke in dream state and my hands were burning and as I looked at them there was a huge lump growing on the back of each hand which was a little bit freaky. It didn't hurt as it grew and I was also aware that someone else was with me, so I asked who was there. "Gabriel" is all I heard then fire started coming out of my hands. I was shocked but it did not hurt or burn me and I got up out of bed and the flames set the bedroom wall on fire, though it did not spread. I turned around with my hands held up and green and purple flames of energy flowed out of my palms and across the room which was amazing. I was then told that this was the power I had and this was its strength, and then it stopped after about five seconds or so. I was like, wow, and started to take a step forward but instead of walking I bounded with a leap of about thirty metres or so. When I landed and looked back I said, "What was that?" (It was like a space leap), and I was told.
"You can do what you want when you're not in your physical body".
I said, "Is this an outer body experience".
The reply was "Yes, you have many powers here".
Then bang, just like that, I was back in my bed again, mulling it all over.

I could not get back to sleep as my brain was racing with what had just happened, so in the end again I asked for the Angel's help, asking them to take me back to dream state which they did, and then the following occurred.

I was on a very long flat ship in the middle of the sea, there was nothing on the deck but me, and a hatch stood open which dropped down below. I looked around and wondered where on earth I was and what I was supposed to be doing, there was nothing or anybody else in sight. Suddenly the sea started to roll and I became a little edgy as the ship was very low to the water and the waves began lapping over the sides as it got rougher and rougher. I started heading for the hatch and, as I did, I could see an enormous wave rising so I started running, fearful of being knocked over board. The ship lurched with the wave and I just managed to jump down through the hatch, but there was no door to it and the waves started pouring in, filling the deck I was now trapped in.

I started to panic a bit now for fear of drowning, as the hatch was too high to climb out of. I thought, I'll just have to wait until it fills with water and hopefully swim up and get out before it sinks, and with that a huge sense of calm came over me and as I looked up there was a beautiful Pegasus standing over the hatch, peering in with his mouth open. He pushed his head further down towards me and I held on to his lower jaw and teeth as he pulled me up and out. I started to thank him but there was another large wave coming and he told me to climb onto his back, so I did so quickly and off we flew. The wave was getting nearer though and Pegasus was really fighting to keep ahead of it, but he told me not to worry. With that the wave crashed down on his rear end but instead of taking us down, it propelled us forward, pushing us towards a large brick building which we safely entered. I have to admit I was a bit dumbstruck and asked Pegasus who he was again. "Gabriel" was all I heard, and then we started walking and wandered around the building. I don't remember what was in the building or anything else that happened after this. I just woke up in my bed and remembered what I am sharing with you now. It was a strange night indeed and never had I seen things so clear and real as I did then.

Some people will say that I was just experiencing a dream and nothing more, and if I didn't know better and hadn't experienced this and now many others myself, I would be inclined to agree. I wanted to mention this specific meditation, dream state journey or outer body experience though because I know they are not just unique to me or psychics, but to most people. The difference is people like me are not so dismissive of them or the reality, and when strange things happen to us like this there's usually a reason? There are hundreds of books with various explanations and interpretations of what you dream about. I've read some and most do make some valid points. My own story I relayed to my good friend Nelly Moon though and this is what she interpreted for me.

Nelly - *"This journey is very interesting as it brings in the four elements of earth, fire, water and air, plus the spirits are showing you your strengths, weaknesses, abilities and fears."*

"The fire from the hands is showing you your gift of healing and the strength of your gifts. You don't doubt your abilities regarding the healing and that shows by the fact that you were not frightened of what you saw."

"The ship is a reflection of you, the person, and water usually is a symbol of emotions. So by the waves your emotions can be very turbulent and it is here where your fears lie. You don't doubt your abilities but sometimes your emotions take over and you doubt yourself. The fact that you thought you would wait for the waters to rise and swim out shows you are patient and willing to wait, but then the emotions take over again and you panic thinking that maybe you are not as patient or as strong as you first thought."

"The Pegasus is your inner strength that will guide you through those times of emotions, but I also think Pegasus is the spirit animal you should use when you are feeling stressed or over emotional about issues. His energy will bring you calm and take you to a safe haven, hence the building which again is symbolic of your body and soul."

"I think it's wonderful that spirit have shown you a way to deal with those inner conflicts and emotions. I also think, maybe, the ship on the ocean is the place to begin your journeys, (meditations). We all need a starting point, like a doorway. For me I start at the edge of the forest but for you, heading for that ship on the water seems a good place to begin. You can let the ship guide you to places you need to go. It could be further down the line your starting point will change".

"Regarding the energy change, well maybe that is a sign of the journeys beginning? But there is something definitely changing at the moment because I keep getting reminded of things that happened years ago, spirit jogging my memory for whatever reason?"

"What I would like to do is send you daily healing on your back if you don't mind. I definitely don't have the same abilities as you but if I can help I would like to try. Also which made me smile is the name Gabriel, I always work with Gabriel when I'm sending healing. He's not always regarded as the best Angel to use, but he has always served me well and I find his energy vibrations work well with healing. So maybe he is also the Angel you should work more closely with?"

"It will be so exciting to see how your journeys develop because that is indeed what you have experienced. Journeys are more descriptive than dreams and you usually remember them clearly, even years after the event. As an example I vividly remember 'dreams' I had as a small child where I would fly around the neighbourhood at night, but now I realise they were not dreams."

As I've mentioned, Nelly's a great friend and very insightful and I could completely take on board what she was telling me. As complicated and scrambled as my journey may have seemed to me, simplified it made a lot more sense. This is also why meditation time can be so important to us to get us through things and to help us deal with many different life issues. Our spirit guides are always there trying to help us but we don't always see how or hear how because of them being on a higher vibration to us. Meditating and connecting with spirit for guidance, direction and answers though can help us a lot, even if we fall asleep through the meditation. This is because I have found if you go into a meditation with a specific question you will get the answers inputted into you. So just because you may come out of the meditation and wake up with no recollection of anything at all, usually over the next few days things become clearer about the question you had for them. A lot of people will just put this down to coincidence or luck but it isn't, its spirit answering your call, and like anything, the more you do it, the better you get at it.

I am not the most visual person or quiet minded person when it comes to meditation but I still do it. Probably not as much as my spirit guides would like but then I've been doing what I do a long time now and I get their guidance in others ways. When I sit or lay to meditate I tend to have that monkey mind that just won't shut off because I'm always thinking of stuff, relevant or irrelevant, but it is a nuisance and I usually give up after five minutes or so. What I've found though is when spirit really have something to convey to me, they just put me to sleep through the meditation and input me. I can't usually remember a thing when I wake up but as I said, you can guarantee their guidance and wisdom comes through over the next few days.

They also tell me things when I'm at my most relaxed or when my head is empty of thoughts. I remember as we were building the Spiritualhart home I was painting fence panels on my own one day. It was raining so I had to paint them inside and I had forgotten to take a radio, so I was in for a pretty boring and quiet day. As it happened it was probably one of the longest communications with the spirit world I've had and the time just flew by. For six hours nearly they constantly filled my head with thoughts and images, guidance and wisdom about all different things happening in my life. The mundane job of painting in silence was a blessing in disguise for me. Not only did I receive all this wonderful knowledge, the time seemed to elapse quickly too and I barely remember painting at all, let alone how many panels I managed to paint.

They also tend to talk to me when I'm in the shower though, which felt a little awkward when it first started happening I admit. I know why though. It's because I'm not concentrating on anything and my mind is open, so it's an opportunity for them to get through to me. Some people may find this intrusive but it's not like there's a bunch of them all staring at me and I certainly can't see them, I just interpret the thoughts and images they present to me in my mind. To be honest I use a lot of my shower time as meditation time and ask many of my questions to them whilst showering, and have done for quite a few years. There's no right or wrong to how you connect with your spirit guides, it's just finding your own comfortable way and this way works for me, and apparently for them too, but I'd recommend meditating first if you're a bit shy!

12

People often ask me about how I manage to do a lot of my work via the computer, and one lady who contacted me through Facebook, and asked to have a healing session with me, we conducted through Skype. She had just been diagnosed with cancer and was told that she must have a hysterectomy as a matter of urgency in order to try to deal with it. The operation though had been cancelled twice and the lady was suffering a lot of pain. She was desperate for some kind of relief which had prompted her to contact me as a mutual friend had told her about what I do and how to contact me.

After speaking to the lady through Skype (an online communication system), we set up a time and date to do a distant healing session, as she was in Essex. The lady was a healer herself so she had no doubts about receiving healing this way, but the negative clearing I said I would do first was new to her. She was happy when I explained what would happen and what I wanted her to do and luckily I have a copy of our Skype conversation from that day, so you can see how easy it is for me to set distant healing sessions up with people –

Dean – Hi Catherine.

CD – Hi Dean.

Dean – How are you feeling?

CD – Good today thank you.

Dean – Did you read my email about the clearing?

CD – Yes I did.

Dean – Did it make sense?

CD – Yes it does thanks.

Dean – Okay, we know where we're at then. This first clear will take about 15 minutes okay?

CD – Yes that's fine.

Dean – Are you going to be laid down for this, have you got some quiet time?

CD – Yes I have a reclining chair and an empty house as Trevor (husband), had to go out.

Dean – That's fine then phones off etc?

CD – Yes indeed.

Dean – How long do you need to ground, get in meditation mode? (I normally do this for patients but because she is used to meditating and healing she could do this for herself).

CD – I have been doing it whilst we talk and I am ready.

Dean – Okay, lie down now and I will start in 5 minutes. Please don't come back to the computer until 240pm. Okay?

CD – Okay.

Dean – Bye for now, speak soon.

CD – Bye for now.

And that was it. I slipped into my sanctuary, did my preparations then zipped onto the astral plane to be with Catherine down in Essex. Once it was all over we were back on Skype again to resume our conversation at the agreed time.

Dean – I am done, how was that?

CD – That was amazing. I felt the air change and saw the bright white light and then vivid colours.

Dean – Glad you enjoyed it.

CD – Yes I did, very much so, thank you.

Dean – That was just the clearing though.

CD – It was powerful.

Dean – Did you feel the pressure in your chest and forehead?

CD – Yes funnily enough, especially around the 3rd eye (brow chakra in the centre of the forehead).

Dean – That was negative energy, I was feeling it too, it didn't want to leave you but it has now, which means you are good to heal, a clear channel.

CD – That's good to hear.

Dean – No good trying to heal someone who has negative energy, it needs clearing first for healing to take serious effect.

CD – Yes of course it does.

Dean – You feel okay?

CD – Yes I feel brilliant.

Dean – Good isn't it?

CD – Yes it is indeed, energised as well.

Dean – There's a lot of guides (spirit), working with me, they are awesome and I am truly honoured.

CD – As well as healing I feel that I will be learning much from you too. You have Native American guides (spirit), and a lady with red hair?

Dean – My spirit guide is Ben Black Elk, Sioux tribe, correct. My gatekeeper is Cloud Man, Assingaboine tribe, part Sioux, there are many others too, though I don't see much of them.

CD – They are amazing.

Dean – They certainly are. So, would you like to proceed with the healing?

CD – Yes please Dean very much so.

Dean – Okay, do you wish to use the loo or anything first?

CD – No that's fine.

Dean – Then I shall start in 5 minutes again and I ask that you get back to me after 3.45pm, is that okay with you?

CD – Yes that's great.

Dean – See you then, bye for now.

CD – Bye for now.

And that was it again. I popped back into my sanctuary, did my preparations again then travelled back onto the astral plane to be with her. About 50 minutes later we were back on Skype to discuss what had taken place.

Dean – I am done hope that was okay for you?

CD – That was fine, I feel that I fell asleep but I also certainly felt the healing.

Dean – Falling asleep is usually down to Cloud Man. When he stands in front of you and waves his hand across you that is it, game over, sleepy time. However it's for a reason, so that I can get my hands inside the body to break things down.

CD – That's understandable.

Dean – Did you have pain in your stomach because I was really feeling it, really sharp, like a stitch but right up the middle?

CD – I did indeed it was like you were pulling on something, trying to tug it out, sort of to the left hand side.

Dean – Hopefully we did some good then?

CD - Yes I think so.

Dean – When is your scan again?

CD – I have had those as far as I know, but I will know what they intend to do on Friday when I have the next appointment. They want to discuss treatment and different alternatives?

Dean – But they'll keep it scanned, monitored?

CD – Yes I certainly hope so.

Dean – I would too, I'd hope to see a difference? It was a very cold energy in your womb.

CD – Yes indeed, that's probably because I'm always so cold. I supposedly have a suspected under active thyroid too?

Dean – As the saying tends to go, heat indicates sending healing to the problem, cold indicates taking it away? Read into it what you will?

CD – Oh, I didn't know that? When I send healing people usually get very hot and are likely to fall asleep.

Dean – It seems the norm, going inside the body is different though.

CD – Yes, I don't think I have ever done that. When my guide (spirit), operates I can see what is being done and can tell people, but don't actually have anything to do with it as such.

Dean – We all work differently I guess?

CD – Yes indeed so.

Dean – It's all for the greater good, which is fine by me.

CD – Yes exactly.

Dean – I'm glad you enjoyed it anyway and obviously I don't have to tell you about drinking plenty of water to flush your system.

CD – That's right. I do drink a lot of water as I am diabetic. I'm full of aches and pains that nobody has ever died of, in fact both my husband and I are.

Dean – I'm afraid I must go now as I have another healing to do, sorry for running over.

CD – No, not at all I have taken up enough of your time, I will say goodbye for now and a very big thank you.

Dean – Thank those above, I merely put my hands out. Take care my friend and stay well. You'll probably find you have a better focus over the next few days as ridding negativity clears the mind.

CD – Thank you and your guides (spirit).

Dean – Namaste.

So that was it, all over, job done, simple as that, not a lot to it really. Not the most mind blowing experience for her as she fell asleep through a lot of it, but that didn't matter at all, most people do. It's the after effects that the clearing, healing or both has on a patient that's the real eye opener. Which is why later after her recovery from the operation, she wrote a nice testimony about her experience with me, and how it had helped her.

Testimony

Last September, after two years of illness and pain, I collapsed for the third time and was rushed to hospital. After many tests I was diagnosed with cancer and was advised that the only way to deal with it was to have a total hysterectomy as soon as possible. I had no problem with this after all I was 57 and my children are all grown up, the youngest being 16, and I had no quality of life at this point. I had lost control of my bladder and was constantly bleeding, so I agreed.

I have a very good friend who put me in contact with Dean in the hope that he could help with healing for me, because by now there had been problems with hospital appointments and cancellation of the operation twice. All the time the pain was getting worse and the morphine dosages I was taking were getting bigger and bigger, but finally my operation was scheduled.

Dean contacted me and explained what he wanted to do, as this was going to be a distance healing via Skype. I just had to have the pc open and sit comfortable in a quiet room or lie on my bed, which was no problem as this is where most of my time was being spent anyway. I am a healer myself but self healing wasn't the answer here, but I did know what to expect, but nothing could have prepared me for the strength of the energy that came from Dean that afternoon.

I found myself travelling out of my own body and my body heat rose. I was tingling and I met spirit guides in this space that was also part of the healing process. As the session ended and I came back to my body, I felt energised and the pain had been reduced. I could visualise the cancer and when Dean had finished it was half the size of when he started.

This gave me the strength and energy to go through to December when I had the operation to remove (what was left of) the cancer. This turned out to be two rare types, one of which only 15% of the population get. I am sure that without Dean's healing my chances wouldn't have been so good, nor would the healing process afterward have been so fast, as Dean continued to send me daily absent healing.

Thank you Dean, blessings, love and light.

CD, Brentwood, England

Cancer is a terrible disease that can really eat away at a person, and it certainly was having its fair share of CD at that time. I don't know how much exactly was removed from her in that one session but the fact that it did reduce in size some would say is quite miraculous. I don't find it miraculous though, I just find it a reality of what healers can genuinely achieve by being a pure, positive channel for our spirit guides to work through. Choosing to take my negative clearing and healing worked brilliantly for CD to get her through to her eventual operation, which I'm pleased she came through well. But could we have got rid of all of the cancer with further sessions? Maybe I guess we'll never know? The fact it helped to ease her pain and helped her through the months leading up to her operation though speaks volumes for the power of healing energy.

13

As we drew to the end of that year I was prompted by my spirit guides to create some empowerments for people to use to help them. I'd been doing what I could for people through healing but this was another way for me to do something more and for everyone to use as and when they wished. I liked the thought of this as I had taken many over the years myself, but I didn't know how to go about creating one, so meditation time was dedicated to asking how. When thinking what to channel and what to call the empowerment it came as no surprise to me when spirit said, "Doesn't everyone need a cuddle from time to time?" Who was I to argue? My spirit guides know best and so it was a pleasure to create it for all who need it. I hope the "Spiritual Cuddle" and all the other empowerments that I have since made are enjoyed for many a year.

The "Spiritual Cuddle" has received some terrific feedback since I made it publicly available free of charge. My spirit guides helped me understand that unfortunately in life we tend to get down for any number of reasons and the world can feel like it is on our shoulders. The empowerment when called upon would help to give people all the love, peace and cuddles they needed to help them through things, whether they were knowledgeable of spirit or not.

For anyone taking the empowerment, it simply lets the spirit guides take a person in their arms and give them the lift they need in the most loving and caring way, helping them to a more positive state of being. All they have to do is relax and ask for it, as my short empowerment manual instructs, then they can just bask in spirits embrace and feel all of the love they have to bring them. It really is that easy to do. Here's one lady's first experience with it.

Testimony

The Spiritual Cuddle Empowerment

When I called upon this empowerment I was aware of being taken upwards, and it was a half hours meditation of peace. I was so aware of all the Angels around me, they even in my mind put a picture of feathers there, a beautiful creamy white colour, but the feeling was one of pure peace.

The impression I got from the empowerment was of how loved I and we all are, also how special we all are. I also felt different parts of me, (Chakra's, Heart, Arms), being moved or stroked, many colours were also put into my mind.

As I received the empowerment it was like time stood still but when I looked at the clock half an hour had passed of peace and tranquillity. It is some hours later that I am writing this but my mind is still so peaceful.

It's nearly Christmas and before this empowerment my mind was a buzz with everything I had to do, but that's all gone now because I know it's all going to be okay and get sorted. Please, please will you give me this empowerment just before Christmas again, and I just know it will be absolutely fine.

I don't know what or how you've done this, but it is such a lovely peaceful feeling and a welcome relief from the stress I'd allowed to build up and just letting me re-assess what's important now.

Thank you Dean, what a truly beautiful gift you have and I feel truly blessed you chose me to receive this.

MB, Hull, England

The Spiritual Cuddle Empowerment

www.spiritualhart.co.uk

Unfortunately in life we tend to get down for any number or manner of reasons and the world feels like it is on our shoulders. This empowerment when called upon will give you all the love, peace and cuddles you need to help you through.

Let spirit take you in their arms and give you the lift you need in the most loving and caring way, helping you to a more positive state of being. Relax and bask in spirits embrace and feel all of the love they have to give you.

****

This is a free self empowerment and to call upon its help and energy simply take your self into a meditative state and say clearly and with pure intent –

"I ask for the spiritual cuddle empowerment, created by Dean Kingett, for my highest and greatest good". (Repeat x3).

****

You can use this empowerment as much as you like and whenever you need it. All I ask is that you pass it on to others so they too can benefit from the gift of spirit. Remember, spirit will always be there for you when you need a cuddle.

****

The Spiritual Cuddle Empowerment

I was compelled to channel and write this manual at a time when a lot of people around me were feeling the pains of life. I'd been doing what I could for them through healing but then spirit prompted me to do something more and for everyone's availability. It came as a surprise to me but then spirit said, "Doesn't everyone need a cuddle from time to time?" Who was I to argue, spirit knows best and it's a pleasure to bring this empowerment to all who need it, I hope you enjoy it?

Blessings

Dean

Spiritualhart

****

For your information

I am offering this free empowerment to the world for everyone's benefit. Please treat it with the respect it deserves and respect spirit when they bring it to you.

YOU MAY NOT CHARGE FOR THIS EMPOWERMENT. THIS IS A FREE EMPOWERMENT GIFTED TO ALL TO HELP WHOEVER NEEDS IT.

Please respect this empowerment, my time and my work in creating it so that everyone can use it for their highest and greatest good.

This manual has been written to help everyone receive the cuddle they need. There is nothing complicated about it, but knowledge of energy work is of benefit to receive its full effect.

This empowerment has been set in the etheric realms for all to receive and there is no certificate. It is simply a gift to enjoy and behold. This manual should not be altered in any way or sold for any cost.

****

www.spiritualhart.co.uk – email spiritualhart1@aol.co.uk

I was incredibly pleased with what I had managed to create with my spirit guides' help. I had been taking empowerments to help me with various things for a long time, but never did I think I would actually be able to create one. My spirit guides constantly simplified things for me though and the more obstacles and barriers that were put in my way, the more I started to move around or over them with each passing year, and not just on a spiritual level, but physical too. Life is not easy by any means, but as I still continue to learn more and grow in my understanding of things with spirit's guidance, I realise a lot of the time my restricted narrow minded views and thinking in the past had hindered me more than was necessary. I had thought I had an open mind growing up and definitely an inquisitive one, but I was still naive in a lot of ways.

Spiritual growth and knowledge though has opened me up week by week, month by month, and year by year in so many different and better ways. If I didn't know better I could be embarrassed for wasting so many years not listening to my spirit guides thoroughly enough in my earlier life. I had listened but the environments I had grown up in were not very accepting of the spirit world, and this had stopped me from acting on their words a lot. I had seen my relations ridicule my father for his healing work when I was younger, and although I am a person who couldn't really care less about people's opinions of me, I had kept my spiritual knowledge quiet and pretty much to myself as I grew up.

I do relish my openness with it now though and have for a long time and despite the mocking and the loss of friends and some family, I thrive on life and live a good, happy and positive one. I live more in the reality of life, and not one of suppression and full conformity to it with a fear of being different from the majority. Knowing what I know and living the way I do gives me more freedom to experience life, and I have learned to drop the mundane things from it that don't serve any good purpose. I keep positive things around me to keep up my mood and vibration. The negative things are kept at bay or dealt with positively, which is something many people struggle with unfortunately because they don't know how. This is a reason I very much enjoy teaching people, so they too can learn to help themselves and enjoy a better, more positive way of living.

The second empowerment I created was called "The Courage of Spirit", and I was compelled to channel and write that manual at a time when a lot of people around me were being bullied and victimised as I myself had been in my working environment before. I, at that time, had had the strength and guidance to deal with my victimisation but it dawned on me that not everyone has the spiritual guidance I had been lucky to receive. After asking for spirits' guidance and listening to their words again it was a joy to create this second empowerment for all who need it. Unfortunately there are those that lack the strength and courage to deal with every day life and the problems it throws at them. Sometimes the timid and the shy are classed as weak but this is far from true and they can be unjustly stereotyped. This stereotypical labelling can lead the bullies of the world to use it to their advantage making a person's life miserable, so this empowerment when called upon will help to give them all the courage, strength and bravery they need to help them through their personal fears and difficult situations.

It's a chance to let the spirit guides empower you and build your confidence to face and take on what holds you back, stifles you and stops you moving forward. By calling on this empowerment, as instructed in the manual, you allow spirit to lift you up in the most loving and caring way, filling you with the courage you need to move on positively. Here is one lady who really got the most out of using it and I guess it was just at the right time to help her move on.

<u>Testimony</u>

<u>The Courage of Spirit Empowerment</u>

Well that first empowerment blew me away but this was something else, I think I've been on some kind of crusade? I asked for the empowerment, (as instructed), and right away I heard Archangel Michael's sword, or so I thought but it was mine. I was in full Angel warrior dress with the biggest sword and I'm sure I was taller too? There was a path before me and I walked down it passing people I have known, and to be honest some I have forgot about too until this empowerment. You, (Dean), and a friend were there in full armour too walking in front of me, swords held upright and you both began cutting the cords that were holding people up. This was something I had to do, it was why I was dressed this way, time to let go for good. These people from my past have all been instrumental in making me the person I am today, good things and bad.

As I walked behind you I watched and you were slicing away at the cords for me. I wasn't as quick at doing it I have to say. I looked at each person as I passed and tried to think why I had to let go? Some were easy, others were not, so many memories of emotional times gone past, all the rejection throughout the years. It made me realise that I've been rejected so much more than accepted in my life.

I began swinging my sword and they did look quite funny dropping to the floor in a heap. I was thinking, "take that", as I cut the cords one by one. My Mother was there too and she was the hardest one to do, but you, (Dean), came and stood next to me and said, "be strong". It wasn't very nice to finally face the fact that my Mother had been rejecting me for all those years while she was alive, but I suppose I knew it deep inside so I cut it, and when I did she didn't fall down like the others, she flew like an Angel to stand behind me.

I think her role as my Mother is finally done, now she watches over me in a different role. Anyway she was the last to be cut down and I feel like I just chopped half of my life away and said goodbye to it. I know another phase is about to begin because the lane we were walking on was being cleansed by Rattle Man my spirit guide.

These empowerments are so powerful Dean, good job they're not in a bottle or they'd explode.

AD, Hull, England

At the end of this book you can find all my other empowerments (Appendix 2).

<u>14</u>

So an eventful year ended with a well earned holiday in December to Puerto Banus, Spain. Relaxing was the plan and when I go away I don't like to take anything spiritually related with me as I like a complete break from my work, so most of my reading material was for pleasure not studying. However, my work always manages to creep into my life at some point and this holiday was no exception, as Susan got talking to a lovely couple from Watford about what I do one evening. I wasn't with her at the time as I had gone off to one of the local bars that was showing the El Classico football match between Barcelona and Real Madrid. I had always had a soft spot for Barcelona so to watch it in a Spanish bar packed with both supporters really added to the event, and the atmosphere was brilliant. Even better for me was the 5 – 0 score line that Barcelona won by that evening.

Susan though had got chatting in our hotel with this friendly couple and the lady in particular was very interested in what I did. It was the end of our holiday week though and I never got chance to really talk to them myself other than polite hellos at the remaining breakfast and evening meal. Susan had given her one of my business cards and told her to have a look at my website when she got back home to England. I'm glad she did as the lady (AR) did read my website and got in touch with me very soon after arriving home.

She was interested in my work but not for herself it was for a friend's son who was going through a very tough time. The boy (LF) was about 9 or 10 years old and was suffering mentally and physically. He had been diagnosed with ADHD amongst other things and also had a brain tumour. His state of mind and body were deteriorating rapidly and the doctors were struggling to stop his decline. Sadly they didn't think he would be alive much longer given his condition. AR desperately wanted to help her friend's son and so told me about him to see if I could do anything. I told her (after meditating and consulting with my spirit guides) that LF was carrying a lot of negative energy. How much I did not know yet, but I told her it could be removed and hopefully it would help his condition.

We set up some dates and times for six sessions to work on LF, all distantly. The first one was to be the longest as we would be doing the negative clearing on him first, as well as a healing after it to start the repair and reconstruct his mind and body. These sessions had to be done late at night when LF was asleep as I needed him to be at his most relaxed. Also his mother didn't want other people to know about our private sessions. The negativity had been controlling his state and illness for quite a while now and this is why he was starting to go downhill fast as it had really took a hold. Our hope was once we removed the negative hold, we would have time for the healing to start kicking in over the next few weeks, and we may start to see some improvement if it wasn't too late.

Removing this negativity was going to be a tough job my spirit guides assured me, but it would be done. My only concern was how much damage it had already done and was it repairable. I knew my spirit guides would do everything they could to help and my hope was that we could stop the tumour from growing, maybe even shrink it enough so it could become operable.

Negativity is a kind of controller and it had been working against his medication such was its strength, making it futile. This is why he had become progressively worse quite quickly and his doctor's couldn't understand it, because they couldn't see it or the way it was feeding off his energy.

Negativity is an intelligent energy and it knew exactly what I was planning to do so on the day of the clearing I sent some of my spirit guides to be with him, to keep the negativity contained and to keep LF as safe as possible until it was time. This negativity really didn't want to leave him but I knew we could do it, and I prayed LF would be asleep when we did.

This may sound a little far fetched but this is sometimes how it is with people who are carrying strong negativity. It's a reason why I would love to do some negative clearance work in psychiatric hospitals and prisons. Not all people in these institutions have mental health issues, they can just be carrying a lot of negativity for one reason or another and it can be cleared. Medicating these people only subdues them as a person, but it doesn't affect the negative energy. You read it in the newspapers or see it on the news every now and then when they let someone who has been locked up for ten or fifteen years back into society. They say they are completely rehabilitated but not long after their release they go and commit another horrendous crime.

This is because negativity is not stupid and it knows it cannot do any damage when the physical person it is occupying is medicated beyond natural function. It is clever so it bides it's time and behaves and doesn't use its control over the person, which doctor's see as progress and lower medication dosages accordingly. Over time they gain a model patient and though it may take a few years, they eventually release them as stable and reformed. Once free that negativity bites back though and unleashes itself fully on the poor host, controlling them again and causing terror for innocent victims.

Earlier in this book I told you about a negative clearing and healing with a lady called LC. If LC hadn't have had that negativity removed from her when we did, then it would more than likely have continued to grow within her and drag her down even further over the weeks and months. In the end she may have lost all control of her life to it and that's not something I want to think about. But it does happen and I have had many cases to deal with like LC's over the years. Luckily, we removed the negativity from them too and got them back on the right track and in control of their lives again.

I didn't speak to LF's mother directly but AR was acting as our communication link and I told her it was up to her what she divulged about his situation. I knew it was going to be a tough one but I told AR that he would be cleared of it that night. If we had enough weeks after that to do something about the tumour, great. But if not, at least he would be free of the negativity, and some of the pain and turmoil for a while if there was nothing else the doctors could do. I don't get emotionally attached to patients but maybe because this was a child it was playing on my mind more than usual and I couldn't wait to get started and to pull the negativity out of him.

I started the session on LF about 10pm and I didn't finish until after midnight. LF unfortunately had three awful negative entities with him, which meant it was a lot harder to deal with than just negative energy. They were very big and it took a good forty five minutes to get rid of them all, and this posed a few questions to me. Why would such a young boy be carrying such severe darkness? He had picked this up from somewhere but how and why? What were the circles and environments this poor boy found himself in? Who does he stay with etc? I felt a good look back over his life needed to be addressed from when his illness started or from when it became worse and a major problem.

As I worked on LF on the astral plane he knew exactly what I was doing and what was happening. He was incredibly brave and knew he was being helped. He grimaced a lot but felt no pain through the clearing, but I knew he probably wouldn't remember it the next day as all of this was done on an energetic or spiritual level if you prefer. After the clearing I started the healing and I was glad to note he was very calmed by it. I like to give my students practical experience in my classes but also now and again if my spirit guides permit it, I will involve them with the real work too with strict instructions under my guidance. I had let two student friends join me in this session to provide extra energy and LF gave one of them a cuddle in thanks as we all healed him. My spirit guides worked hard on him that night as there was a lot of damage done by the negativity, leaving a lot for them to repair.

I emailed AR about it the next day telling her it had gone well and he was now free of the negativity. We had set up times and dates for his next few weekly healing sessions but I told her I would also now be sending healing to him daily to keep the healing process ticking over. I hoped she and his mother would start to see a different little boy now that he was free of negativity. I asked her to keep me informed of his progress and also if there were any thoughts on how or why he may have picked all of this up. The entities were not of this world and were extremely dangerous. One is bad enough, but to have three, that raised a lot of questions.

When AR replied she said LF's mother had told her that he was tossing and turning a lot as we worked on him. The next day though had been a very good day for him and he hadn't been sick once. This was very good news and just shows how immediately a person can start to change once negativity is removed from them. She also told her that I had had to remove three negative entities from him which were causing him all the problems and, with regards to this, she stated she had had three bad men in her life, all useless, and all were a bad influence, but could they have affected LF that badly? I felt the road ahead for poor LF was going to be a very rocky one, even if the doctors could do something about the tumour. This boy had been through a lot in his short lifetime and there was going to be much emotional and mental healing needed if he did survive the tumour.

The next healing session I had with LF started earlier then I expected. I was still teaching my Thursday night psychic development class when I was aware that spirit were working on him and preparing him for what I had to do later that evening. My spirit guides were inserting things into his head so that when I started at our scheduled time at 10pm he would be more than ready to receive all the healing they could give him. When I eventually did finish teaching and got to work on LF that night there was a lot of breaking down of what I can only describe as sludge like jelly which was removed from him, and it took a fair amount of time. As the session ended though a pure white cleansing light was filtered through his body to purify him and rid him of any unwanted energy. There was also a Kestrel with him which must have been some sort of spirit animal guide, protecting and watching over him.

As well as having the tumour, LF's speech was also slurred. His left side was not working well, and he was being treated with Oramorph, Lansoprazole, Ibuprofen and Paracetamol amongst other medication to try to help him. AR assured me he was being a very brave boy but the next healing session threw up some quite shocking revelations regarding his mental and emotional state. Again I had allowed my student friends to assist me in the healing session, but we were not expecting the visual images or the information that was to come through to us that night. The healing session started nicely with wonderful energy as always, but after about twenty minutes or so, LF appeared naked and frail looking to us in our minds eye. I do not wish to go into detail here, suffice to say that LF had encountered some serious abuse through his young life which I am sure will have had a lot to do with his ongoing problems. I don't think you can put the tumour down to his abuse but who knows? I am not a Doctor and it would be wrong to speculate about that, but his mental and emotional state had been seriously affected by it. As you can imagine it was quite upsetting and disturbing for us. But I talked to LF and told him we would do all we could for him to help him, and that he must try to keep strong and be brave, and with that he disappeared, leaving us to bring the healing session to a close after about fifty minutes or so.

The information we had received was very delicate but it was in the past. What had happened had happened and there could be no changing that. My focus was purely on helping LF now, in the present, however that would be, physically, mentally or emotionally. I briefed AR on the night's events the next day but without going into too much detail. She told me she too had the same thoughts and suspicions, but LF's mental state had meant nothing had ever come out in the open about any abuse he had endured. I told her I would continue sending healing to LF daily, until our next full session, and that was one night that will stay in my mind forever.

My student friends had, like I, become attached to LF and asked if they could help me again in my next healing session with him. I understood their passion to help LF as they had seen so much of this little boy's pain, and their compassion to be a part of his healing process was obvious after what we had discovered. One of them had a son of his own, roughly the same age as LF and he desperately wanted to help him, but I reminded him that the healing was out of our hands and what would be would be. With this in mind a few days later we were ready to heal LF again, and it was to be one of the most emotional healing sessions I have done to date. I don't expect to see or hear things through my healing sessions as I have mentioned, that doesn't seem to be a strength of mine, but with LF it had been different so far and this night was to be no exception. We prepared as usual and started sending the healing energy from my sanctuary and all was peaceful and calm as we felt the vibrations and sensations flowing through and around us, as my students sat at the opposite end of my healing table to me. After about twenty minutes LF started to materialise on my healing table. He was sitting cross legged and facing me and my students were aware of him being there too, but they couldn't hear the telepathic conversation that LF and I were having.

LF told me he was scared and didn't know what to do. He knew we were trying to help him and he thanked us for that, but now he was confused as he needed to make a choice, a choice that was very sad and very hard for him. He told me he was frightened of the dark monsters and he pointed outside my sanctuary, and sure enough, I could see all the dark negative entities desperately wanting him back, but afraid to come too close with all the pure spirit guides that were there guarding and protecting us all. I told him he didn't have to be afraid of them anymore as they would not harm him now as we had freed his physical body from them. That's when he shocked me and said, "That's not the choice, my choice is do I live or do I die now?"

He said his time as a physical being was over and that he was ready to go now and be free of all the pain, but he wasn't sure he was ready yet to leave his mother and this was making it very hard for him. I was stunned with this conversation and the dilemma facing him and I felt quite inept to answer. I couldn't make this decision for him I didn't even know what to advise him. I had never been put in this position before, so I called on all the spirit guides to help us. I cannot remember word for word what was said after this as it was such a long time ago, but I know I told him that only he could make the decision and whatever he chose that the dark and negative side would not harm him. This was such a sad and profound moment for us but I was aware at how comfortable I was with it all. I knew I should be very upset at LF taking his final steps to leave this Earth, but I wasn't. I was just more pleased that if it was his time to go then at least we had got rid of all the negativity from him, making his passing a lot safer and easier so he could step into the light confidently and unhindered now.

There was more communication between LF, myself and the spirit guides but it was at a higher level than my physical brain was privy too. What I do know is it lasted a while as I just waited there and stared at LF, sitting cross legged on my healing table. After a short while though I knew the dialogue was over as LF moved forward towards me and placed his small hand to the centre of my chest and on my heart. The love and power I felt from him was unbelievably strong as it spread through my entire body and he said thank you to me and smiled. I was about to reply but Archangel Michael appeared from nowhere, took LF up in his arms and vanished from the sanctuary, and as he did the energy that had been filling the room around us all abruptly stopped. My students and I looked at each other then I finally said, "I think LF has gone", and they agreed. There was going to be no more healings for LF, he had made his choice and it was an amazing but sad thing to be a part of.

I didn't know what to say to AR the next day. I didn't really want to have to say LF has found his peace, so I was surprised when she emailed me first and said LF wasn't doing so well. This came as a bit of a shock to be honest as we were all so sure last night that Archangel Michael had already spirited him away and he had passed over. He didn't stay on this Earth plane much longer though and he did finally pass away a few hours later, just as we knew he was going to, although we did think it had happened there and then the night before.

I could have omitted this incredible healing journey with LF from this book but I felt it relevant for a few reasons. Firstly, because it was such a relief to free LF from the negative entities that plagued him. If he had have died under their influence I dread to think where he may have ended up on the other side. Secondly, it shows a strong working with not just our spirit guides, but also with our own higher selves, our spiritual self if you like. When LF appeared to me that last night and spoke of his choices he was not the physical LF his family and friends would know, he was his higher spiritual self which is why he knew what was going on and he didn't speak like the afflicted physical child he was. Yes he was very scared of the negative entities that wanted him, but he didn't have any real concern for dying. He knew that would just free him from his pain. His only real concern was at leaving his mother which was understandable as he knew she would be very upset and there was an obvious mutual love for each other.

I also wanted to put this in the book because it shows it is impossible to know everything about the spirit world and the multidimensional worlds that surround us. I do not class myself as a psychic I never have. I am a healer first and foremost and that seems to be where my spiritual strength lies. I get told what I get told from my spirit guides but sometimes it's a bit like a cryptic crossword and you have to somehow piece it altogether. I and my student friends were quite sure in our minds that when Archangel Michael came and took LF away he had decided to help him make his transition from his physical life there and then, which was not the case. For this you would say we were wrong and you would be right in saying so. However, about a week later the spirit that was now LF visited me one day during a meditation. I wasn't searching or asking for LF, I never do that for anyone who has just passed over. They have their own things to do in the spirit world and I don't wish to interfere with their new learning process shall we say, for want of better words. When he came through it was a pleasant surprise and as we greeted each other I asked him if he was okay. He told me that he was and he thanked me again for helping him make the right choice. He also told me he had to return to his physical body first though as he wanted a few last moments to say goodbye to his mother. This made perfect sense to me now and explained why he hadn't passed over that night, but a little later after seeing his mother again. It made no difference to LF that he couldn't speak at the time and she couldn't hear him, it was just simply something he chose to do before he left this Earth plane. It was a huge show of love from him and I completely understood why he had done it.

So my student friends and I had been just a little ahead in our thinking about LF's passing at the time, but what we had been shown was what was inevitable, he had made his choice and his physical life was coming to an end. LF just had his own personal agenda to see to first. Seeing his mother for one last time as a physical being, which was quite a beautiful thing to do. This allowed LF to come to terms with his passing, free himself from the pain and move onto his next phase in the spirit world. We, as psychics, mediums, healers and such cannot know the reasons behind everything, that's impossible. But knowing LF was safe, at peace and happy made me smile at what we had done for him.

Some people may see this as a healing failure, but I certainly don't. There was a far bigger picture at stake here than just living in the physical world. I understand only what I have managed to learn over my years working with the spirit world and sharing information with some of my like minded friends around the world. We agree on a lot of things and our opinions differ on a lot of things, but what I have found is there is no wrong or right in how we all work and do things. We are all just at our own stages of learning and understanding small pieces of how this infinite universe works. With regards to LF, I am positive in my mind that AR connected with Susan on holiday because spirit guided her to us, and they knew I could help free LF from the negative entities tormenting him. Of course, I wanted to do more than that for him, I always do, but I have learned and I understand that peoples' lives are completely out of my control. I'm just here to do what I do and that's to be a channel for my spirit guides to work through to help people as they see fit, not how I do. It's frustrating at times because I always want the best for everyone I heal. But I am just Dean, a physical human being at the end of the day, and I am immensely honoured, as I have said, to have my spirit guides working through me.

15

Talking about negativity is not something I particularly like to do and I really didn't intend to put anything about it in this book, but my spirit guides thought otherwise. I'm happy to comply with them though as without their help this book wouldn't have even got started so as always I'm just following their guidance and sharing with you what they want you to know. So without further ado let me tell you about a powerful little girl I met a few years ago called RP.

I was contacted by a lady (SP) who knew a friend of mine, one of my psychic development students at the time. He and his wife had told SP about me as she was having trouble in her home with some kind of negativity and it was causing her 9 year old daughter a lot of distress. I told her what I did and that I would come to her house to get rid of whatever was there as she didn't live too far away from me, and that it would probably take an hour or so to do it. She agreed but was a little apprehensive about telling her husband as he didn't believe in all this "mumbo jumbo" as she put it. I understood what she meant. She was not the first person to have a partner that doesn't believe in what I do, the spirit world or life after death, and I'm sure she won't be the last. I promised I would keep my conversation minimal when I visited if he would agree to me being there, which I'm pleased to say due to all the problems they were having, he did.

One of my student friends (DD) was really coming on with his psychic development work and I decided to take him with me, or rather my spirit guides prompted me to. He was being shown a lot of negative stuff and how to deal with it in his meditations and it seemed they wanted to give him a taste of what could become part of his work in the future. I myself had a little bit of a problem with this at first as I like to work on my own. I know what I'm getting into when I visit negative properties and that's fine, but to take a student with me would be a first. It became very much apparent though that he was to come and assist me one Thursday evening in my development class. I brought the psychic development group back from their meditations and we were sharing experience's which were all pleasant as usual until I got to DD.

His meditation had told him what was in the house I was due to visit and it was extremely unpleasant. As he shared this information my own intuition kicked in and we started bouncing our thoughts and visions off each other, much to the astonishment of the other students present. My own spirit guides showed me a quick flash of what awaited DD and I, and I also got the confirmation from them that he was to go with me. I still wasn't overly happy about this but I could not argue with my spirit guides. If it was time for him to learn and understand more I couldn't deny him his journey on his spiritual path.

On the day I told DD to come to my sanctuary about an hour or so before we were due to arrive at the house to clear the negativity. I wanted to make sure that he was fully protected for what we were going to face, and I also wanted him to fully understand that he was there to observe and push energy out, nothing more. He understood completely. He was excited but also a little nervous which was to be expected. Once we were both ready we set off for the house in good humour, but as we got nearer the property we knew we were being psychically attacked by the negative force. We both started to feel pressure building in our heads, like a headache coming on and I told DD that the negativity knew we were on our way and he concurred. It was trying to put us off going, trying to frighten us, and I had already told DD that he must not fear it, whatever it tried to do, or it would feed off that fear and we would be in serious trouble. That was not something I could have happen and I never have yet, but this was new to my student friend and I needed him to remember and stay focused.

When we arrived at the house SP greeted us and let us in. Her husband was at work and her daughter was still at school, but she told us their daughter couldn't wait to meet us when she got home. I told her we were under attack and the negativity really did not want us there, and without being rude I asked her if it was okay to get straight on with the job in hand. She obliged and led us upstairs where I had already informed her I would be starting and the loft hatch was ready and waiting. Every house I have ever cleared negativity from always seems to start in the loft or attic. It's like the negativity thinks I won't go there and they'll be okay until after I've left or because it's dark and they think I'll be too afraid. They're wrong on both counts, and as far as I'm concerned a dark loft is just a dark room, it may as well be an unlit living room to me.

We climbed up into the loft to start our work and no sooner had we entered and started to fill the room with pure white energy we heard a scream. I saw very briefly in my minds eye what looked like the Golem creature out of the film Lord of the Rings, quite nasty looking. It was running scared though and fled the loft immediately as DD and I proceeded to protect the area from any other negativity getting in there. When we came down from the loft we went into all the upstairs rooms one by one protecting them and shutting down any mirrors, televisions, computers and anything else that could be used as portals to travel around the house. It all seemed very quiet though and I was getting suspicious. This negativity had been attacking us on our way here when we were several miles away. It was obviously very strong, so I wasn't convinced that the thing we had encountered in the loft was the end, there had to be more to it. I asked DD what he felt and he agreed. It felt too calm for what we had seen in our meditations and thoughts, so I told him to stay on guard as we continued our search and protected each room as we went.

There were two rooms left upstairs for us to do, one was RP's bedroom, who this negativity was causing so much fear, and one was what looked like a guest bedroom opposite that. I told DD we'd do the guest bedroom first and I asked him to go over to the widow wall and draw some protective symbols on it, and I would start on the opposite side to him. We had barely started when I said to DD, "I know where it is".
   "Where?" He replied.
   "It's in the cupboard next to me" I responded.
   "Oh sh*t" said DD.

I asked him to come over to me then and stand behind me. I wanted him to direct as much light energy as possible at this negative force when I opened the cupboard door. Then I asked him if he was ready. He said he was, and I reminded him again, "No fear", and he nodded. Then I opened the door.

What shot out of the cupboard and wrapped itself around me was far too quick for me, nor could I see it, but I sure could feel it as it tried to squeeze the life out of me. I was held in a vice like grip and my breathing became very short and very fast, and I couldn't expand my chest fully such was the hold it had on me. I started pushing as much light energy at this negative entity as I possibly could whilst remaining calm. It would not win and I would not fear it, for fear is a sure way to be overpowered when dealing with negativity. I looked at DD who was obviously quite shocked now. He had not seen or felt anything like this before and again I said to him, "No fear, just push the light at it" and, credit to him for his first encounter, he stood his ground wide eyed and did.

This negativity had me in its grip for about thirty seconds, which isn't a long time I know, but it seems like it when you can't breathe properly. Eventually though the light and the energy we pushed at it weakened its hold and it fled, but where to we weren't sure. I asked DD if he was alright and he said, "Yes, just a bit shocked". Then he described what he had seen take a hold of me. He said it was like a huge insect, like an orange centipede with lots of tentacle like legs which it had wrapped around me. It was quite vile to look at. This is why I am glad I am not the most visual person, especially when dealing with negativity. It's bad enough at times feeling and sensing it, but to see it too I can mostly do without. We continued to protect that guest room so it couldn't get back in there. Next we did a search and protect of RP's bedroom before venturing back downstairs. We were both buzzing now with energy and adrenaline and wondering where we would encounter it next. This you may think sounds quite an inappropriate reaction after what we had just been through. But what you have to remember is when you have all your spirit guides with you, they fill you with such strength, courage and confidence that they really do eliminate any fear that you might normally have about such things.

As we entered the living room I asked DD to go to the front window to start protecting that area. I started to do one side of the living room and as I did I got the strange feeling I was being watched. I looked around me trying to sense where it was coming from and as I did I caught sight of myself in a mirror to my right hand side. What stared back at me was like me, but it wasn't my true reflection. The face staring back was one of pure evil and it was grinning quite manically at me. I, on the other hand wasn't grinning at all, nor I'm sure, did I have that mad look in my eyes, so I promptly threw some protective symbols into the mirror dispelling the image and closing it down as a portal. This was certainly proving to be an interesting case and as we moved from the living room to cleanse and protect the kitchen and dining room, it only left one place where it could be hiding and waiting for us, the conservatory!

I warned DD that this would probably be the last showdown between the negativity and us. All rooms in the house had now been searched, cleansed and protected so there was nowhere for it to go. It had to stand and fight us if it wanted to stay, and that it did! It threw its' negative strength at us as soon as we stepped inside the conservatory and we could really feel the throbbing pressure inside our heads again as it attacked, giving us a nauseous feeling too. We hit back with our own positive light energy and it was not happy with us at all as it flew about the conservatory, desperately trying to overpower us. It didn't last too long though and we soon began to realise it was weakening as the pressure inside our heads started to subside, eventually disappearing altogether, and then we knew it was finally over. It was gone. Our spirit guides had captured and dealt with it as necessary.

I have no idea what happens to negativity when I deal with it as I don't wish to get involved and make any decisions for its whereabouts. I know of some though who will send it back to people if it has been conjured up through hatred or black magic and such, but I think this can leave them open to some possible bad karma so I don't do it. I prefer to just leave it all up to my spirit guides. They are far more knowledgeable than I about these things and I trust it is always dealt with justly and accordingly. What I do know is that it doesn't belong inside people or their properties affecting them adversely and ruining their life, which is why I'm glad now that I accepted my path to work against negativity a good few years ago. My spirit guides persuaded me well.

The reason this household was hosting all this negativity though I discovered, was because of the little girl RP. She was such a bright shining light and energy, and she was so perceptive and in tune with the spirit world, that the negativity had picked up on her and was desperate to shut her down as a spiritual light worker of the future. Children are far more perceptive than adults, but conditioning and conforming to life can knock it out of them as they grow up. If you have ever watched a baby or toddler seemingly mesmerised by something or giggling at something you cannot see, it's more than likely that a spirit guide of some form is entertaining them. The trouble is when young children start to tell their parents about what they can see, it's all put down to their over active imagination. Most parents and teachers alike will tell children that there are no such things as fairies, pixies, ghosts, goblins or monsters and more which they can see, yet expect them to believe in the Bible which speaks of spectacular miracles and Angels as well as all of its' political fear as an example to live their life by.

If we are expected to read the Bible and believe it as true, then why is it that so many adults don't believe in healing energy, life after death or the spirit world? It's written for us to read in many different languages and Jesus is even quoted in the Bible as saying we can all do as he, so why is it so disbelieved. Jesus rose from the dead and many saw him after his resurrection. When you go to church preachers tell us about the afterlife and heaven, but still the majority disbelieve it. For the biggest selling book in the world it's a shame that for many it holds no significance to their life at all, not even when they lose someone they love. As I have said I am not the greatest fan of the Bible. I found it not very interesting to read. But I did not as a child, and I certainly do not now, doubt in healing, life after death or the spirit world.

This is why the negativity wanted to shut RP down. She was a very gifted child and I have no doubt that if life's conformity, teaching and peer pressure doesn't knock it out of her thinking, she will be a very strong and powerful woman come her adult life. In fact I know she will as my spirit guides told me so. After the house had been cleared I healed the entire family one at a time to check nothing negative was residing with them, as sometimes negativity can jump into a person to hide. I doubted it had because I had placed the family in protection before I even arrived at the home, but I always like to make sure. I guess that's just the perfectionist in me. The husband had arrived home by now and although he was very sceptical of what I did he was pleasant enough and agreed to a short healing session.

I spent about fifteen minutes on him and SP and found nothing unusual which I expected, but when I healed RP, wow. This little 9 year old was so powerful she started healing me back. The energy was amazing between us and I was so relaxed with it I was struggling to stay awake. RP certainly was special and when I ask her how she had managed to keep the "monster" away as she referred to the negativity, she replied, "I light up my torch". I thought this a bit strange at first but then she explained it was her special torch inside her body. It soon became apparent to me as we further discussed this that she meant she lit up her chakras to keep it at bay. How brilliant was that! It showed that despite her lack of knowledge at her tender age, her spirit guides were certainly helping her to keep safe, and she told me about Daisy, her Unicorn guide and their special place where they would go to keep her safe. This little girl was fascinating but I had promised to keep conversation about such things to a minimum, and so I left them all safe in their home as DD and I bid them good day.

Later that evening SP emailed me and this is what she had to say about our visit and the day's events.

Hi Dean,

Firstly THANK YOU so much for today. We went out earlier and for the first time in a long while we found it nice to return home. RP has just gone to bed in her own bed and settled much quicker than usual, I have had to sit with her until she goes to sleep for a while. She's taken the stone you gave her to bed with her and it's under her pillow, its apparently healing her duck.

She has done nothing but talk about you all day, before you arrived and after you left, she really liked you.

She showed me what she had drawn for you in the envelope she gave you as she was looking for her Unicorn stickers. She never draws Daisy for anyone EVER, and that is a picture of her Unicorn in the place they both go. A very special gift I think.

She asked me this morning for my crystal that I wear around my neck and sat with it as she often does as she told me it needed charging. She said that I have been surrounded by bad things but I am a good person, they are there because of her and she is sorry. She said that when she breathes she makes souls? The souls she makes she gives to me to protect me but she said they do not last forever and sometimes she can't make them quick enough and the bad people get to me.

She told me I have a fairy, an angel, a monk, a unicorn (which I knew about) and Mars! When I asked her what she meant she started telling me about planets aligning that make energy and when they do they help me. She said Dean doesn't need help because he's tough.

Dean it hasn't stopped all day constantly telling me stuff, what I'm telling you now is just a little bit. She hasn't been fazed by anything she has seen or heard today, she's just taken it all in.

So once again thank you from all of us here it was so much appreciated and would you thank your friend too xxxxxx

I guess RP was quite intrigued and pleased with our visit and the work done for her family. I replied to SP and explained a few things, also about what had happened during our work there, as I had been unable to say much whilst at their home.

Hi SP,

It must have been nice to return home to a house you no longer have to fear. I hope RP slept well and in time she will understand the power and value of that stone I gave her. I'm glad she liked me and I understand how personal the picture of Daisy is to her, it was a lovely gift.

Do you know how to charge crystals, if not I can tell you?

The breathing of souls seems to me that she knows she is God, a part of anyway, we all are. I too use God's breathe in some of my healings, particularly when clearing negativity.

The planets carry immense energies some of which I am attuned to and use myself, but for RP to know this at her age is quite mind blowing.

As I promised I didn't say much in front of your husband as I know he doesn't really believe in what was happening. I hope it didn't seem like we were dashing off but we just needed to get the job done and leave so as not to offend his views. It was nice to meet him though and to be fair I think his ignorance to things that have been happening has helped to keep him free of most of the negativity.

The Golem looking thing in the loft screamed as soon as we stepped inside causing us a minor headache, but it didn't last long as it fled. There was a heavy energy in the bathroom which soon cleared, but it was the bedroom opposite RP's where the first major attack was.

DD was doing the window in there and I the door wall when I felt its presence in the cupboard. I opened the door and it jumped me and DD saw an orange centipede looking thing with lots of tentacle like legs. It wrapped these tentacles around me and tried to squeeze the life out of me and my breathing became a little difficult as my chest started to get tight and my heart started to race faster under the pressure. We stood firm though and continued to push light at it and after about thirty seconds or so it had to flee, this time downstairs as we had already cleansed and protected the other rooms.

When we came downstairs and entered the living room DD started to do the front window area and I the wall where the settee is. That's when I sensed it was watching me and I noticed the mirror it was using as a portal. I had no expression on my face as

I looked into the mirror, but the reflection of me staring back was one of pure evil, mad eyes and a menacing grin. I smiled into the mirror to show I had no fear but the image did not change, then I closed the mirror down just like I had the others around the house.

As we continued our work it told me I was pathetic and that it was going to smash my face, but it was running out of places to hide and we finally nailed it in the conservatory. The energy was very thick and heavy in there as it tried its last frenzied attack on us, again causing us minor headaches. It could not go anywhere else from the conservatory as the house was surrounded and it daren't go outside, nor dare it try to get into the kitchen because RP was there and for all its' loathing of her it feared her too and she was too well guarded.

Obviously I didn't want to explain this yesterday in front of your husband, it was just a case of get the job done and leave you all in peace. Nor did I wish to frighten RP with these facts. If there's anything else I can help you with then please don't hesitate to ask and I will try to answer any questions.

LNL

Dean

SP replied to my email and she confirmed a problem with the bedroom where we had encountered the first big negative attack.

Hi Dean,

My husband surprised me yesterday by letting you heal him and he also commented on the calmness of the house too. He finds it hard to believe but he said it was nice to meet you and that you and DD were genuine blokes.

We all slept really well, even Poppy (the dog), and I had to wake all of them up this morning. RP was on top form today and I really feel for her poor teacher.

I am very aware of what happened here and the severity of what you got rid off. It has scared me for so long and over the last few days I haven't been in that bedroom unless I have had to. That room used to be RP's room but she kept getting upset in there so we moved her to where she is now and she has slept better there.

When I first had RP and she was just hours old I told her that one day she would change the world, and I truly believe it. For 9 years I have seen a little girl struggle with what no one else understands, I feel like a mad woman when I tell anyone. No one understands her even I have no real idea what she is capable of, but I hope you will be around when she needs you because she will. She's already asking when she can see you again.

I saw what happened on the table yesterday, she almost blew you away when you were healing her, you were meant to meet.

On a lighter note I would like some healing on my back please and would you mind me bringing RP.

Once again thank you for what you did, the shift here is clear for all to see.

SP

SP did start coming to see me for a few weeks of healing on her back which started to bring her some relief. She started feeling the pain ease immediately and it improved steadily over each week. She also started to bring RP with her

too and I had some wonderful conversations with her that I just couldn't help but laugh at, but I was equally quite amazed by them too. RP couldn't understand one week why I couldn't see Jamie a Unicorn guide of mine stood in my sanctuary when she could. She told me he was friends with Daisy her Unicorn and that they were stood right in front of me I had to explain to her that her gift of psychic sight was far better than mine. But then one week whilst healing her mother I whispered to her, "Hey RP, Jamie is here isn't he?"
"Yes", she replied smiling at me, "Can you see him this time?"
"Yes", I answered, "I can see Daisy too, she's red isn't she?"
She positively beamed at this and I gave her a knowing wink as I continued healing SP.

After the healing I asked SP if she could stay a few minutes longer as I would like to do a bit of work with RP, providing she would allow me to and RP was happy to. She said that was fine and when we asked RP she was more than happy to take part in some energy work with me. We sat opposite each other and I talked RP through channelling healing through her body. I hardly had to though, she knew exactly what she was doing and loved it as we played with the energy. What was more amazing though was that she could see and describe lots of my spirit guides stood around me, and she had a particular fascination with the Ascended Masters I worked with, as she had never seen anything like them before. This was one perceptive little girl and I knew she had a big and important future ahead of her.

Over the next few weeks SP visited the sanctuary for healing occasionally with RP and there were many, many questions (mainly from RP), and I was really starting to enjoy the fact that RP was slowly becoming a student of mine. She was definitely the youngest I had ever taught and told about the universe and spirit world. Unfortunately though it wasn't to last for long as RP's constant talking about what she knew and what she was learning was understandably taking its toll on family life, and so both SP and RP eventually stopped coming to see me. It was a shame but I understood why. RP still had her school years ahead of her and obviously her parents wanted her to focus on that. As SP wrote in her email about RP to me though "No one understands her, even I have no real idea what she is capable of, but I hope you will be around when she needs you because she will". I'm sure I will be around for her too when the time is right and when RP is ready, and my spirit guides tell me I will be. So given the short time we spent together conversing, teaching and learning I will just have to wait until she is ready to find me again. Until that day I'll have to wait, then we can begin it all again. But I think she will be showing me more than I show her if she keeps on the spiritual pathway she has already been walking, I'm sure it will be very enjoyable meeting again though.

16

I would rather tell you more about the positive side of my work than the negative side. However, my spirit guides felt it necessary to add some negative experiences though as many people reading this will not have much understanding of why things are going wrong in their life or someone else's. That's not to say all of our ailments and illnesses are caused by negativity, they certainly aren't, but they can be a contributing factor, especially when conventional medication isn't getting anywhere. As for 'spooky' things happening in properties, neither are they always down to negative presences. Sometimes when I go to clear a property of a so called ghost or poltergeist as they are sometimes termed they are not at all, they are simply just spirit trying to make contact. Sometimes they are relatives or spirit guides, or they are what's sometimes known as what I call lost souls.

What do you mean by lost soul you may ask? Well, let me explain an instance that happened with my own family a long, long time ago. You may recall earlier I told you about my first experience of the death of a close family relative, my Nanna. My Mam was so upset at the death of her mother at the time that she sought answers in a spiritual Church, desperate to receive a message from her and some confirmation that she was safe and well on the other side. She attended the Church for quite a few months with my Father and although she got a few messages from the spirit world, there was no proof that any were from her mother. She grew disheartened, the ridicule she was receiving from attending along with my Dad becoming a healer soon took its toll, and she stopped going. This was a shame but I can understand it and if I'd known back then what I have learned through my work I would have been able to help her understand more.

It was a lot of years later that I found out that my Nanna hadn't crossed over properly when she passed away. Yes, she had died and wasn't in her physical body anymore, but she had become lost in the transition process. To try and simplify it, basically when she died and the light came down for her to take her to her next phase, she didn't get in to it. My thoughts on this are that as a living being she did not believe or was far too sceptical about the afterlife. As a brief example of things, when that so called heavenly light, spirit, Angels and whatever else comes down to help you make your transition from the physical body you should get in it, because it only stays so long for you to do so. I am presuming that, for whatever reason, my Nanna didn't understand the concept of all of this and perhaps out of fear or anger chose not to. Her decision left her without a physical body to use anymore to be seen by human beings. It also left her roaming around the Earth plane for a long time as many do, until she finally worked things out and accepted she was not physically alive any more, and could not be the physical Elsie Pearson anymore.

It must have been a bit of a shock for her, so much so that it apparently took her over two years to accept things and finally make her full transition to the spirit world. So through this time for whatever reason she wasn't able to, or perhaps didn't know how to get a message through to my Mam who desperately wanted to hear from her. Obviously this was not in my Mam's comprehension of how things worked and so she turned away from thinking about the existence of an afterlife for a very long time. She had given up on all hope of hearing from her mother after only a few months, and that, I'm sorry to say, caused her a lot of painful and angry years.

This is just one example of what I call a lost soul. Many different psychics and mediums have their own interpretations and that's fine, I do too. But for the purposes of this book, I choose to use this one to share with you. So when I go to clear properties of what people may be afraid of and calling a ghost, it can just as easily be someone who hasn't passed over properly. They mean no harm usually and they also know as they learn that we, as humans, all have the ability to see them and communicate with them, so they sometimes try to get our attention. These souls are no problem at all to move on and I love to help them over to the over side to be where they rightly should be. Not all of them want to go over though and that's their prerogative, they have their own free will too. So I just move them onto somewhere else so as not to keep disturbing the humans in the property.

Sometimes in the psychic development classes I teach, we will finish an evening's work with a soul rescue, as I always have lots of souls hanging around my sanctuary waiting for help. It's very rewarding work for both my students and I, and I find it nice that lost souls of not just humans but animals too find their way to me to be helped into the light. It sounds a bit weird I know, but during these class soul rescue sessions over the years we have helped, dogs, cats, sheep, mice, rats, horses, snakes and even a crocodile into the light, though that one certainly drew a few gasps, plus many more different species.

I do remember also a lad I went to school with coming for help one night and again it was a pleasure to help him make his full transition to the spirit world. Unfortunately Simon had been killed a year earlier as he walked home one night. I don't know the full details and don't wish to speculate on them, but it was in the newspapers about his death at the time. Simon came to me and asked if I would help him get into the light. I said of course but I asked him why he hadn't passed over properly a year ago when he died. He explained to me that he couldn't because his family were devastated at his death and he needed to be around them to help them through their grief. He told me it was a year on from his death and they were coping better so he could finally now make his full transition so would I help him. Of course I would but I was in bed at the time and as I looked at the clock I noticed it was almost 1am. "Right now" I asked, "It's almost 1 o'clock in the morning".
"Yes" he replied, "I'm ready."
"Okay Simon, I'll see you in my sanctuary in about five minutes, just let me get dressed and set up", and with that he disappeared to wait for me.

It didn't take me long to dress and go next door into my sanctuary, and as I started to set up, he sat waiting patiently on my healing table for me to begin. He didn't speak to me again other than to say I'll be back to say thanks Dean, and I knew he probably would. I called in all my spirit guides and helpers and together they helped open that gateway to the other side, realm or dimension, whatever you care to call it or know it as. It didn't take a long time and although I didn't see him go with them, I felt he'd disappeared as I could no longer sense his presence in my sanctuary. I closed the opening and said my thanks to all who had helped me and bid farewell to Simon. He was where he needed to be now, and that always makes me smile. I returned to bed and slept well and later that day I was talking to a student of mine at the time who also knew Simon from school, and about the unfortunate way his life had ended. He had been in contact with her too and she was pleased to know he was now safe and in the light of the spirit world.

Probably about a week or so later Simon was true to his word and came back to briefly visit me as I was working in the sanctuary one day. He didn't stay long, just enough to say thank you as he'd promised and that he was good and well, and that was all he needed to say. So, as you read this, I hope you'll understand that not every bump and noise in the night is an evil ghost out to get you, or a poltergeist that is going to start hurling things around the room. There is much to learn about the spirit world and the universe and for all my time working with it I still know very little, but I do understand more and more with each passing week, month and year. I guess that's what keeps me so dedicated to what I do and my love of helping people however I can, with spirits' guidance of course.

I have also helped a lot of particularly perceptive people, even psychics and mediums to remove or rather move on and help lost souls from their own properties. This isn't because they are afraid of them, although that would be quite the oxymoron wouldn't it, a psychic worker frightened of spirit. It's usually just because they just don't know how or perhaps want to for some reason, so when a spirit comes through asking them for help, they often send them to my sanctuary as they know that I will be able to help them. It doesn't matter where these psychic people are in the world. When they tell the spirits to come to my sanctuary, the spirits know exactly where I am to find me, and they always do.

This is because even if they haven't made their full transition they will have learned how to get around the universe following the death of their physical body. It may have been a confusing and frustrating time learning their new way of life living on the astral plane at first, but when you haven't got a body, I guess you adapt to things pretty quickly. Thoughts are energy, so just like me thinking I need to be in Australia or somewhere to do a healing or a clearing for someone means I'm going to be there in an instant, so too and obviously with a lot more understanding of it can lost souls and spirit. So once they have been told I can help them, all they have to do is think of me or my sanctuary and they will be here with me instantly, it really is that simple.

I must admit I do not help every single lost soul or spirit as soon as they arrive as doing that for every individual one would leave me little time for anything else, if at all. As mentioned earlier I usually get my psychic development students at the end of a class to take part in a soul rescue with me. This not only helps the souls over into the light but also helps my students' understanding and development of their spiritual work. It can be quite an emotional time for some of the students especially if they are helping children over, so I always let them choose if they wish to take part in any soul rescue work. They do find, like I do though, that this sort of soul rescue work is very important and knowing we are helping souls to get where they need to be as we work with the Angels and Archangels to help them brings a lot of satisfaction.

Testimony

Dear Dean, Thanks very much for the cleansing of the lost souls that took up staying in my home for a few days, as soon as I found them I contacted you to remove them. The energy is so much lighter now they have been helped over, much thanks to you and your guides.

LL, Bournemouth, England

17

Help is needed by many people in many different ways whether mental, emotional or physical and I can understand the pressure and stress it must put doctors under. Their own dedication to years of studying the human anatomy and all its' illnesses and ailments is something I am glad I have not had to go through in order to do my healing work. I am lucky that my spirit guides know exactly what a person or animal needs and how best to help them. I have much respect for those who do know how the body works though, and it must be so frustrating for them at times when even with all their knowledge they can't find a cure or treat a patient quickly enough. We, as human beings, are not all the same though. We have different allergies, ailments and pains, so certain things are impossible to know sometimes without many, many tests and getting to the bottom of things can be a long, long process.

This is why I feel healing work and healers in general should be part of the hospital team. Healers could help bring so much pain relief on a daily basis to those suffering, and also help to speed up a patient's recovery after an operation, or perhaps avoid the need for one. This, however I cannot see happening for a long time and probably not whilst I am on this Earth plane, but I can live in hope. Healers do not need a medical background as they are not doing anything to damage a physical body, they are simply being a channel for their spirit guides to work through to help people. A healer being present in an operating theatre could have a tremendous calming effect on not just the patient, but also the surgeons as they send out the healing energy, filling the room with love as the spirit guides assist both patient and surgeon alike.

I have had many patients over the years where unfortunately doctor's haven't been able to help a specific problem, some physical, some mental and some emotional. One lady in particular was diagnosed as peri-menopausal and was suffering quite badly with it. Peri-menopause is the stage of a woman's reproductive life that begins several years before menopause. This is when the ovaries gradually begin to produce less estrogen. It usually starts in a woman's forties, but can start in their thirties or even earlier. Peri-menopause lasts up until menopause, the point when the ovaries stop releasing the eggs. Some of the symptoms experienced during this period are tenderness of the breasts, fatigue, irregular periods, vaginal dryness, urine leakage (when coughing or sneezing), mood swings, difficulty sleeping, heavy and/or longer periods, and possible blood clots.

This lady contacted me early one morning by email, and as I had no patients early that morning I replied to her as soon as I read it. I told her I would send her some distant healing to help her, and to try to alleviate the symptoms she was suffering. We agreed to do it within a few minutes time, and as she was no stranger to healing she knew all she had to do was lie down, relax and let the healing take place. I myself ventured into my sanctuary to set up and prepare and within about ten minutes the healing began, and I could feel the energy flowing through me as usual. I can't remember quite how long this healing session lasted but she contacted me after to thank me for me fitting her in at such short notice. I went about the rest of my day's work so it wasn't until later in the evening when I was checking through my messages that I came across another email from her, which she kindly allowed me to use as a testimony.

Testimony

I have been blown away, but I am sure as a healer you have heard it all before? I have been peri-menapausal for months, well over a year actually. I had a long six month gap in my cycle but then had one, and I have basically had bleeding 24/7 since. Some days I am better than others, but I have had to cancel smear test after test because of this problem.

Due to the whole auto-immune diseases I have I was unhappy with my GP offering a total hysterectomy, after which I would feel apparently, "Right as rain." I was not sure that this would sort it all out and I have avoided going to my GP since.

My symptoms have gotten a lot worse of late to the point of spending my days sitting on a towel at home unable to venture out. Yesterday and last night were horrendous, worse then ever hence my plea for your help this morning.

RESULT! No blood, none whatsoever, like NONE! First time in a year.

Thank you Dean, thank you so much, my whole womb area feels lighter, less bloated and NO PAIN! I feel normal again. Thank you once more my friend, I am smiling inside once more.

KO, Meigle, Scotland

Pretty amazing result for one healing session I thought. I was extremely pleased for her and the relief it had brought her after over a year of suffering. It has to be said though our spirit guides cannot always help heal or cure everything in one healing session through a healer. This is not because they can't, it is because we, the healer, as the channel for them to work through are sometimes not a pure enough vessel.

Every time we breathe, eat or drink we are taking energy into our body. This is a scientific fact, but some of it is not good for us at all as it causes blockages within our body. The air we are breathing is not as pure as it should be for a start, with all the vehicle fumes and aerosol sprays we constantly pollute it with and more besides. Most foods are full of preservatives, E numbers, MSG's and more too, all that do our body more harm than good. And let's not even get started on what's in our drinks. It is quite shocking if you care to do your own research, just what you will find is allowed on our supermarket shelves, but who has time to read the labels?

The food and drink industry is a massive business and the choice range just keeps on growing. But at what cost? None to those who keep producing it that's for sure, they just keep getting richer while the quality of their product gets poorer. But that doesn't bother them, they can just fool our taste buds with their added extras. This, however, affects us as the consumer on a massive scale and is a huge cause of a lot of our illnesses. Again I don't wish to drag politics too much into this book, but I will say one thing if you care to look into things more closely - look at who owns or has shares in which companies and you will soon start to see why it's allowed to be sold to us at our expense and their gain.

I have learned more than just about the spirit world and other dimensions through my studies over the years. When I look back, especially at my teenage years and through my twenties at the junk I consumed on a daily basis it makes me cringe. No wonder I didn't pay as much attention to my intuition back then as I do now, I was constantly blocking myself off from it. This is why as a dedicated healer I now base my daily diet on fruit, salad and vegetables. Even these though are not all as fresh and pure as we might expect. Crops are sprayed with various pesticides, the ground they are produced in is packed with chemicals, and now we also unfortunately have genetically modified food. How insane is that? It's all about money and, sadly, not about our welfare or health.

So how do you beat it? How do you stay an open pure channel? How do you stay healthy enough to be able to help yourself and others? I'll tell you. I heal everything I'm going to consume before I eat it, or rather I purify it with my spirit guides' help. It is no different to healing or cleansing a person, although it is a lot quicker. When a body has toxins in it a person becomes ill so we remove the toxins so they become well again. Most food has at one stage been a living organism just like us humans so we can treat it exactly the same way, purifying it, so that it's better for our body to consume, simple really. This doesn't mean you can live on cake, chips and fizzy drinks for the rest of your life by simply purifying it I might add. Obviously a balanced diet is important. But it does mean that you can make things better for your health.

A lot of the students I have taught are quite amazed that you can heal, energize or purify your food when I tell them they can. But it's nice to listen to some of their experiments as they grow and learn in my various classes. One student who is a psychic medium was so excited when he learnt Reiki with me and finding out all the things he could do with it, put the energy to immediate effect when he left my sanctuary. Here's what he had to say.

Testimony

I would like to thank you for my level I Reiki initiation it was wonderful, enlightening and very therapeutic, and I feel, a life changing moment for me. I would like to honour the Reiki energy by adding this testimony and if this encourages more people to choose you as their Reiki Master on the Earth plane, so much the better because there are a lot of fakes out there, and if people can save themselves time and get themselves properly attuned by a Master who comes from a place of truth, justice and dedication to the art, then better for all.

After six hours learning about Reiki in one of the most chilled out and beautiful environments imaginable, I felt so zoned out when I left the Spiritualhart sanctuary that I felt as though I had gone to the other side, left my body and all my worldly cares behind. On the way home I ate a couple of sandwiches I had bought when I left the sanctuary as I felt hungry. I had not eaten since 9:30am and I decided to Reiki one of them.

Both sandwiches were the same but the one I added Reiki too tasted so much better than the one I ate without Reiki. I have not eaten anything since without adding Reiki to it. When I got home I drank a huge glass of Reiki water, had a shower and went to bed to use the Reiki on myself and self heal.

Awaking the next day I felt wonderful and I had a bowl of porridge that I added Reiki to which tasted fantastic, and some herbal tea which felt like a magic potion after adding Reiki.

I know that the energy is a tool and a valuable gift and I know that I am going to really enjoy and have fun using it, as well as doing a lot of good. The best part is the more I call up and use Reiki, the more Reiki I get myself. I am looking forward to my journey with Reiki as well as achieving some ambitious goals whilst working with Reiki and the spirit world. I fully intend to go all the way with this and more, but I know my true reward will not be the certificates of attainment that will come from doing so, it will come through my experiences of using this power to heal to bring positive changes to my life, those of people around me, and the plant, animal and mineral kingdoms.

Thank you once again for your tuition and the attunement, and I would like to thank Dr Usui (founder of Reiki in the late 1800's), for dedicating his life to the (re)discovery of this wonderful life force and for giving it a name. Had it not been for him there would be no Reiki and no Masters to attune people to it, and we would still be stumbling around in the dark. Thank goodness we are not.

JW, Hull, England

Another student of mine when I attuned her to Reiki, decided to try a great experiment at home and one which I share with all my new students. She was an avid gardener and she grew lots of her own herbs, plants and vegetables in her garden which she also had a greenhouse in. Her experiment was to Reiki only one side of the greenhouse for seven days to see if there would be any significant changes in the plants. This wasn't because she doubted what I had taught her, she just wanted to work with the energy and actually see it working for herself. She was not disappointed, especially when the seven days were over. Her little experiment had worked a treat as the plants she had been giving Reiki too had grown more or less to twice the size as the others. Not only that, she found it quite astounding that the plants she hadn't given Reiki too were actually leaning over, as if they were trying to get the energy too.

I have done many experiments over the years as I am always trying to find new ways to use energy beneficially for myself as well as others. When I create my various energised stones for instance, I create them en masse and when I do this there are many pieces that are too small or broken to use but I do not discard them. I place these small or broken stones around the perimeter of my own property to keep positive energy around my home and also to keep the negative energy or entities away from it. I have also noticed though that because of the positive energy the stones give off, the various plants, flowers, shrubs and trees around the property also benefit too. They seem to grow faster and taller and they are more healthy and vibrant than they used to be.

Another thing I decided to start creating for people to use daily a few years ago is energised water plates. There is much said about our drinking water being hard or soft, depending on where you live and also the debate about the fluoride in it being good or bad for us (I'll leave the politics of that debate to the reader). My Mam had just bought a water filter to keep in her fridge, in the hope of better tasting water. Needless to say she doesn't have any use for it anymore since I started making my Telos plates. I did an experiment in one of my psychic development classes with my students one evening who were pleasantly surprised at the difference my energised water plate made to an ordinary glass of tap water. I brought a jug of water into the class and poured them all a small glass asking them to take a drink of it. I then asked them to firstly swill it around their mouths to really taste it and to also feel the texture of it before eventually swallowing it down.

Once done everybody agreed it was just the normal tasting tap water that they were accustomed to drinking. I then placed one of my water plates in front of them all and told them to place the rest of the glass of water they had on top of it for just five seconds. That done I then told them to take another drink, swill it around their mouths again to taste it and feel the texture, and straight away there were a few surprised faces. My students couldn't believe the change. Not only the taste of the now energised water, but also in the way it felt in their mouth and throat as they swallowed it. Most agreed it actually tasted of something now, not just boring flavorless water and they also said it felt softer in the mouth and throat. I've been making the water plates ever since for people and I especially like to use them in my psychic beginner's workshops, as they are always a real eye opener for new students.

18

When we moved into the new Spiritualhart home, as I mentioned earlier it wasn't quite ready, but the neighbours were very helpful and one couple offered to store some of our belongings in their garage for us. The gentleman (GD) was a very ill man and he suffered with many different problems including chronic obstructive pulmonary disease (COPD), which he had had for many years. His breathing was very poor for someone who was only 42 years old at the time and he had to use various inhalers, nebulizers, oxygen tablets and more every day. His breathing was so bad that he couldn't walk far without gasping for breath, and although he had a wheelchair he pretty much refused to go in it. Pride getting the better of this still young man.

When the Spiritualhart sanctuary was finally ready and open I offered to give the gentleman some healing sessions in thanks for him storing some of our belongings for a few weeks. I explained that I wanted to give him a negative clearance to remove the energy blockages from his body first in the hope the healing we did after would help him to breathe more easily. He wasn't against what I did but nor was he that enthusiastic about giving it a try which was understandable. Most people who don't fully understand what I do can be a little sceptical until they've actually tried it and experienced the healing effects for themselves. He did however, I'm glad to say, come around to the idea that he had nothing to lose and possibly something to gain, and agreed to an initial four healing sessions with me.

Four sessions though turned out to be a lot longer as GD was quite amazed at what the healing sessions did for him and how they made a massive positive impact on his life. GD's health had been on the decline for years and was steadily getting worse, but once we pulled out the negative energy things really started to change for the better for him immediately, and he continued to keep coming for his treatments on a weekly basis. Free of the negativity in the very first session he felt like a huge weight had been lifted and he could take deeper breathes straight away much to his surprise. The amazement didn't stop there though. When he came to me for his second treatment he told me he hadn't needed to use his inhalers or take his oxygen for a week. He couldn't believe it as usually he would need his oxygen three times a day and his various inhalers were usually taken twice a day. He'd also noticed he could get about the house a lot better without being out of breath, and was even managing to go outside for a bit. Walking about was a privilege that had been taken away from him due to the exertion on his lungs and the breathlessness it would cause him, but over the weeks as he continued with his treatments he grew in confidence and started to walk further and further. He even started taking the dog for a walk again such was the change in his condition.

GD went from strength to strength over the weeks and months and not only that he also started attending some of my psychic development and attunement classes. This was so he could learn how to self heal and keep helping himself more and more as he now had a quality of life again, one which he pretty much thought had passed him by. Developing and learning with me also helped to bring out his intuitive side and he started to see his own spirit guides and Angels and even his father started visiting him in his meditations. Emotional as some of his meditations could be they only ever brought tears of joy and happiness as his father would tell him things and advise him of what he must do to keep on top of his illnesses. GD it seemed was probably never going to be a fully fit and well man again. But with the negative clearing and healings with me, and his own self healing, he could start to enjoy life again, and do a lot more than he previously could.

GD has become a good friend and neighbor over the years as has his wife, and I have helped him and healed him with many other ailments that have stricken him down from time to time since our first session together. With all his problems he still has to attend the hospital for new tests and new medications now and then, but in the doctor's efforts to help him it seems that most of their drugs tend to do him more damage than good. The problem is with all these drugs they keep prescribing him are the terrible side effects they keep causing. GD has suffered eye problems, rashes and even the blackening of his tongue to name a few, all caused by the medication prescribed for him to try. This is again why I think healers would be of the upmost value in hospitals, clinics and doctor's surgeries. Medical science cannot help everything and everyone and it probably never will. That's not to say it's no good, it is. There are some brilliant products that can aid us in many different ways.

Our bodies may all be similar but they can and do react differently and this is a problem that science does not seem to fully appreciate. Our thoughts about things, our emotions, the foods we consume, our allergies, fears, phobias and much more make us all unique in our own special way. All of them can cause blockages in a person's mind or body and can cause many different illnesses, viruses, diseases and pains. Yes, some medications do a fantastic job and can be quite fast acting and that's great. However the sooner a person can stop taking any drugs the better. Should people be put on medication indefinitely though, especially when it's causing damage to the body, damage that the doctor's know it is going to cause and rarely tell us about?

We put a lot of faith and trust in doctor's because we perceive them as clever people who know far more about the human body than we do, and that I can't argue with. Why is it though when they prescribe us something that may help, they never tell us of its probable side effects and what damage it may cause? I have done enough research on this subject to know exactly why, and I had the most enlightening afternoon a few years ago when a doctor and a surgeon visited me for healing and told me how much they were actually against the medical profession and pharmaceutical companies corruptness. Once again, I do not wish to take this book down a political route, it's not why I have written it, but it was nice to hear them confirm a lot of things to me.

Long term medication can cause a lot of damage to your internal organs which we seriously need to keep working for us, to help us stay alive. When you start damaging these organs you can cause more illness or pain, sometimes so damaging or painful to the body that an organ may need removing. Operations can be successful and are often seen as miraculous but they often leave a person hindered and on medication for the rest of their life.

I'm not suggesting the implementing of healers in medical centres can prevent the need for operations, but what I am suggesting is if healers were readily available maybe the need for many experimental drugs with people wouldn't be as necessary. Of course that would certainly upset the pharmaceutical companies though wouldn't it, the benefit of our health over their profit.

GD continues to try whatever the doctor's wish to try and that is his and everyone's prerogative. Whether they'll ever get to the bottom of it all though we both doubt. The bonus is he knows I live next door if he starts suffering too much and if the medication experimenting causes him too many problems. He can also self heal as I taught him too, so he's lucky in both those respects.

The marvelous outcome of GD's case though is that he has a quality of life again that was missing for so long and was gradually getting worse. His resentment of needing to use a wheelchair on what looked like it was going to be a daily basis is quite forgotten now as he continues to walk around unaided and even on his own when he walks the dog. GD is to be commended as he put a lot of time and dedication into his own well being and it has reaped rewards for him. He remembers all too well how bad he was before he met me. And even though he is still not at full health, he knows pulling that negativity block out of his chest has helped him to heal and get so much of his life back.

Testimony

I have suffered from chronic obstructive pulmonary disease since I was thirty and I am forty two now. I have been on numerous inhalers, nebulizers and oxygen tablets over the years and I was on six inhalers that I had to take twice a day.

Dean moved next door to me in 2010 and I got to know Sue and she talked to me about what he did. My illness was getting worse and my treatment even with all the steroids and tablets had brought me to such a low at this time that I eventually thought what the hell I'll try it.

I started going for the healing treatments regularly and still go now when I need them. It was the best thing I could have ever done and I felt the effects pretty much straight away after his first treatment on me. My first visit was very strange but also very enlightening at the same time. It felt like a very big jigsaw puzzle that I had all the pieces to but not in the correct order. After speaking to Dean though gradually everything seemed to fall into place, at which point my mind was racing with all kinds of thoughts as it was all fascinating stuff.

Dean then started to do some hands on healing to which my whole body seemed to go from a state of anticipation to a state of complete relaxation in just a matter of minutes. After what seemed like a good couple of hours, but was only about fifty minutes, I felt like a great burden had been lifted off my chest, and to say I could breathe slightly better would be a huge understatement.

My second visit was to be an even bigger surprise! I had my conversation with Dean first though before the healing and I told him I had not used my inhalers or oxygen since our first session, but that the nights had passed with a little restlessness. I was slightly confused by this, but he said that the healing works differently for everyone, it either can make you very relaxed or quite restless as you adjust to the healing energies.

Anyway, after completing this second treatment I sat up and Dean asked me how I felt and to my astonishment my lungs felt even more full of air than when I went into his sanctuary. In fact I told him that it felt like someone had removed my old lungs and replaced them with a new set. I was amazed, full of energy and excited at these feelings and more came over the next month, I can honestly say I have never felt better.

I am now attending Dean's spiritual development classes and learning how to self heal to help myself more. What a ride this has been and so much to learn. It's been the best thing, Dean moving next door, I feel I can do anything.

GD, Hessle, England

19

As well as running my psychic development classes from the Spiritualhart sanctuary I also started running monthly workshops for spiritual beginners. These were great teaching days for me, and great learning days for the new students. The day would start at 10.30 a.m. on a Sunday morning and finish around 4 p.m. with a thirty minute break for lunch. I would take the students through the basics helping them to use their senses as I introduced them firstly to their spirit guides and gatekeepers. I would then explain grounding techniques, protection and working safely to them before taking them through a meditation. And although not everyone sees things straight away through meditating, they did all however feel things, as their bodies were healed, and a great sense of peace and calm came over them. I would give them an attunement too that they could use to help them in their physical daily life and their spiritual work, and I taught them an easy way to give psychic readings, which always astounded them when they gave readings to each other.

The looks on their faces when they gave a complete stranger a psychic reading was priceless at times, as they learnt how easy it was to use their intuition. I also taught them about chakras as not many of these beginners knew what they were. I also got them to heal each other which also astonished them as they could feel the healing energy running through their bodies, especially when I got them creating energy balls in their hands. They might not have been able to see the energy they were creating, but they could all feel it much to their amazement. The workshop ended with one of my empowerments, and also some work with a healing stone which I would let them keep. Everyone received a manual covering all the day's work and certificates too.

I enjoyed doing these fun filled introduction to spirit workshops and still do, whether in my sanctuary or sometimes on my travels around the U.K. I'm pleased to say that many of my own psychic development class students started out in my beginner's workshop, and it's great to be able to watch them grow and learn through the weeks, months and years they spend with me. As much as I teach them though they also help me to keep pushing myself to do more as we experiment and learn together. I must admit I did have some reservations about putting some of these lovely statements from past and present students in this book, but then my spirit guides told me I had to. I am in no way egotistical nor am I an egomaniac, I just loving doing what I do. Sharing these student's thoughts about how they've developed, with whatever I have taught them, I find quite nice that they have chosen to express it. I am truly honored by their kind words though and to know they have grown under my guidance is quite humbling, I hope I can help many, many others too.

Here's what a few of my students have to say about their own development and learning with me.

Testimony

I first took part in one of Dean's "Beginners workshops" and I was so impressed in the content and the way Dean worked I joined his weekly development classes. I have never looked back and have grown so much spiritually. Dean is an excellent mentor, very genuine and completely dedicated, he is also a truly amazing healer, and this is something I have experienced first hand.

I know of no other place like the Spiritualhart sanctuary or of anyone like Dean. It's very hard to explain, you have to experience it for yourself, whatever your spiritual needs you will not be disappointed. The cost is minimal, Dean's certainly not in it for the money, unlike some?

LJ, Cottingham, England

Testimony

I have had tuition in meditation from Dean for almost a year and found his classes inspiring, informative and relaxing. Dean's passion for the work he does is an absolute credit to himself and can only benefit those who pursue the same path of enlightenment. I have thoroughly enjoyed my experiences within the classes and can whole heartedly recommend Dean's classes to anyone who wishes to walk the same path.

CH, Hull, England

Testimony

I met Dean at a mind body and spirit fair. The name Spiritualhart had been mentioned to me twice before and so meeting Dean seemed timely and as great believer in the power of the number three, inevitable. We began talking but very quickly the fair was drawing to a close and I found myself asking him if he had any spaces in his psychic development circle as I would be interested in joining. No one was as surprised as me as I have resisted sitting in circles for all sorts of reasons for years. I would therefore like to tell you a little about my experiences on two aspects.

Dean as a teacher – He is one of the most genuine and generous psychics and healer I have known. He works without ego or affectation and is totally focused on helping his students to be the best they can be. He is always working and developing himself and is keen to pass on his knowledge to everyone. He encourages the group, and questions never seem silly. The circle which he has created is a warm group of people with lots of different skills, all of them encouraging each other to develop. The group is developed and helped by Dean constantly and we give back with absent healing, soul rescues and other psychic gifts.

Dean as a healer – I went to Dean to receive a healing and balancing of my chakras. His healing is powerful but energising and the experience was very deep. It left me feeling refreshed and very relaxed while at the same time I felt as though I had done a lot of work on a spiritual level. Dean is very practical and matter of fact, which makes it easy to relax and get the most benefit from the session. He is easy to talk to and has empathy with people and their situations. I would recommend him to anyone who wants healing or to move forward with their life. He has the power and the willingness to help them to move forward positively.

CR, Beverley, England

Testimony

I heard about Spiritualhart by word of mouth. I am a qualified hypnotherapist and a medium and I have been involved with spirit from a very young age. When I found out that Dean was a Reiki Master I rang him to find out more about his practice. After a brief conversation I was sold, because I was more than satisfied that he "came from the right place", for want of a better way of putting it.

I wanted to be attuned to Reiki as an energy healing modality to complement the other things I do. What a pleasant surprise the sanctuary was, a lovely chilled out environment that was hard to envisage. I spent a really enjoyable day learning and being attuned to level one Reiki.

Dean is an excellent teacher and what he has told me has stuck with me first time. Despite his accomplishments he is disarmingly humble about them, and is unbelievably down to earth. He explains things perfectly. Dean is the only person I know who gets a kick out of his job, (a guarantee of excellent service), and I myself cannot see a more pleasant way of earning one's living, than by doing healing in such lovely surroundings.

I also attended a workshop on psychic protection and once again I learned a lot and had a super chilled out day. I strongly recommend that you experience the sanctuary for yourself. There is a wide repertoire of healing available for those who are stressed, in pain, depressed and broken.

Dean is a star performer at what he does and if you go to see him, you cannot be anything other than enhanced by the experience.

JW, Hull, England

Testimony

I first met Dean on a very wet and windy day. He came recommended by a good neighbour who had taken her dog to Dean for some healing. It was nearly a year later though before I plucked up the courage to go and see him and I have never regretted doing so. Initially it was for the healing but I soon found myself wanting more information about the work Dean does.

The more I talked to Dean the more I realised this was a very special young man, with a very positive outlook on life which is infectious, he really made me want to learn. I attended his psychic development class and this whetted my appetite for more, so the next step was to attend his "Mystical Evening", and that too was exciting.

Sitting in the audience I felt the power of the energies all around me and I then decided to take Dean's Reiki attunement class. This was the most awesome experience and I will be grateful to Dean and spirit for the rest of my life. He is truly a good ambassador for the spirit world and will always be a part of my life, as he makes the work he does accessible to everyone.

Bless you Dean xxx

CT, Hessle, England

I am learning constantly as I work and I hope not to be caught out in the future by any negative experiences. But I certainly was one day when a very upset and nervous lady telephoned me and asked me if I could fit her in for a healing that day. It was a Saturday and I had things planned but the desperation in her voice made me change them to accommodate her. I told her to come to my sanctuary at 12 p.m. and when she arrived she was very tearful. I talked to her for a while to help her relax as I didn't want her to be tensed up during the healing in case she blocked the energy off, which people sometimes can do. She had lots of issues, some of them stemming from her childhood years and some from her marriage which she had left but was still causing her problems.

When she'd settled down I asked her to lie on my healing table and explained what I was going to do as she had not had healing before, but I had been recommended to her. She was happy with what I told her and so I asked her to close her eyes and just concentrate on nothing at all, simply to relax and enjoy the healing energies as they worked within and around her body. I moved around her to start at the head end of the healing table and started channeling the healing energy as usual, but as soon as I faced my palms towards her I got a huge shock. She was riddled with negativity and it pushed back at me with such a force that it hit me smack in the chest and almost took my breath away. Her body started to contort and her arms wrapped around herself, squeezing so tight it was like she was trying to crush her own body. This was a very strong negative presence and also very clever as I had no idea what she was carrying when she entered my sanctuary.

I did now though and stopped the healing as I calmed her down and told her what I needed to do. If I'd have told her something was in her at the beginning she probably would have thought me mad and left, but she'd experienced its power and presence now and she took in all that I quickly had to tell her, telling me to go ahead and please get it out of her. I understood why my spirit guides had not let me sense it while we were talking now. This woman was nervous and frightened enough when she came in, telling her about what was inside her would probably have seen her run a mile. But now she knew it was there and desperately wanted it removing.

My plans had now changed from a simple healing to a full on negative clearing and I moved around to the foot end of the healing table. I started to channel the purest, brightest, whitest love, light and energy up through her feet in order to flood her body with it. This was to push the negativity up and out of her for my spirit guides to deal with. Her body started to buck with this purity and she started to cough, and as I watched her face changed into one of pure hatred as the negativity took over, then it grinned and mocked me as it exerted its power and showed its strength. Her arms stretched out to the side then and twisted back, and her fingers seemed to become elongated. What happened next I will never ever forget in my entire life and I can still picture it clearly now. She started to arch her back off the table at an impossible angle and as she did I could see her rib cage pushing through her clothing and her breasts seemed to disappear as her body continued to contort backwards in a V shape. I have never seen a human body go so misshapen. It was like something out of a horror movie.

You would expect panic and fear to kick in when seeing and dealing with this sort of thing and, as the physical human being I am, I would too. I couldn't afford to though, nor did I have time to and my spirit guides gave me all the strength and courage I needed to stay there and help her. This is why I have so much love, trust and respect for them, they never let me down. I started talking to this negative presence telling it that it had no place in a child of our creator, the great white spirit, and it would leave her body. I told it of my own strength and who I was, not just Dean, but as I am known by some in the multidimensional worlds, the "eight rayed torch", as I continued pushing the love, light and energy into her to force it out.

It took a while but eventually I managed to connect with the lady and talk her through, talking to her own spirit guides and Angels, which bless her she somehow managed to do in a further attempt to weaken its hold on her. This was by far the worst and the strongest negative clearance I had ever done so far, and it took me over forty minutes to finally push it out of her so she was in control again. I must admit I was relieved when it was all over as it had been quite disturbing watching it all happen. I still can't get the images out of my head, I don't think I ever will. I found out throughout the ordeal though why and where it had come from and I told the lady who agreed with all that I had picked up on and was feeling. It was all to do with the end of her marriage and her ex-husband's hatred of her. He still wanted to control and abuse her as he had throughout the marriage, something she hadn't told me. But when I told her, she confirmed he was still trying to ruin her life even though they were not together anymore.

Hatred, violent thoughts and evil wishes are all energy and can do an awful lot of damage when aimed or sent to someone. Also the darker side of the spirit world is always ready to play with those stupid enough to invoke and use their help, all of which was what had happened in this poor lady's case. I healed and repaired her after the negative clearing and she left much relieved and in high spirits. Unfortunately though a couple of hours later she telephoned me again and told me she could sense something in her home. We had freed her of the negativity but it seemed there was something still lurking in her house that she couldn't sense before, but now her body and mind had been cleared she could. I agreed to go round to clear the negativity from her house the next day, and she told me she was going to sleep at a friends that evening as she was frightened of being attacked or of anything getting back inside her, as that was an experience she didn't want to go through again.

As she didn't live too far away from me I drove around to her home the next day and met her outside the house, as she didn't dare enter it again until I had been in and made sure it was safe for her to do so. She let me in and said she would wait outside for me in her car, so I closed the front door behind me and headed off up the stairs to start the clearance and protection of the entire property. All went smoothly and I couldn't actually feel anything too negative, stale energy yes, but certainly not any entities as I did my rounds. When I got to the living room though, that's when my spirit guides gave me a nudge and said, "It's in the car".

This was good in one respect because I now knew where it was, and also the fact that it had decided to leave the house as I'd entered probably meant it was in fear of my spirit guides and I. The bad news was that if it was in the car, it was with my client. I finished in the house making sure that it couldn't get back in then I went outside to the car where she was still sat waiting for me. As I got in the passenger side I told her I had to clear and protect her car and she said, "I know, I was going to ask you to, it's been in here a while". And so I did. The energy was far stronger than that in the house had been and it started to play it's head games with me causing me a headache, but eventually it passed as it's presence disappeared from inside the car. A good thing you may think but unfortunately it wasn't. I had to tell the poor lady that she would have to accompany me back to my sanctuary, as some entity had gotten itself inside her to hide from me. She agreed as she didn't feel good but she was understandably frightened as she had already been through quite a traumatic time the day before and was obviously dreading it being the same.

We drove to my sanctuary and as she knew what I was going to do this time there was no need for explaining much and we just got straight on with the negative clearance. As soon as I started channeling energy into her though she went into spasms quite a few times and it was not pleasant to watch again, let alone guessing what she was feeling. The entity was really mad at me and it was determined not to leave her, so after a while my spirit guides told me to split myself into my multidimensional self so I could also get inside her body and fight it out with the entity in the hope it would lose its hold on her. My physical body had one hand on her stomach and one hand between her shoulder blades constantly filling her with love, light and positive energy as my multidimensional self, my spirit self, if you like, left my body. My spirit body moved to the soles of her feet and also started pushing energy into her then it started to walk right through and up her legs constantly pushing love and light at the negative entity. The lady was still having spasms and her breathing became very short and fast but I knew I couldn't stop. We had to get the entity out now or she would just have to go through it all again.

I talked encouragingly to her throughout it all, telling her how well she was doing and that we would beat it together, but she had to stay positive with me and not give in. To her credit she started reciting prayers out loud and this gave her something to focus her mind on rather than her twisting, writhing body. My spirit self moved through her pelvic area and waist now and the entity started to move upwards in her body trying to keep away from me but all the time fighting back. I continued to walk myself through her stomach and her chest and as the entity became confined to her head I continued to push it up and out of her. It was of much relief to both of us when she finally gave a huge gasp as we over powered it, and it left through the crown of her head, and she was free of it at last.

There were a few tears of joy from her at the release she now felt and we spoke for quite a time after it about a lot of different things regarding her situation and her past. I taught her a few things too to keep her safe and protected and also to help her keep the energy vibration positive in her home. She came to see me for healing for a few weeks after too as she wanted to really get herself back on track and in the land of the living again. She had lost a lot of her life due to negativity. Not just from the entity but from her childhood years and throughout her adult life. She had suffered massive amounts of abuse that is personal to her, but through the healing sessions she started to gain more control over herself and my spirit guides further helped her to discard a lot of unwanted baggage. She was able to confront things that had happened to her more positively with each passing week and she started to get over the guilt and shame of the things she'd been through. It was a huge learning curve for her and I was happy to help her through it. To see her change from the poor defeated wreck, to the much more confident and happy woman she became is just another reason why I love doing what I do so much to help people.

20

Experimenting and having fun is a big part of my ongoing development and spiritual growth. It helps me push boundaries that most normal human thinking wouldn't consider possible. I was bored one day flicking through Facebook when I saw a female friend of mine from Scarborough had been making her own herbal soaps. I am a big fan of natural products and as I was at a loose end I thought I'd try something different if my friend agreed. I sent her a message and asked her if she would like to take part in a little experiment with one of her new soaps. She replied promptly and said she would like to, so I told her what I wanted her to do. I asked her to take a picture of a bar of soap and send it to me, then place the bar of soap on a table or worktop in her home for about thirty minutes. I told her I would energise the soap so that when she held it or used it to get washed with, it would also heal her, uplifting and refreshing her. I don't think she was overly convinced it would work but I was and so once I received the picture, which gave me something to focus on, I set about energising it with Reiki energy.

As I looked at the picture of soap on my computer screen I asked my spirit guides to work through me and to place the Reiki healing energy into the real soap in my friend's house to energise it. I had my hands open, palms facing upwards as I said this and immediately I could feel the energy flowing out through my palm chakras in the centre of my hands. This made me smile and confirmed what I already knew, that it was going to work, and also give my friend, JU, up in Scarborough a pleasant surprise. I channeled energy into the soap for about twenty minutes and then I finally brought my hands together to close down the energy, thanking my spirit guides for working with me and ending the session. I then sent a message to JU telling her it was ready and that she could now conduct her own experiments with the soap and tell me her experiences later if she didn't mind. She didn't mind and here is what she had to say about our little soap experiment.

Testimony

I was introduced to Dean a couple of years ago through a mutual friend, and although I haven't had the pleasure of meeting him in person we've often interacted online. When I mentioned that I'd started making my own natural herbal soap he promptly said he, "had an idea", Hmm. I was intrigued so, as asked I sent him a picture of a bar of my lavender and sage soap which he then energised with Reiki.

The only experience I have had with Reiki is with some healing stones some time ago so I genuinely didn't know what to expect or feel. Firstly, as advised, I held the soap in my left hand and closed my eyes. I felt a soft touch along my arm as if I was being touched very lightly with a feather. Afterwards I went for a walk with my husband and I felt light, bright and vitalized. I felt as if I had a definite spring in my step.

On returning home I laid quietly on the bed holding the bar, and as I drifted off to sleep I could feel the vibration along my arm. It was the same sensation I often have when using my crystals. I awoke after two hours completely refreshed I don't think I'd realised how tired I had become lately.

So the next experiment was bath time. It was a lovely feeling using the soap, both healing and cleansing. It was such a tangible hands on way of receiving healing, and very easy to imagine the healing energy entering my body. I slept well again that night *and I woke up with that same vitality. My mind feels clearer and less stressed and physically I have a feeling of well being.*

I asked my husband if he would like to try the soap, expecting at worst skepticism, and at best, him just humoring me, so I was so surprised when he said he felt really revitalized and as if a ton weight had been lifted from him.

A very successful experiment indeed.

JU, Scarborough, England

As I mentioned earlier I created some empowerments to help people and I continue to make them. So nice was some of the feedback from people who had used them, that I have created forty three so far as I write this book, which are all freely available on my website www.spiritualhart.co.uk . It was especially nice to receive an email from Germany one day though asking me for permission to translate them. This I granted and a few weeks later I was sent copies of my empowerment work in German. I couldn't read a word of it, but it was wonderful to see and know that what I was creating was being used and well received in another country. I do not know if my empowerments have been translated into other languages, but I have had emails from people from many different countries around the world thanking me for them and the help it has given them.

This did my confidence the world of good at the time as I had been told by my spirit guides that I was not to just keep making empowerments for people to use, I was also to create new energy systems for them to use too. I was not worried about creating these new healing systems as I had every faith in my spirit guides and I knew they wouldn't let me down. My main concerns were writing the manuals for the attunements, who or what to do them with, and would they be strong enough for people to use to help themselves and others.

The first attunement system I created is very special to me as it was with my own spirit guide as we created the BEN BLACK ELK SHAMANIC HEALING SYSTEM together. It took me several months to write it as I wanted to make it as simple as possible for people to understand, so not just advanced healers could use it, but also beginners too. I could not have been happier when the chance to channel this healing system was presented to me by Ben Black Elk. A true medicine man of his time, his trust, patience and faith in me was never more prevalent than when we created this Shamanic healing system together.

Ben was never a chief and never claimed to be one, he would only ever honour himself and his people by wearing a single feather as part of his head dress and who he was as a Native American Indian. A dedicated herbalist, he had studied well from his father's teachings (Nicholas Black Elk), and taught many people the simple ways of life and remedies until his own transition to spirit.

I created this healing system with his help and guidance as a 'stand alone' system, but it will also work in conjunction with any other healing modality you may choose to use with it, for instance Reiki.

Knowledge of Shamanism is not a requirement to take this attunement as Ben and I brought this energy and healing system through for the benefit of all to use. The attunement not only brings energy into your being to use it will also bring you a sacred ethereal Shamanic rattle and wand to use if you so wish, and give you the ability to open a vortex to enable you to recycle negative energy into positive, by using the simple symbols in the manual, once attuned.

However, you do not need to use the symbols at all to perform a healing session, simply channeling the energy either hands on or distantly with your pure intent is enough. They are simply something people may like to work with to help enhance their own spiritual experience, especially if they have a good knowledge of energy work, and from my own personal point of view it shows respect to Ben Black Elk and other Shamanic guides when you use the tools they bring to you through the attunement.

Rattles were the perfect accompaniment to Native American Indian ceremonies, which often included dancing. The rhythm of the rattle during a dance is something that resonates to the very soul, helping make the ceremony a very special experience. The Native American Indians realised that spiritual energy can be derived from a trance like state induced by music. The rattle causes our body and mind to respond to it, as the sound and our pure intention can unblock energy within our bodies, helping to heal us. Shaking the rattle also helps to break up negative or stagnant energy that blocks the natural flow within the body and aura, and it can also cleanse and purify rooms or objects.

When using the ethereal sacred rattle during a healing session you would just need to state your intention to activate the Black Elk Shamanic healing system first, then draw the symbol on your hand or call it mentally into your hand. Whether you can see it, feel it or not is irrelevant, as it will be there if you have been attuned to this energy system. It's just that your psychic perception may not be high enough yet to see or feel things. By shaking the ethereal sacred rattle over and around a person from the crown of their head to the soles of their feet your intention is to clear any negativity, and to repair any rips or holes in the aura. You can also ask mentally whilst doing this that any negative energy may be safely grounded and recycled into positive energy, so it may be safely given back to the universe, to be used for the highest and greatest good, so that nothing is wasted (If desired you can also place the vortex symbol beneath them to suck down the negative energy).

Doing this will not only repair and cleanse the aura, it will also help it to grow and expand, giving a patient more protection around them as the aura will be filled with the beautiful colours they need. This is a great purifying and cleansing way to start any healing session as you prepare the body, mind and spirit for treatment.

When using the ethereal sacred rattle for cleansing a room or object of negative energy you just state your intention again to activate the Black Elk Shamanic healing system, then draw the symbol on your hand or call it mentally into your hand, again seeing it or feeling is irrelevant as it will be there. When you shake the ethereal rattle around the room or an object, you can ask mentally that it be completely cleansed and purified of all negative energies, again asking them to be safely grounded and recycled into positive energy, so it may safely be given back to the universe. Once done you should be able to feel the difference in a room or as you hold the object. As you increasingly and intuitively work with this energy system you should not be afraid to experiment with the ethereal sacred rattle especially with guidance from your own spirit guides. This system has been channeled to give you the freedom to explore your own creativity and expand on your own spiritual path.

Wands have traditionally been used to direct energy for many, many years by asking the creator, Wakantanka or God to direct energy through our bodies and out through the wand with our purest intentions. Wands are often made with crystal tips to direct the energy as they are a natural source of energy straight from Mother Earth. The Native American Indians paid enormous respect too and valued her for her gifts and nourishment. When using the ethereal wand during a healing session you would state your intention to activate the Black Elk Shamanic healing system, then draw the symbol on your hand or call it mentally into your hand, again whether or not you see it or feel it depends on your perception, but it will be there. I find a good place to start a healing session on a person is by aiming the ethereal wand at the patient's seven main chakra points (base/root, sacral, solar plexus, heart, throat, brow and crown). Starting at the bottom, the base chakra and working your way up to the top of the head to the crown chakra. As you do this you can mentally ask that the chakras be balanced and aligned as you begin the session.

You can also aim the ethereal wand at any specific places you know need healing or are intuitively drawn to asking mentally that these troublesome spots may be paid attention to, in accordance with the recipients highest good. The ethereal wand can also be a great aid when hands on healing may not be appropriate. Things like burns or any severely painful areas that cannot be touched you can simply point the ethereal wand at, asking mentally that the energy may travel through you and the ethereal wand as you direct it to the affected area.

Using the vortex symbol can be used to help take negative energy away from people, objects or places. Much caution should be used though when opening one for spiritual purposes, only doing so with the purest of intentions. When wanting to open and use a vortex during a healing session, once connected to the Black Elk Shamanic healing system energy, you can either use your hand or your ethereal wand to draw the vortex symbol underneath the patient's body or feet depending on whether they are seated or laying down for the treatment. Seeing or feeling the vortex open is irrelevant again as you will have done so with your sheer intent of drawing the symbol. Once the vortex is open ask mentally that any negative energy from the patient may be safely sucked down into the vortex as you heal them. When the treatment is coming to its end ask mentally that the vortex be closed and removed safely from underneath them, recycling all the negative energy in it into positive energy so it can be given back to the universe, so nothing is wasted.

When using a vortex to rid negative energy from a room or object, once you are connected to the Black Elk Shamanic energy use your hand or ethereal wand to draw the symbol on the entire floor or under the object. Once done ask mentally that any negative energy may be taken down into the vortex with the intention of it been recycled into positive energy. Channeling the attunement energy for as long as you intuit until it is cleansed. As you come towards the end of the cleansing ask mentally again for the vortex to be closed and safely removed, again offering it back to the universe.

I thoroughly enjoyed creating this first of many attunements and I was guided to channel it and write the accompanying manual with Ben Black Elk. Also because my many students had been asking me to do something Shamanic as many of them, like me, had Native American Indian spirit guides. I think they really expected an empowerment as they were used to using so many of mine already, so this was as much as a surprise to them as it was to me, but a very welcome one. I had never actually taken a shamanic attunement myself to pass on to them, but Ben helped me see to that and create his Shamanic healing system. Under his guidance and wisdom he helped me to bring this energy into use as a powerful energy attunement for anyone to use and benefit from. Adding the rattle, wand and vortex symbols into the attunement was a wonderful extra to the system, so people can use them just like I use my physical tools for healing in my sanctuary.

As with my empowerments it was nice to be asked again from my German friends if they could also translate this attunement which of course I agreed to. I guess I need to start brushing up on my German though because as nice as it was to receive the German copy of it, I still can't read it!

I was so excited when this attunement was written and channeled that I couldn't wait to try it and so I set up a global event on Facebook. I invited lots of like minded friends to take part in a distant healing session with me using the energy, and they in turn invited their friends too. The event took place one Tuesday evening at 7 p.m. (GMT) and I sent the Ben Black Elk Shamanic healing system energy out to them all for thirty minutes. I'd also invited people via email too, so several hundred people took advantage of my offer.

I sent them some simple instructions of what they were required to do to receive the healing energy at either the designated time or after the event at a time more convenient to them. This was because many of them taking part had never received healing before, so I wanted to make it clear to them how easy it was to be healed and feel the energy. I set a lot of my various work up this way because of time differences around the world. When you understand energy and you work with the spiritual realms it's quite an easy thing to do. It's just a case of placing the energy in the ethereal or spiritual realms for people who can't make the exact time to call upon when they wish. All they would then need to do is go into a meditative state after the event, and ask their spirit guides and higher self to receive it. They could do this by simply stating something like, "I now wish to receive the Ben Black Elk Shamanic healing system distant healing, prepared for me by Dean Kingett, for my highest and greatest good". The healing energies would then start to flow to them and they would receive their thirty minute healing session, easy.

The information I sent them was very straight forward as receiving healing energy is effortless, but the effects can be quite remarkable. All they had to do was simply sit or lay down somewhere comfortable about five minutes before I was going to send them the healing energy. This is so that their body would be nice and relaxed when I started to send it. I told them to just close their eyes and work with their senses throughout the thirty minute session so they could experience the vibrations and sensations of this wonderful healing energy, as it healed their mind and body. I also explained after the healing was over that they should make sure that they were fully awake and alert before doing anything strenuous, as their body would be in a state of total relaxation.

After the healing session was over I received some wonderful feedback from lots of those people who took part at the original time and also those who took it in their own time, some of them several days after the event. Everyone who sent me messages had positive and fulfilling experiences from the healing session and if I'd had any doubts about letting Ben Black Elk down they were soon cast aside. The energy attunement I had created with Ben was a huge success and I've enjoyed attuning many people to it since, helping them to learn and grow on their own spiritual paths. Here's what three people who took part in the healing event had to say about their own experiences with it.

Testimony

Before taking your Ben Black Elk healing I couldn't even be around three people at once because I just had too many sensory problems. Well I just went to a family party and before I would have to take something like a tranquiliser and I would still have to leave early. I went this time though and it was the best party in my life, I didn't have any sensory problems. Three people called me after it to say they couldn't believe it was me and asked what I had done that changed everything.

I just can't thank you enough but I had to tell you I was really surprised, everyone was.

LS, Salisbury, Maryland, USA

This lady also took it but ninety minutes after my event had finished. This just helps to prove the point I was making earlier, about being able to place energy in the ethereal realms for people to use at their own convenience.

Testimony

Your healing night was amazing, I felt heat rushing up my spine, across my shoulders, down my arms and up and around my neck and at the back of my head. There was also a tall spirit guide standing behind me and I could see his big white hands on my shoulders whilst the healing was taking place. I just sat and let the healing come in and around me.

The healing was only for thirty minutes starting at 9pm but when I finally opened my eyes it was 940pm. It proves how powerful distant healing can be by just sending a healing thought and proof we are all connected to the Christ consciousness, the one conscious energy.

MM, Hull, England

There were a lot of people taking a healing session for their very first time too and this couple and even their dog benefitted from it.

Testimony

Your Ben Black Elk Shamanic healing system was the first time my husband and I have tried this kind of thing. What a result!

I saw many colours and symbolic visions and my husband experienced tingling in his fingers. Afterwards we had an amazing feeling of peace and calm. We felt questions were answered and now we have the ability to deal with problems. Our little dog has been so calm and happy too.

Thank you so much for the invitation and we hope this will be the first of many new wonderful experiences with you.

Love and light.

AB-T, RB-T and Billy the dog, St. Albans, England

21

I have no idea how many I have healed over the years all together and it's not something I'm keeping a record of. I do have my patient files in my sanctuary, but as I have done and will continue to do, a lot of my healing work through Facebook, emails, demonstrations and such it is impossible to know the exact number. What I do know though is that I love doing it and helping as many as I can. I can't list every single healing experience I've had either because there are too many for me to remember. These next few excerpts are from my own notes that I have made through the years and what my spirit guides have allowed me to know and to do through my work with them. There is no order to them, just a few random ones to help you understand our capabilities as not just healers, but as human beings, because we can all do this work and more.

Ten short excerpts from my diary notes

I began healing EM today and was guided to use the Atlantean energies. I made a contact with her shoulders to start the session and then moved to her head, but as I moved to the right hand side of her body things started to happen. I tried to move my hands over her throat chakra but as I did my left hand shot down to where her right ovary is. This didn't surprise me too much as I know she has tough menstrual cycles and I could feel her pain in my own body in exactly the same place. I left my hand there a while and the heat intensified as my patient promptly fell into a deep relaxing sleep.

After a while her spirit body rose up from the physical body and the spirit Doctors and surgeons started to cut stuff away from her. I was then urged to place my hands in her spirit body to start scooping out what they had cut away, as they opened a vortex in my sanctuary floor to ground it in. This was very interesting and shortly after I stopped I asked my spirit guides if there was any more I could do to further help her and them.

With this, an ethereal needle appeared in my hand with white light flowing from it and I was told to sew. I said I didn't know how or where to but my spirit guides said it doesn't matter, just sew, so I did. Soon after I stopped sewing I was given some ethereal gauze to place over the stitching to protect it, and as I did this I realised the pain I was feeling in my right side had gone. With a smile on my face I uttered, "This is insane", and my spirit guides replied, "It is not insane little fish, this you know".

When I'd finished the healing session EM confirmed that the side I had worked on was in fact the main cause of her problems. She also said that she had just started her period today and that side was causing her severe pain, so much so she had driven to visit me with a hot water bottle on her tummy. The pain now however was gone, what an awesome healing session that was.

~~~~~

I was working on T distantly today (a gentleman from near Leeds) when my spirit guides brought his spirit body to my sanctuary table, not unusual as this has happened many times before. What was unusual though was my spirit guides told me to lay my physical body within his spiritual body to conduct the rest of the healing session, so I laid upon my healing table merging myself with him. As I did this one of my multidimensional selves left my physical body to lay inside T's physical body at his home, then we began to remove some cancer cells from his lungs.

~~~~~

I had a lady visit me today who went through a messy separation about two years ago and unfortunately he had started to send her nasty emails and text messages again. When I was healing her today I asked my spirit guides if there was anything more I could do for her and they told me to put my ethereal hands inside her head. I said, "What for, what do I need to do?" and they told me to just rummage around, so I did, and I ended up scooping out her negative energy thoughts to clear her mind of him.

She emailed me later that day and said how much she had enjoyed the session and how much it had helped her and enlightened her. She said she was in a completely different mood to how she was earlier, anger and frustration had been lifted from her. Another lesson for me to stop questioning my spirit guides and just do what they guide me too.

~~~~~

As I was healing LJ today I saw a foot in my mind's eye that looked to me like it was covered in blood, but I couldn't really tell as I was only seeing the image in black and white, it did look a mess though. I also felt a stabbing pain behind my right eye and had pains in both my wrists.

I told LJ about the things I had been picking up through healing her and she confirmed that her foot is covered in psoriasis (not blood as I thought), she has recently started getting stabbing pains behind her right eye, and she has painful arthritis in both her wrists. She had also been doing some painting and the pain had got worse.

She was quite amazed with my diagnosis of some of her symptoms.

~~~~~

When C came to see me today I placed my hands on his shoulders to start the healing session, but after a few minutes one of my multidimensional selves left my physical body to lie inside his body which has happened with patients before. Shortly after though five more of my multidimensional selves left my body to place their hands upon and within him doing whatever was necessary, it was quite fascinating to see.

129

As the healing came to its end the multidimensional self that had lain within his body rose up, taking some of C's ailments with it, which I saw as dark spots. As it moved away from him it stood to the side and safely grounded what it had removed from him, completely cleansing itself of all energies that were not ours before returning back to me with the other five.

~~~~~

I cleared MI of a negative entity today which was a shape shifter, but as I did so my spirit guides made me aware of a presence in her home too. I told her about this and she agreed to let me clear her home of negativity also as she had two small children.

As I started my rounds of the house MI went for a drive as she didn't want to be in the home whilst I did it. I encountered nothing upstairs but when I went into her living room I was hit in the stomach by some force that literally took my breath away and I had to run into the kitchen as I thought I was going to be sick. I was retching but nothing was coming up, but I knew the negative entity was the cause as it tried to get inside me, so I placed my hands to my stomach and started channelling light energy at it to get it out before it took root.

My hands were vibrating so strongly and fast as I did this they were a blur to me, and after about sixty seconds of intense pain it finally left me and I collapsed to my knees with the relief. My first reaction was one of anger at what had just happened but I quickly got a grip of myself as I knew that was no way to take on a negative entity, for it would simply overpower me if I attacked it with hate and anger. So I strode back into the living room where it was waiting for me and told it how much I loved it and was there to help it. Needless to say it didn't react well, but it didn't do me anymore harm as my spirit guides soon dealt with it and got rid of it.

I told MI afterwards about this and she asked me how long ago I was retching. I said about twenty minutes ago and she couldn't believe it, she too had had to pull the car over about twenty minutes ago and started retching. When I told her it had all happened in her living room she told me she hated that room and hardly ever went in there. She also confessed she had tried to take her own life in that room and it always felt dark. This made some sense now as to what had happened as her own attempt at suicide had sullied that room which is why it was so negative. When it attacked me it was also attacking her because she had given me permission to get rid of it, proving again how clever energy and entity can be.

~~~~~

A friend from Wales was suffering from high blood pressure which she had had for a very long time. I told her to find a stone so I could channel emerald crystal energy into it for her to try to help bring it down. She said the results have been absolutely amazing from something so simple but extremely beneficial.

~~~~~

I gave a private tarot reading today for one of my students who said she found it very deep and emotional. She said everything I told her was spot on and felt so true to her and that I had helped her so much not just with the tarot reading but over the last two years. Others had mocked and laughed at her but she felt she had lost the baggage she was carrying little by little which had held her back, and now she was glad to be who she was. She said with my classes and the help of spirit she felt healed and truly loved.

It has been a long journey on a lot of different levels for this student but seeing her transformation on a weekly and monthly basis is just one of the reasons I love doing what I do.

~~~~~

A stranger to healing decided to take advantage of one of my free healing events. She had been suffering from her diverticulitis and gall stones for the past four weeks, and was in bed nearly every day. She had finished her antibiotics to no joy and was really at her wits end as she struggled with the pain it was causing her.

The lady said she saw my free healing offer and initially thought, "I don't think this will work for me" but decided to try it anyway. She said the healing felt funny at first as she tried to relax, and it felt just like a little tingle which kept on going. She slept brilliantly that night though but the pain did return in the morning and she thought, "Oh well, just a one off".

She did however decide to try it again and the pain faded so much that by the third day she had no stomach pain at all, she said it was her best day for a month, and now she has full faith in the positive effects of healing energy.

~~~~~

A lady said I had been recommended to her by a mutual friend and wanted to have a negative clearing and healing with me. She didn't really know what it entailed but her friend had assured her that to get her out of her rut and get her back in the land of the living again it would do her the world of good.

The lady lived down in Leicestershire and so we set up a mutual time and date for me to do it distantly for her. She said she had not enjoyed her life for many years and felt she was just existing in it rather than living it. She felt stuck but she knew she had to do something and when her friend told her about having a negative clearing and healing with me that had changed her life, she decided to give me a call.

After working on her I'm glad to say it has changed her life too, as she told me she has not felt so at peace with herself for over a decade. She cannot believe she now has such clarity of thought, such a still mind and a feeling of inner peace. She told me she feels much more energized too and that she is sleeping like a baby now.

~~~~~

People's emails, telephone calls, text messages, Facebook messages and testimonies are always nice to receive. Not to swell my personal ego though, I have no interest in that, but it's always great to know how well people or animals are doing and what my spirit guides have done to help them. It's also nice on occasion when I bump into people who I've worked on in the past and haven't seen for months or even years and they tell me how well they have been since their time in the sanctuary with me, and the various things that have changed for them, physically, mentally and emotionally.

One email I was especially pleased to receive though was not to do with healing at all, but an attunement and was from a Reiki Grand Master in Australia called Brenda H. I had come across Brenda's website quite by accident as I noticed she was advertising one of my free empowerments and curiously wondered, but was secretly pleased that it had found its way to the other side of the world. When I got in touch with her I realised she was a well renowned creator of many empowerments and attunements and she was part of what is known as the International Light Worker's Association. This group has some very wonderful and gifted people who have made a lot of their work freely available, like I have, to help others but on a much wider world scale.

Brenda is a lovely lady and originally from England but had moved to Australia a long time ago. As we emailed each other we talked about our passion for our healing and spirit work and she sent me lots of manuals and empowerments to help me and my students. I reciprocated her kind gesture by sending her some of my own work which she was happy with too, but I also sent her one of my new attunements to try that I had just created. This was quite a brave offer from me but I had to know whether what I was creating was good enough. Brenda had been doing this work and creating empowerments and attunements for years. She was very knowledgeable and I thought good or bad, I would know exactly where I stood regards energy work if she would take my attunement.

The Ben Black Elk Shamanic healing system apart, my spirit guides had taken me down a completely different route for channelling most of my attunements than what they had done with my empowerments, and although I was happy to do so, my physical brain was a bit dubious. Angels, Archangels, Ascended Masters and animal totems seemed to be the normal way for people to create energy systems, but my spirit guides had me creating mine with some very strange and even prehistoric creatures. I had loved working with them. It had been fun of course, but the real questions were, would they be accepted by people to use and work with, and would they be strong enough to heal and help people? I was hoping Brenda would answer these questions for me. They would either be a success or I would have wasted many, many months of my time. But I doubted that, my spirit guides had put too much time and effort into me for them to fail.

Brenda agreed to take my Abaia magic attunement. The Abaia is a type of large eel which dwells at the bottom of freshwater lakes in the Fiji, Soloman and Vanatu Islands. The Abaia is said to consider all creatures in the lake its children and protects them furiously against anyone who would harm or disturb them. It is said that those who are foolish enough to try to catch the fish from a lake containing the Abaia are immediately overwhelmed by a large wave caused by the thrashing of the Abaia's powerful tail.

Many Magi are interested in the Abaia as they have existed for far longer than humans have. So when a new species is discovered, its arrival is met with great excitement because it may unlock some mysteries of the past. They are a strange, long forgotten race that has managed to survive for countless generations. These fish are beautiful beings, so very different than any others that exist today.

Scholars believe them to have originated four hundred million years ago, when no people walked the Earth. During the day, these huge creatures hide away in deep caves, slowing down their hearts and metabolism to save their energy. As night falls, the Abaia resume their activities, finding food and navigating the watery depths. Being nocturnal is to their advantage, as their large eyes can easily see without light. The Abaia are stunning creatures, with strange scales harder than most metals. These scales seem more like armour than anything else, and some think they are somehow related to dragon scales.

Other fish stay far away from the Abaia, as if they know that the Abaia are not from their time. Indeed, these beasts are a threat to all but the largest sea creatures, eating all smaller fish. As one would assume the Abaia are not particularly loving companions and they remain on the ocean floors, content with their own company. Their colouring, either a deep green or blue, makes even the youngest Abaia difficult to see, and although they come into the world as incredibly small creatures, Abaia age and grow like all others. They are larger than almost any other fish though, just another odd trait that sets them apart, and Abaia can reach up to eight feet in length, well over the size of any grown man.

The Abaia possess a strange magic and when in trouble, the fish will shine a bright white for an instant, and then where there was but one, there will be many according to the wish of the Abaia. They will act as one, perhaps attacking a foolish enemy, or helping a human companion, but when the fish has tired of using its power, there is another blinding light, and all that remains is one Abaia. If this extremely valuable magic was ever to be understood by cruel people, the world would surely suffer, but as it is, this magic is lost to our understanding. Even young Abaia can call upon this power, though they can only duplicate themselves a few times. As they age, they grow more sure and capable of wielding their magic. Once an Abaia hatchling has reached adulthood, it is quite a powerful companion.

These fish swim impossibly fast, with the help of unique hollowed bones and powerful fins which allow them great maneuverability, and they can change their direction in an instant, even swimming upside down. Abaia rely on currents to travel, using fins as rudders to guide them, and unlike other fish, they use currents to move vertically, rather than forward and back, giving them yet another advantage.

This strange yet wonderful creature and attunement that probably not many people have heard of I'm happy to say, went down very well with Brenda, and she thoroughly enjoyed taking in its energy. Her email to me telling of her experience of my attunement put a huge smile on my face and she even did me the courtesy of writing a short testimony for me to put on my website. Coming from a fellow Reiki Grand Master and a member of the International Light Workers Association I was and still am very humbled by her kind words.

Testimony

This morning I called in the Abaia attunement you so kindly sent me. I can honestly say I have never felt anything like it before, it was amazing!

The only way I can describe it is that although I knew my body was here, I was not in it. It was as if I had become an energy of my own, above and beyond physical realms.

I loved it, it was a feeling of complete freedom and knowledge, just awesome.

Brenda, Reiki Grand Master, Wollongong, Australia

As I mentioned, I have created many attunements which you can find available on my website www.spiritualhart.co.uk. Some of them, like the Abaia are very strange and some of them most people won't have even heard of or even knew existed. Why, you might ask, would I want to create attunements with such ferocious looking creatures and carnivores? I did wonder this myself until my spirit guides explained things to me simply.

When in existence on the physical plane it is true some of the creatures I have created attunements with hunted and killed to survive, but so do many animals today. You would not wander through a pack of Wolves or a pride of Lions and expect to be ignored would you? In the physical world you would be easy prey for them to attack, eat and survive, nothing more as their natural instincts would dictate to them. There is no difference now to how certain animals think and behave to how say a Tyrannosaurus Rex did over sixty five million years ago.

What my spirit guides pointed out to me though was that we all have animal spirit guides and duly indicated my own Tiger, Bear, Wolf, Dragon, Unicorn and Pegasus guides to name but a few. This was when the penny dropped and I realised of course that animals in the spirit realms do not need to eat or attack us, they come to us with much guidance, wisdom and healing just like a spirit guide does. Therefore some of these attunements my spirit guides wanted me to create with weird, wonderful and seemingly scary and intimidating creatures were nothing to be concerned about. It was all about the strength of their energy to help people either through healing, guidance or protection. Even if people wanted to try to use my attunements to harm others it wouldn't happen, because they were created in the light with love and compassion and only for good use. They would, however, protect you to some extent just like an animal guide would, especially through meditation and other spiritual work.

I have an incredibly open mind due to my years working with the spirit world but a lot of people haven't, even those who work spiritually can be very naïve in their thinking. This is another reason why I had to leave the spiritual Church years ago as it was stifling my progression. As much as spiritual Churches are a good place to start if you want to receive psychic messages, healing and perhaps learn to meditate, many of them are too blinkered in their thinking and cannot move far away from religious indoctrination and the Bible. The spiritual Churches I visited were very much like this so I kept a lot of my thoughts to myself as some of them would argue to defend the Bible and its teachings. It seemed they had educated themselves with one book and that was the way it was, so there wasn't any point in offering your views because they didn't count or fell on deaf ears.

My Father was very much this way as he attended the spiritualist Churches for many years, but he has seen my progression and heard my knowledge which has opened his mind more, and I really enjoy it when he sits in some of my classes as he wouldn't for a long time. I think this was down to the fact I'm too open and honest with people and I like to do a lot of practical work with the students. I see no point in me doing everything every week in the classes. That's not the way to help people grow and trust in what they are doing and learning. My Mam also sits in my weekly classes too which is nice and she gives some very accurate psychic readings, considering she turned away from spirituality all those years ago.

There are seventy four attunements that I have created so far, which I have listed at the end of this book (Appendix 3).

135

22

Psychic surgery had always amazed me but when I started doing it myself under my spirit guides' supervision and direction I was amazed even more. I must admit though the first time my spirit guides asked me to put my hands inside a patient's body I panicked a little. I was just about to do it and my hands were inches away from the patient's body but then I pulled back and told my spirit guides I couldn't do it. It seems silly to me now given the trust I have in my spirit guides, but back then I guess my physical brain was still kicking in too much telling me certain things were impossible. Years later I know very differently as I have been a part of countless psychic surgery work with my spirit guides. No, I can't perform heart transplants or brain surgery before you ask, but I have removed foreign objects from the body, removed cancerous cells and performed minor surgery numerous times.

One of the first minor surgeries I actually did was during a distant healing session. A friend telephoned me saying he was in agony with his stomach hernia and would I send him some healing to ease the pain. He had planned on going shopping with his girlfriend and his mother that day, but they had had to go without him because he was in so much pain. I agreed to try to help him and told him to lie down and not get up for at least forty five minutes whilst I sent him distant healing. On ending our conversation I went into my sanctuary and called upon my spirit guides as usual and felt the energy start to flow. I knew by now my friend would be lying down so I asked my spirit guides to bring his spiritual body to my healing table for us to work on. Within a few seconds I felt my friend's energy on my healing table and placed my own physical hands over his stomach where the problem was. This was all I planned on doing at the time to help relieve the pain for him, but my spirit guides had a better idea.

My hands were guided to push the hernia back into place as we worked on his spiritual body. I have no in depth knowledge of how the human body works or indeed where most things are within it, but I did as I was directed, trusting in my guidance. Once the hernia was pushed back in place I was told to hold one of my hands palm upwards and some ethereal gauze was placed in my hand. My spirit guides then told me to place the gauze over the hernia to keep it in place. It was a very surreal moment but I did as I was asked never doubting that it wouldn't work. Once in place I just kept sending the healing energy into my friend's body until the healing was over and then my spirit guides took his spiritual body from my healing table back to his physical body. What I had done in my sanctuary on his spiritual body was replicated in his physical body and although it may sound quite unbelievable to some, that's exactly what happened.

After I had finished the healing session I was talking to Susan about it when the telephone rang. It was my friend again and he couldn't believe the pain had completely gone. He said that before the healing he was struggling to walk around his home because of the hernia pulling and the pain, but now it felt fine. He could even stand up straight with no feeling of pain. I advised him he still needed to go to the doctor's though to get it checked out, as the gauze we had placed over it was only a temporary measure to keep it in place and ease the pain for him. He said he had an appointment booked already so that wasn't a problem. He was just glad to be pain free again and thanked me profusely.

As fantastic a healing session as that was for both of us it actually got my friend into trouble. When his mother and girlfriend arrived home from their shopping trip, and found him walking around as if nothing was wrong they accused him of pulling a fast one. He explained he had telephoned me in desperation and what had happened, but it seemed they were less than impressed and totally disbelieved him. They argued that if he had been in that much pain it could not have just disappeared in less than two hours. I did verify his story a few days later to his girlfriend though, but I'm still not sure whether she fully believed us.

Some of you reading this may say that's not psychic surgery because there is no cutting or sewing involved and that's fine with me, I'm just a healing channel at the end of the day and not a qualified Doctor or surgeon. To put your ethereal hands inside a physical or spiritual body and alter things accordingly though is more than just luck, and this is why I class it as a form of psychic surgery.

I have done psychic surgery on myself which was a long process but it got the job done, saving me an operation and more than likely having to be on medication for the rest of my life if I had agreed with the Doctor's recommendation. After having an MRI scan it was found that I had a hole in my heart. The various doctor's I saw said this was not uncommon and apparently about twenty five percent of people have one and many don't even know it. They said, however, that in later life it could cause me problems and possibly lead to a stroke or heart attack, and as my hole was particularly large they wanted to perform what they termed a minor operation.

To close the hole in my heart the Consultant wanted to use a catheter procedure. This is where the surgeon inserts a catheter (a thin, flexible tube) into a vein in the groin area and they then thread the tube to the heart's septum. A device made up of two small disks or an umbrella like device is attached to the catheter and when the catheter reaches the septum, the device is pushed out of the catheter. The device is placed so that it plugs the hole between the atria, and once it's secured in place the catheter is withdrawn from the body. It seemed ever so simple as they explained it to me and showed me the hole in my heart on a monitor. You could see the hole quite clearly as the heart pumped away and I watched it as I had my ultrasound scan. I wasn't very happy at this, as you can imagine, but life is life and I'd been born with it and lived with it all my life. I just hadn't known about it until now.

I asked many questions of how the operation would possibly affect me. This was my heart after all and I was very concerned about how it would affect my daily life. Surprisingly they said it wouldn't really affect my life at all.

Apparently having to be on medication to thin my blood, lower cholesterol and more was no big deal to them. I had to bite my tongue then as administering drugs is a big deal in my eyes, especially when they expect you to take them for the rest of your life. I was 40 years old at this time and I had no intention of being on medication for the rest of my life, nor did I plan on having the procedure. But I didn't tell the Consultant there and then, I needed time to do some serious thinking.

I am not totally anti-medication. I know sometimes our body does need certain things to help us fight disease, but I am also well aware of the problems medication can cause especially if taken long term. Again I am not a Doctor or a Chemist but I do know that drugs have side effects, and weighing up the combination of medication for the rest of my life and surgery, this operation didn't seem worth it. I listened to what the Consultant carried on telling me that day but with little interest. My mind was now pre-occupied with how I was going to change things for myself. As we left the Castle Hill hospital in Cottingham, Susan turned to me and said, "You're not going to have the operation are you?" I think the look on my face said it all as we walked back to the car together.

With doing what I do and knowing what I know and have learned over the years, having the operation and taking medication for the rest of my life would seriously affect my abilities as a healing channel. Medication is a toxin and whether they help an illness, virus or disease they are still poisoning or damaging something else in our body at the same time. This may be minimally at first but over time it can be very extensive. Medication can damage our organs and cause other illnesses and ailments or allergic reactions and I can't have that happening to my body if I want to keep healing people at the level I've so far achieved. I need to keep my body as free of toxins as possible to maintain a good channel for my spirit guides to work through. I also need to keep positive and healthy and drugs can often lead to lethargy and depression as side effects, and that's a road I don't want to go down.

Some of you reading this may agree or disagree with my thoughts on medication and again that is your prerogative. I have no desire of talking people out of taking drugs if they think they will help them and that's the way they want to go. For me though there was more at stake here than just being on medication for the rest of my life. I had my work to think about, and if that was going to suffer and stop me working and helping people as well as myself it just didn't seem worth it. If I couldn't constantly heal my own back pain enough that would also probably mean more medication and more than likely I would eventually become dependent on a wheelchair. As I pondered these thoughts I realised my quality of life would be seriously hindered and I was not prepared to let that happen.

I rationalised that my spirit guides had put too much time and effort into me, and that they had too many plans ahead for me for this hole in my heart to just ruin it and bring it to an end. I meditated a lot on this issue and I was constantly asking for guidance over the following few days about my situation and what I could do to avoid this operation and the long term medication I would need. My spirit guides never let me down assuring me my path would not be hindered or ruined and they told me exactly what I had to do to ensure this. It was to be a long process but it would be worth my while and they knew I had the dedication to them and myself as a healing channel to do it. They were right as always and I kept their guidance to myself, but I did everything they told me to over the next few months, trusting in them and how they could assist me.

Four months after finding the hole in my heart and the consultation about the planned operation, I was called back to the Castle Hill hospital. The Consultant wanted to do another ultrasound scan to check exactly what needed to be done, and to book me in for the operation they presumed I would be going ahead with. I had barely spoken to Susan about it since our last visit and she knew it was pointless trying to make me change my mind about not having the operation. She knew me too well once I had made a decision about something, but she did want me to attend this appointment and so I did, on a very cold December morning.

I was the first appointment of the day so luckily we didn't have to wait long before a nurse asked us to follow her into a private room to do the second ultrasound scan. She told me I only needed to take my shirt off and to lie down on the bed then she left the room for a few minutes, leaving Susan and I alone. I looked at Susan as I lay there and I said to her, "I'm going to tell you something now, I've been doing a lot of work on my heart over the last four months".

She looked at me curiously then replied, with a grin and shaking her head, "If that hole has disappeared what are you going to say to the nurse?"

I smiled back at her shrugged my shoulders and said, "I have no idea, but I guess we'll soon find out won't we? Either way, you know I'm not having this operation and ruining my work and spiritual path". Then I told her briefly about the psychic surgery I had been doing on myself every night when I went to bed, healing my heart and using ethereal light to sew up the hole.

With that the nurse returned and started to smear a jelly substance over my chest to begin the ultrasound scan using a transducer or probe. An ultrasound scan is a painless test that uses sound waves to create images of organs and structures inside your body. The lubricating jelly is put onto your skin so that the probe can make a good contact with your body. The probe is connected by a wire to the ultrasound machine, which is linked to a monitor. Pulses of ultrasound are sent from the probe through the skin into your body, and the ultrasound waves then echo or bounce back from the various structures in the body. The echoes are detected by the probe and are sent down the wire to the ultrasound machine where they are displayed as a picture on the monitor. The picture is constantly updated so the scan can show movement as well as structure. For example, the valves of a heart opening and closing during a scan of the heart or in my case finding a hole, as the operator moves the probe around over the surface of the skin to get views from different angles.

Susan stared intently at the screen that started to show my beating heart as the nurse rolled the probe across my chest in search of the hole. After five or six minutes of trying though the nurse said the words I was hoping to hear with a nervous laugh, "I can't seem to find it". I looked at Susan and she looked at me shaking her head in disbelief and I must admit I had to stop myself from laughing as she silently mouthed to me, "I don't believe it".

The nurse continued searching and rolling the probe over my chest for a few more minutes but still with no success, so she asked me to sit up straight and to raise my left arm up so she could work from the side and through my ribs. This, she said, was so she could try to locate the hole from another angle, but again after a few minutes she couldn't find one. In a final attempt the nurse then asked if I could lean forward so she could work through my back. It may be, she suggested that my lungs were blocking sight of the hole in my heart. Again nothing showed up on the monitor after several minutes of trying. I was grinning like a Cheshire cat and so was Susan even though she was still shaking her head in disbelief, but she knew exactly why the nurse couldn't find it. Out of ideas the nurse excused herself and said she would be back in a minute, which gave Susan and I a chance to finally start giggling. "Unbelievable!" Susan said, "But how?"

"I told you", I replied, "I have been constantly working on it every night for the last four months. It's taken a long time but it looks like it's been worth it doesn't it?" She agreed still a bit in shock but then the nurse returned with two doctor's behind her as they introduced themselves to me. The Doctors were from Greece and India respectively and they both performed the procedure to close holes in people's hearts. One of them took over the ultrasound probe and began rolling it over my chest again as the two Doctor's, nurse and Susan looked closely to find the hole. As there was no sign of the hole through the chest, they did exactly as the nurse had done first working through my side and ribs, then through my back, but again there was no sign of any hole, which gave both the Doctor's puzzled looks.

After a few minutes discussion they decided it would be best to inject me in my arm and push air through my vein which would travel into my heart. This they said would show them where the hole was and we would be able to see it on the ultrasound monitor. My smile waned at this but I knew I had to let them do it, but I still remained confident that the work I had done with my spirit guides had been a success. It was a bit of a messy job as they tried to do this, and as the needle came out of my arm my blood sprayed over one of the Doctor's, the nurse and the room. This later caused me to think about something I had been told in a consultation earlier that year, that my blood was too thick and that they needed me to take certain medication to thin it. I'd refused the medication of course much to the Doctor's disappointment, choosing instead to work with crystal energy to rectify it, not that I had told the Doctor this. It certainly didn't look too thick then as it shot out of my arm but most doctor's I have found just want to put you on drugs for anything and everything. No wonder the pharmaceutical companies put them on commission, but let's not travel down that road.

As the air was sent through we all waited and watched the monitor in anticipation for the hole to appear, and after several minutes the tiniest hole could only just be seen as a pin prick of air passed through it. Was I disappointed? Not at all as the two doctor's then looked at each other and said there was no need for an operation on something so small, returning the smile to my face again. They couldn't understand though when they looked at the ultrasound pictures from four months previous how it had closed up. There was a massive difference between the two sizes. We didn't offer an explanation either, I just wanted to leave with the good news and pay my thanks and gratitude to my spirit guides for what they had done for me. They had saved me having not only the operation, but spending the rest of my life on medication and any side effects that they would bring. They had also saved my work as a healer so I could carry on doing what I love most with them helping all.

We left the hospital that day with big smiles obviously. It was a definite victory for spiritual healing and what can be achieved with time and dedication. As healers we can be part of some seemingly miraculous changes but we are not Jesus, we cannot just heal and cure people or animals with one touch or one healing session every time. Minor ailments and illnesses yes, but not major, we are just not working at that higher vibration yet, but we can help to change things given the time. On leaving the hospital that day I did not stop healing my own heart daily and I still do, because as tiny as the hole was I did not want it to get any bigger again. If my own self healing and psychic surgery had managed to close that gap to a pin prick size in four months, my hope was that it could be fully closed with more time. This I would never know without another ultrasound of course, but I'm happy in the knowledge that my spirit guides did what they did, so every time I self heal now, I always continue to do a little bit of work on my heart to make sure the hole stays closed.

It is nice to share some of my healing experiences with you in this book, but it is also nice to share my own personal healing. There is no pain with spiritual healing even on such a major organ as the heart. I feel very little as I self heal a part from very pleasant vibrations and sensations running through and around my body and a sense of total relaxation and calm. Just like most of my patients though I often slip into a peaceful, relaxing slumber.

Carrying on the work of psychic surgery, I have also fitted many ethereal gastric bands for people to help them cut down on their food intake and lose weight. A physical gastric band, also known as a stomach band or a lap band, is an inflatable silicone ring that is placed around the top of the stomach. It is often known as the ultimate portion controller or the gastric band diet, keeping a person feeling fuller for longer. It works by restricting the capacity of your stomach, so that you eat less and over time lose weight. It is the most popular weight loss surgery option, but unfortunately is does cost a few thousand pounds to have one fitted privately in a hospital and is not always available on our National Health Service. Gastric bands are made to suit weight loss requirements and to ensure a realistic, achievable weight loss of one or two pounds a week. When a stomach band is fitted it compresses the top of the stomach sending signals to the brain to generate a sense of fullness.

There is a high risk of complications though as the operation, while simple in theory, involves making massive changes to the way that your body functions.

These changes have to be done so as not to cause the body to damage itself or reject the surgery. Our digestive system is a complex series of interconnections, and altering one section can have huge effects on the rest of your body. In general most of the complications that can arise through band surgery are correctable through a relatively simple procedure, but most of the serious complications will result in the need to remove the band. This means another operation and obviously nothing gained but a severe dent in your bank account.

There are many things that can go wrong with having a band fitted through surgery including band erosion, which is when the band pushes or grows into the lining of the stomach. This can cause significant health complications if the lining of the stomach is compromised and the band must be removed. Band intolerance can occur because like transplants, your body has a chance of simply rejecting foreign objects placed inside it. Gastric bands are not a normal part of the human body, and our immune system has developed to reject foreign bodies from inside us. If your body starts to reject the band the person will feel extremely unwell, and may start vomiting regularly. Band leakage can happen too as sometimes your gastric band will not seal off the entrance to your stomach appropriately and it will leak. This means that the effectiveness of the band will decrease over time, probably returning your original appetite. If this happens your Doctor can investigate and minor surgery may be needed to remedy the situation. Other problems that do occur are band slippage, blood clots, bowel dysfunction, esophageal dilation, indigestion and more. Gastric band surgery also puts you at a higher risk of developing gallstones and gall bladder disease.

My spirit guides brought this gastric band procedure to my attention when helping a patient in her sixties who was having difficulty with her breathing and struggling to walk far. Her breathing had become so bad over just a couple of years that getting any exercise had become impossible for her, and even walking thirty yards to her car to visit me for healing, she needed to have a rest half way. The healing sessions she was having with me were doing her the world of good though. Her chest felt clearer and she could breathe more easily, but she was concerned about all the weight she had put on and how easily she became exhausted through lack of exercise. This was when my spirit guides said we could fit a gastric band on her temporarily to help her to cut her portions down and to lose some weight. I suggested this to her but at the time had no idea how to fit one. But she, like me, trusted in my spirit guides to help her.

I studied the gastric band fitting procedure which seemed fairly simple from my point of view as we just had to remove the patient's stomach, fit the band and then replace the stomach. That sounds absurd doesn't it? But that's how simple healing and psychic surgery is. No need for an anesthetic or lengthy operation, no blood, no pain and no long recovery period after. If you would have told me this kind of thing was possible twenty years ago, I wouldn't have believed it either, but it does work. Also with an etheric band there isn't the issue of rejection, or a risk of any complications with erosion, intolerance, leakage, slippage and such. I know some of you may say well what about the long term effects like developing gallstones or gall bladder disease but that isn't a problem either. Spirit guides would not allow me to channel anything that would jeopardise a person's life, which is why etheric bands are only temporary.

The etheric gastric band simply helps a person cut down their food intake for a few weeks or months then disappears from the body. Hopefully by this time the person has got used to being fuller quicker, reduced their portions accordingly and are able to continue their diet on their own. These gastric bands are a motivator from my spirit guides to help them start to lose the weight they need to, as sometimes they know we need a lot of help to get us started with things that seem impossible for us to do. I do, of course, explain all this in depth to my clients as well as the need to exercise and eat a proper balanced diet to further help themselves. Just because you have a band fitted doesn't mean you can live on fast food and cakes, that's not the point, the point of them is to help your health.

When I fitted the gastric band on the lady who was struggling with her weight I started with a complete negative energy clearance. This was to ensure nothing negative would prevent the band from being fitted. After the clearance I healed her as normal but about halfway through the session I moved around to the side of her as she lay on my healing table to start the procedure. As I have mentioned already I am not a Doctor and I have very little knowledge of the human anatomy, but that makes absolutely no difference at all when you work with spirit guides. I mimicked my intentions with my physical hands above her stomach area whilst my ethereal hands went inside her body and removed her ethereal stomach, placing it in my physical hands. I was then told to circle her stomach with one of my hands, and as I did white light started to come from my hand, and this created the temporary band to shrink the stomach for however long was necessary.

Once the band was fitted and my spirit guides were happy we placed her ethereal stomach back in her body, then I continued to heal her for the rest of the session as normal. When I ended the healing we talked a while and the lady said she could feel wonderful tingling sensations in the stomach area still. She also said that during the band fitting she could feel pulling sensations in her stomach but they were not uncomfortable, just feelings she had never experienced before. She was also breathing better again so all the healing signs were good. The lady at the time of the band fitting was twenty two stone and in her working years she had been a chef. She thoroughly enjoyed her food but could not believe in the first week after having the band fitted how much she had cut down on her intake, and started to lose some weight. It didn't stop there though, she continued to lose the pounds each week and after just eight weeks she had lost two and a half stone, taking her weight down to under twenty stone for the first time in a long time. This enabled her to move about more easily too.

As I said I have fitted quite a few gastric bands on clients to date and people's experiences with them vary. Some lose weight very fast and some gradually, some lose centimeters or inches off the body quite quickly too, but all those that I have heard from after a gastric band fitting have said how their portion intake had cut down considerably and how fuller they felt. One lady who saw speedy results on both weight and inches was kind enough to write a short testimony about it which I will share with you.

Testimony

I have struggled with my weight and I am under 5ft tall, so every bit shows. When I heard of Dean Kingett and the psychic surgery he could perform, I knew this was for me. No waiting months or years and no big price tag. I had an ethereal gastric band fitted with no stitches, no pain and he also wiped all the negativity I was carrying away from me.

He talked me through everything first and guided me through all that he would be doing, and basically all I needed to do was relax. In the first six weeks of the gastric band being fitted I lost nine pounds, and in the second week I lost another six pounds. To date six weeks later I have lost nearly two stones and seventeen inches off my body.

TH, Hull, England

23

I will continue my work to help and educate people regardless of any derision and I remember doing a short talk at a friend's psychic demonstration at "Ye Olde White Hart" in Hull where some of the audience were very sceptical and even quite rude that night when I began. My friend Nettie was hosting an evening of clairvoyance and unfortunately the psychic medium she was supposed to be doing it with couldn't make it, so she asked me if I would do a short talk and bring some of my healing stones to show people to start the evening. I agreed and took a variety of my creations to show them but they had little interest in what I was showing or telling them that night. I don't, as a rule, do my own demonstrations in pubs or clubs as when I do energy work with an audience they need to be aware of their senses, and obviously alcohol in a persons system numbs their senses. This was just a talk though, but most of them just weren't interested. All they wanted were the psychic messages they were hoping they would receive.

After twenty minutes or so I thanked them for listening (those who were), and told them I would be in the next room with my creations if anyone wanted a chat or to ask any questions in the interval. When the interval came everyone just headed to the bar and no one came in the room I was in for quite a while. As I was talking to Nettie though a family of seven ventured into the room to have a look at what I had on offer, so she left me to talk with them as they started to ask me a few questions. They were quite disbelieving of what my creations could do and help them with and a young gentleman who was with them said, pointing to a lady and sniggering, "She's got a headache, can you do anything for that"?

I looked at the lady and asked her how long she had had the headache for, to which her reply was all night, starting before she arrived. I pulled out a chair and asked her to sit on it and let me try to remove it, to which she shook her head but was eventually talked into doing so by the rest of her family. I told her to close her eyes and just relax as I held my hands to the back of her head channelling the healing energy into her. After about sixty seconds I moved to the side of her and with one hand gently touching the back of her head I began reaching into her forehead with my other hand in an attempt to remove the pain. My physical hand obviously stopped as it met her forehead but my ethereal hand went straight into her head, repeatedly pulling out the bad energy and pain. Her family watched me work on her giggling at my actions as they whispered to each other, but after about three minutes the lady said, "Oh my God, it's gone, I don't believe it!"

Her family soon stopped their giggling and whispering at her statement, and they watched me work on her for a few more minutes with interest now. When I eventually finished and the lady opened her eyes again she was quite at a loss for words apart from saying thank you, as her family members questioned her, asking her if the headache really had gone. It was the end of the interval though and the second half of the evening was about to begin, and so they made their way back to the main room to take their seats again. I thanked my spirit guides for healing the lady with a wry smile on my face as they had certainly put an end to the giggling and whispering, and I was sure they would be talking about it after the demonstration had finished.

As it turned out, not only were they talking about the headache removal after the demonstration, but during it too, as word had gone around the audience about what I had done. So as the demonstration ended about half of the audience came straight through to see me. I didn't heal anyone else that evening but there were many questions now and a lot more interest in my creations and my healing work. The derogatory whispering I'd witnessed from my short talk earlier was now a thing of the past. Proof in their eyes, had now been given to them, as they told me about their own ailments and asked if I could help them.

I enjoyed the change in their opinion of me and about what I had conveyed to them earlier, but it just showed how ignorant people can be about things they don't know about or can't understand. I don't fully know how electricity works but I know if we plug a television set in we can see pictures and it makes a sound. How can we see those images though and how can we hear the sounds. Most of us don't know the answer to these questions but we accept the television as a major necessity in our homes. A radio is pretty much the same, how can we just turn a dial or push a button and have access to lots of different stations from different parts of the country or the world? Yet again we accept this without knowing how it works exactly, just that it does.

I suppose, to simplify, I view healing energy in much the same way as I view electricity. I know it exists because I can use it, just like a television or radio. It's a frequency, a vibration that I can tune into to help people. Energy is everywhere and everything is made of energy, a fact scientists are well aware of. Scientists are brilliant for helping us to understand a lot of things, but they prove that much, that a lot of it just gets ignored by people unless you are really interested in it. I have been interested in healing and the spirit world and other dimensions for many years so I have chosen to study it, that's why to me and millions of others it is very real. Just because many people can't see or feel what psychics, mediums, clairvoyants, healers and others can, doesn't mean it doesn't exist. After all, you can't see electricity or the frequencies floating through the air all around you can you, but you know it's real and accept it.

There is a scientist called Dr. Robert Lanza who was voted the third most important scientist alive by the New York Times, who has written a book called "Biocentrism: How Life and Consciousness Are the Keys to Understanding the Nature of the Universe". The book sets about proving that life does not end when the physical body dies and that it can go on forever. Dr. Lanza is an expert in many scientific things and he is involved with physics, quantum mechanics and astrophysics. This mixture has come up with the new theory of biocentrism which teaches that life and consciousness are fundamental to the universe, and that it is consciousness that creates the material universe, not the other way around.

His theory implies that death of consciousness simply does not exist. It only exists as a thought because people identify themselves with their physical body. Most people believe that the body is going to die sooner or later and think their consciousness will die with it. If the body did generate consciousness, then consciousness would die when the body dies, but if the body receives consciousness in the same way that a cable box receives satellite signals, then of course consciousness does not end at the death of the physical body. Consciousness exists outside of the limitations of time and space and it is able to be anywhere at all, either in the human body or outside of it.

Dr. Lanza also believes that multiple universes can exist so that in one universe the body can be dead, and in another it continues to exist. By this he means that a dead person while traveling through the tunnel of light ends up not in hell or in heaven as many have been taught to believe, but in a similar world to the one they once inhabited, but this time alive. This theory by Dr. Lanza now has many supporters. Not just people who want to live forever, but also by some well known scientists. These are the physicists and astrophysicists who tend to agree with the existence of parallel worlds and who suggest the possibility of multiple universes. A multi-verse is a well defended scientific concept as scientists believe that no physical laws exist which would prohibit the existence of parallel worlds.

Data has also been gathered from the Planck space telescope which supports the idea that our universe is not alone. With this data scientists have found that the universe has a lot of dark recesses represented by some holes and extensive gaps. This means that there is an abundance of places or other universes where our soul could migrate to after death. According to scientists our souls are said to be constructed from the very fabric of the universe and may have existed since the beginning of time. They say our brains are just receivers and amplifiers so that there really could be a part of your consciousness that is non material and will live on after the death of your physical body.

With scientists proving so much though year after year still the majority of people will not accept that we do not die, and that we just discard our physical body when we make our transition from this world to the next. When our time here expires for whatever reason the energy of our consciousness just gets recycled back into a different body at some point. But in the mean time it exists outside of the physical body on some other level or dimension that we commonly may know as the spirit world. This is why when we open our minds enough we can connect with loved ones who have passed over, because they are not dead, only their physical body is.

Bringing awareness of all I do is why I enjoy teaching psychic development and doing psychic demonstrations to open people's minds. At my private demonstrations, particularly in my sanctuary, I sometimes do what is referred to as a transfiguration. This is when I ask some of my spirit guides to come into my physical body and as they do most of the audience can see my face change, as it takes on the appearance of men, women, children and animal spirit guides. It may sound quite unbelievable to some but it happens and some people also refer to this as trance. When I do it though I do not go into a trance, as that is a state in which you are awake but not really conscious of where you are. I know exactly where I am when I do a transfiguration, and I am aware of everything throughout it.

There is one transfiguration in particular that stands out to me which I did a few years ago when working with my good friend Eileen Akrill, a very talented and popular psychic medium from North Cave, East Yorkshire. The transfiguration we were going to do together was at the end of the demonstration, and as I was putting the stools out for us to sit on, Eileen said to me "Is Susan coming in to watch the transfiguration tonight?"
"I don't know, why?" I replied.
"Go and get her" she said. So I briefly excused myself as I popped out of my sanctuary and went next door to find her. Susan was in the kitchen when I entered and she said "Have you finished already"?
"No", I answered, "Eileen just asked me if you were coming in to watch the transfiguration."
"What for?" was the response. "I've seen it loads of times."
"I don't know, she just asked if you were coming in."
"Okay, I'll be through in a minute then".

With that I went back into the sanctuary and started to explain to the audience what Eileen and I were about to do. I always give the audience the option of staying to watch the transfiguration or not, as some people are very scared of the spirit world even though they believe in it and come to the demonstrations to listen to the psychic messages. Whilst explaining what was about to happen Susan entered the sanctuary and stood at the back, then we dimmed the lights and Eileen and I began.

It's a strange but powerful experience doing a transfiguration, but one I enjoy as it really opens people's eyes when they see the different spirit guide features coming through my face. I can feel their energy within my body and I am aware of sensations on my face as it changes, but I do not know who or what is coming through me until people tell me who or what they saw after. Doing a transfiguration requires ultimate trust in your spirit guides to keep you safe and protected throughout it, and this I have, but I do not recommend others doing it unless you're of a high vibration and have a very good knowledge of the spirit world. Eileen and I did the transfiguration for about ten minutes as usual then I felt her squeeze my hand to signify she was ready to bring it to an end. I was ready too but as I thanked the spirits for working through me in my mind and asked them to leave my body, I could still feel an energy presence within me. This was unusual so I kept with it knowing there must be a good reason why, and so I continued to stay in transfiguration mode a while longer. The energy didn't stay with me too long though, maybe about ninety seconds or so and then left as I opened my eyes again.

As usual the audience was quite amazed at what they had witnessed through Eileen's face and mine. Native American Indians, Oriental people, Aborigines, Ascended Masters a Wolf and many others were mentioned as being seen, as

our features changed throughout the transfiguration. It had been another good demonstration and we thanked them all for coming as we ended the evening and said our goodbyes. When everyone left and Susan and I were putting the chairs away and tidying up ready for the next day, she stopped me and said, "I know why Eileen told me to come and watch tonight".
"Really? Why?" I enquired.
"I saw my Dad tonight, he came through you at the end of the transfiguration" she said.
"Ahhh, so that's who it was." I said with a smile.

Susan smiled too as her father had only six months previously passed away after a stomach aneurism. "I saw him and he knew I could see him" she continued, "but he wouldn't leave you, so I had to tell him I really could see him and that he had to leave you now".

We were both smiling and Susan had tears in her eyes as she told me more and we talked about her father, and as we did flashing energy lights could be seen around the room and the familiar feeling of spirits touch was all around us, confirming Eric, her father, was with us, and that she had indeed seen him come through me that evening. Tears of joy are a great sign of release of the emotions and Susan, like I, understands that only the physical body dies, but it doesn't stop us missing people being in our day to day lives. The general belief that we die completely is reinforced throughout our life and very few places, particularly educational and religious establishments will not teach about life and death from a spiritual view. Knowing about and understanding just a little bit about the spirit world and the afterlife can be a huge consolation when we lose someone, and it's why we should be taught about it from an early age so the grieving process can hopefully be dealt with a lot easier, I know it has certainly helped me.

To explain further and put it in simple terms, when people emigrate to another country, for whatever reason, it can be a very heartbreaking and emotional time for those they are leaving behind. However, the progress in the world of technology means contact can still be made with them through the telephone, an email, skype, webcams and other more traditional means such as a letter. This is wonderful for those involved as friendships and relationships don't have to end because of the distance that has been put between them. This is pretty much the same when you are in touch with, and understand, your psychic abilities. You don't have to lose touch with the people you love as they're still available to contact if you open your mind and stop believing it's impossible. It has saved me a lot of heartache knowing my friends and family are not dead and gone forever, and knowing they are safe and not suffering, just living in another realm, time space or dimension. I know it's not quite the same as having them here with me but at least I can still have some contact with them however minimal, and their advice and guidance just like my spirit guides is incredibly valuable to me.

24

The world we live in is a beautiful place and can provide us with everything we need to live and thrive. Unfortunately, the human race is, it seems to me, quite flawed. Power and greed have become more and more prevalent in today's societies and people's values have changed over the years. The media portrays 'pop stars' and sports personalities as our ultimate role models. Many of them behave in an appalling way, making power, money and control the things to aim for, while having narrow minded shallow views and beliefs.

The Earth is an enormous space, enough room for everyone to live harmoniously alongside all the other wonderful creatures that also inhabit the Earth, or it was until power and greed took over. The Earth doesn't have any borders, just man-made countries, division and ownership, making true freedom a myth. We could live our lives full of peace, understanding and love, but that's not what we are taught.

Human nature is to love, it makes us feel happy and needed, but society teaches us from a very young age to hate, own, be angry, seek revenge and use violence to get what we want. Everything, from some nursery rhymes and children's books, T.V. and the media all carry messages of hate and violence, bombarding us on a daily basis and nothing is done by our Governments to stop this. By the time we reach our teens it is indoctrinated into our nature, making it easy for manipulation by the powers that be to continue.

Compassion, love and respect are pushed way down the 'agenda' and war, greed and corruption portrayed in a positive light. There is no wonder there is so much conflict in the world, politics and religion, power and control, money and greed all play their part and have a lot to answer to!

I don't have all the answers to all the problems of the world, but I am glad I am more aware of the issues and the reasons behind them and I now think more carefully before I act or react to situations brought to my attention. There are hundreds of books and websites that you can read to help you understand the corruptness of the control in our world. How you view the way the world around you is run is up to you, all I am saying is that sometimes it is better to research and dig a little deeper when faced with the news and articles in the media relating to world issues. The choice is yours but it is well worth doing your research if you want a better understanding of life for you and your family.

People are in recent years, however, starting to listen to their intuition and asking more and more questions and are getting in touch with their spiritual side but many of them don't know exactly why. What they do know though is something is not quite right with the world around them and that they are seeing that they are being forced to live in an unharmonious way which isn't helping them, or anything else living on this planet. I feel that this is because their consciousness has been raised and their own spirit guides are helping to make them more aware of how things are or could be. We are supposed to have free will on this Earth, so we should be free to choose how we want to live and what we want to do. But we only seem to be entitled to this as long as we conform to the government's laws. Our spirit guides wouldn't encourage us to go against the law of the land but can make us question why the law is as it is and they can show us a way of achieving peace, being happy and content and to live our lives in a more constructive and compassionate way. All we have to do is listen, get in tune with them and let our intuition guide us.

The more people that realise this and are open to change, the more people will question what is being sold to them as right and wrong, instead of conforming to the views of whichever political party happens to be in power. From what I have seen politicians promise the earth and deliver very little yet still people vote in the hope that things will change. Sometimes you need to question who actually runs a country – is it the Government or is it the people with all the money who have the power, the large corporations, pharmaceutical companies and the like.

We are brought up to be patriotic, to love our country and to defend it at all costs, perhaps after years of listening to the propaganda on our T.V. screens, many will be ready to fight and die for their country but maybe won't actually know the real reasons that war has been declared. You may have noticed that Government after Government always want to cut budgets. It doesn't matter which political party they are, but they always have enough money to go to war. I would like to think that more people are asking how/why?

I have over the years learned to deal with the anger and hatred that I had in the past, and with my spirit guides help and guidance I live my life in a much better and happier way. I choose not to be dictated to, manipulated or prejudiced, which is why I do my work without any qualms, I just love helping people. I am not perfect, I am human after all and I know I have a lot more to learn for however long I am here. But the more I do learn and grow, the more peace and tranquility I bring into my life and those around me. I am so glad I listened all those years ago when my Father told me about the spirit world and the after life, and that I continued to learn and study this subject throughout my life.

25

My healing life so far has been quite a ride and I've enjoyed it all immensely and I hope to for many more years to come. The growing, learning and experimenting never stops and neither does the fun, so it never really feels like going to work, which is a real bonus to me.

For the people I have lost in my life through me doing this line of work though, I have gained many more in the form of students and clients who have learnt and felt the reality and benefits of what I do. Unfortunately what I do draws a lot of derision from those people who don't really understand the Universe and how it works. Some people are embarrassed by what I do, some fear what I do and others think I have gone completely mad and all religious when the truth of what I do became public knowledge. As mentioned previously I don't do religion. It is far too political, manipulative and constrictive for an open mind like mine.

So, not surprisingly, I kept my spiritual knowledge and healing abilities to myself for a long time before I shared it with my close friends and I wasn't thrown by their shocked reaction when they did find out. They all knew me as Dean the party guy, the wild guy, the funny guy, so when I finally listened to my spirit guides and took my divine path and purpose on this Earth seriously, I knew most of them would fade away. I don't have a big family but a lot of them too are dismissive of my work, but I don't mind, I know they will all understand it one day, although it's a shame that, like many, it will come through their transition from this world to the next. This is why I enjoy teaching my psychic development classes so much. When people learn, understand and know they are just energy and cannot actually die then death of the physical body is nothing to fear anymore. Being educated and knowing this also helps people deal with the physical death of friends or family. Yes we can still cry at the loss of a loved one, that's natural emotion. But knowing they are not actually gone forever is a great comfort. Knowing that we can still, through our psychic abilities, communicate with them or see them again is of great solace.

I have tried to keep politics and religion out of this book and skirt around the edges as much as possible, but it's hard not too because I feel they are the main reasons most people disbelieve in the spirit world and/or energy work.

I have not written this book with the intention of converting people into my way of thinking. I hope it will just help them better understand what can be achieved and the things they are capable of if they choose to follow a spiritual path. I know my path and place in this world but, unfortunately, many do not. I sometimes wish I had taken it all more seriously when I was younger because perhaps I would know even more than I do now, and maybe I could help people even more. I understand though if I had taken it more seriously I wouldn't have learned all the valuable lessons I have learned, and that knowledge has been priceless to me and my patients and clients throughout the years. Some things you just have to experience to truly know how they make you feel or react, because if you haven't lived it, you do not know the full joy or pain of the experience or situation.

So I guess that's it as we come to the end of this chapter and indeed this book. I have enjoyed sharing some of my experiences with you and I hope you have enjoyed the journey with me. I have had so many wonderful experiences throughout my work and I have tried to give you an insight into some of them here. My only regret is that I can't remember them all. This however is why I have been getting reprimanded (in a nice way) whilst writing this book by my spirit guides as they tell me to document everything from now on, because apparently this will not be the only book I write. Time will tell I guess, but as I have said my guides are never wrong!

As a parting gift if you are open to healing energies then you may like to try this. On the back of this book is a photograph of me. Look into my eyes and then just sit back for five or ten minutes with your eyes closed and see what you sense or feel. You will receive the healing energies that you need at that time. Please feel free to use this as often as you wish. I hope you enjoy it!

LNL

APPENDIX 1

The Life Improvement Interview – from Redondo Beach, California, USA

OCTOBER 2010

Angie – Hi everyone, welcome to Life Improvement I'm your host Angie Anderson and shortly my co-host Cat McIntire will be joining me. On today's show we have Dean Kingett a Master healer. Dean is a Master of many healing modalities and he does one on one healing sessions and also teaches classes on healing and spiritual transformation at his sanctuary in Hessle, near Hull over in the UK. Dean offers a lot of incredible information and inspiration on his website which is www.spiritualhart.co.uk (this website was not the one used in the interview, but is the correct one to use if you wish to find out more about me and what I do).

Dean has a raw passion for helping others, he's devoted his life to help facilitate healing for others as well as teaching others how to call upon these healing forces for themselves, and he does it in a most respectful and loving way. I'm sure some healers do their work simply because they can do it, because they've been trained in it, but Dean clearly does this work because he loves it and he truly cares about people.

My personal experiences working with Dean have been absolutely incredible and on a spiritual level transformational. I can't say enough about him really, there's a lot I would like to say but I think I would rather see if we can get him online here and just get started with the interview.

Angie - Cat are you there? Can you hear me?

Cat – I can hear you now. I'm here now. Remember now I'm calling from Belgium (laughing, as this isn't true).

Angie – Ok we're going to do this now with the Skype, I'm a little nervous because I'm not sure what's going to happen? But hopefully he'll talk back to me any time now as we pull him in?

Cat – If not we'll just talk to his spirit (laughing).

Angie – He works with his spirit guides. I think he has another name for them?

Cat – He's got a whole bunch of them.

Angie – Right.

Cat – Like his little gang.

Angie – He tends to give credit to them rather than to himself, I'm like you know, you do incredible work, this is awesome, he's like no, no it's not me, they do all the work, so he's very modest in what he does, which is pretty cool.

Cat – I think I remember Ben Black Elk and Cloud man.

Angie – What?

Cat – Ben Black Elk, that's one of his guides.

Angie – Oh, okay, I think we have him online now? Dean, are you there?

Dean – I am indeed can you hear me?

Cat – Uhuh, we got you this time, yayyyy.

Dean – It actually works, it actually works (laughing), hello to you, how are you doing?

Angie – Well, I'm very good, Cat how are you?

Cat – I am enjoying the sunshine.

Dean – Lucky you it's a bit grey and miserable over here today.

Cat – In England really? (Laughing).

Dean – Yes, well just for a change (Laughing).

Cat – We've actually been having, well, it will be raining and dark skies one day, and the following day sunshine, and then the day after that grey skies again.

Angie – It's been weird lately I dressed for winter yesterday all bundled up, went out and ran my errands and I was boiling, people were running around in sundresses, I'm like wait a minute someone didn't give me the notice (laughing).

Dean – I definitely need to move to sunnier climes I think, I really don't like the cold, its not me.

Cat – Right, that can really make a difference on how you feel.

Angie – Okay Dean, lets get started are you ready?

Dean – Ready as I'll ever be (laughing).

Angie – Okay, well before we get started on just basic questions, what's in the name Spiritualhart?

Dean – Spiritualhart is written how it's written without the E for good reason. When I was trying to put together a team to do the demonstrations and the charity work we do, obviously we wanted spiritual as a word in it somewhere but there's many, many different groups out there, and it was my own spirit guide Ben Black Elk who actually give us the name and spiritual obviously because of the work we do and the Hart is because the male Elk is actually called a Hart. So that's how we sort of put it together, not my idea it was obviously given to me by my good friend Ben Black Elk, so we've used it ever since, which is the same reason for the picture coming together as well with the two Elks on the logo and the heart in between, so a little bit of a story behind it.

Cat – You just stole my animal titbit that I was going to throw in.

Dean – I'm sorry (all laughing).

Angie – So you mentioned Ben and I guess you have basically a gang of folks who you work with, considered on the other side. Do you know them all like by name or maybe visually or is it just kind of a sense you get that there's a force there with you, how does that work exactly for you?

Dean – I see a few of them, but I don't see all of them, I work with far too many to be honest. A lot of them, my medium friends and psychic friends have told me that certain people are working with me, things like that. I work with obviously my spirit guides but I work with the Angels as well. The Ascended masters are a big sort of influence in a lot of the work I do too. To get complicated you can go into the multi-dimensional world things and I have guides from

Atlantis and Lemuria which I can't even begin to tell you about that sort of stuff that's way beyond my knowledge but it is just an honour to have these people working through me doing what they do, which is a lot of good stuff. Ben I do get to see occasionally, he will show his face or guide me in certain ways, and with practicing Reiki, Dr Usui who founded the Reiki back in the 1800's, he's around a lot as well. It is good it's nice to see them now and again but I must admit I'm not very visual and I'd be lying if I said I was, it's not sort of my thing, and what I definitely am not is a medium, I just get guided. When I'm healing they just tell me to put my hands wherever they need to be and we just let the energy flow. Leave it to them, it's the best thing, they know what there doing I haven't got a clue.

Angie – Wow, so do they actually say, you know, there's something going on here, is it something like that or do you just get a sense for where things are kind of going on and it needs to be cleared?

Dean – It happens a few different ways to be honest. Sometimes when I'm healing a patient and I'll be talking to my guides saying where do I need to be, they will present the problem on my own body. I will feel a pain in my leg or in my stomach or in my head or wherever so they sort of let me know that way so I can move my hands to that certain area, but if I'm doing like an absent healing, which if I'm working on somebody from the USA or wherever, which is, you know, you can't do a hands on (healing) then it tends to go a little bit different because your working on the persons spiritual body then, and they allow me to put my hands inside that spiritual being as its lying in my sanctuary, so you can put things back like hernia's and remove things like congestion, things like that. It's very strange it's very weird it's all very fascinating to be honest. It's hard to believe, it's a seeing is definitely believing thing. I just listen and sometimes like I say they will just move my hands automatically, whatever. It is a very intuitive thing and I do struggle with it a lot because it does get very, very confusing at times, but it seems to work and results have been good over the last few years so I'm not knocking it, they know what their doing.

Cat – He brought up one of his guides Dr. Usui and I've been personally trying to live by his spiritual principles and I falter. I'm human but it's made a huge difference in my attitude towards myself, towards other people and the way that I handle grid lock. Usually I just try to steam roll through them and now I'm either finding a way to flow with them or flow around them. So I wondered if you could share these spiritual principles with our listener's.

Dean – Yes, they're very good to live by, but you're right we are a fallible breed, unfortunately we are these physical idiots we are. It's very hard to reach them sort of levels of perfectness shall we say, but it can help you along. Its' looking for the good in everything which is hard to find because the world is a very negative place unfortunately, but if you can see through it, things like honouring your father and your teachers and your mother and stuff like that you don't always do. Were not the most respectful as children are we, and were not the most respectful as we grow up. Being kind to every living thing, what child doesn't step on a spider or something like that because we are completely inferior of these little tiny creatures? I was terrible to be honest, spiders absolutely petrified me, but when I started working with energy and spirit, they really don't bother me anymore and they're just something I can pick up and put outside now when they've come in the house. It does give you, trying to live that sort of way, it gives you a better understanding and perception on life and what it's actually about. We take a lot for granted particularly insects and things that appear ugly to us, but like spirit says, everything has a reason and everything has its purpose. We shouldn't deem something so little and insignificant to us as a life worth wasting, but we do unfortunately. Spirits guidance has changed my life massively. Don't get me wrong I'm not a big pusher of religion or anything like that. I don't knock any religion, but I can't really live by one. I was born church of England so I'm supposedly Christian, but I've studied the Bible, I've studied Buddhism, I've studied a little bit of Hinduism and certain other things. When all these guides come in to help you from all these different religions then how can I choose a religion?

Angie – Yes.

Dean – It's very difficult and to them (spirit) it seems to me like they don't really care about religion up there, they're just all about love, respecting your fellow man, your fellow woman, your fellow animal, respecting everything basically. The more you work with it (spirit) that's the kind of outlook you get. It comes with a lot of respect obviously. When I'm out of the sanctuary I'm Deano, same kid everybody knew back in school, back when I was a teenager and all the rest of it. I don't pertain to be any sort of religious guru or anything like that, that's not for me I'm not one for preaching, I'm just honoured to do what I do basically.

Cat – I think it's really wonderful that you offer people free healing for them self, for their animal companions, family or friends if they just ask to be added to the list for absent healing. I think that's so loving and giving that you offer that physical, emotional, mental (healing), and that's including also our fellow animals the four legged and the winged and such.

Dean – I think everybody, every thing deserves it really. I mean to me again, my healing sessions can last anything from forty five minutes to two hours depending on what I'm dealing with. Obviously some problems are more severe than others, especially when you are dealing with negative energies as well and things like that. The way I see it and the way my guides and Angels and everybody else who works through me and does so much to help me help others, then for me to give the free healing and add people to the healing list and just send out that bit of healing to them all every day, then that's just like me paying some respect back for what they allow me to be for others basically, which is why I like to do it.

Angie – So, where did this all start, like basically where did the interest start, when in your life did this really become not just an interest but a total calling, because I know it's a complete and utter all encompassing calling for you at this point, but maybe not always?

Dean – Yes, it definitely has become that, it's definitely taken over my life. I first sort of understood it a little bit, as I remember being 12 years old and on a Tuesday night my Mother used to play for a local darts team. It was one of her girl's nights out sort of thing and it used to leave me and my Dad sat in together on a Tuesday night. We used to just chew the fat and mumble about certain topics and things. I really used to enjoy them he used to make me feel like a grown up, like an adult. We used to have these great conversations and stuff and he'd let me have a shandy now and again, I felt like a proper adult (laughing), it was quite nice. I just remember on this one occasion sat down, I don't know how it came up I haven't got a clue how it came up, but I remember him talking to me about spirit and the afterlife, and I remember him being so embarrassed by telling me about it, and I think he was just waiting for me to start laughing or just totally disbelieve it. But he got the exact opposite, what he got was an incredibly intrigued child and I just questioned and questioned and questioned, and he told me about my Grandad who was a medium himself and a few other people. I just lapped it up like you would, why would you disbelieve your Father? He was my best friend as well he still is to this day. I sort of left it then, we talked about it, but that was it, it was over and I never really thought that much about it again until I was 15 about 3 years later and that was the first time that I ever experienced the death of a family member, which is not a great time for anybody. But all this knowledge my Dad had given me, we'd spoke about it briefly over the years in between, and so when my Mams mam died, my Nanna, I just couldn't cry. I tried my hardest to and I know it sounds silly doesn't it, sounds quite callous, but I just couldn't. I even closed myself off in my bedroom and I stared at photographs of my Nanna and all I could do was smile, I just remember the great times and the good times. I just knew I'd see her again, I knew she'd be back and I knew I'd see her whenever, and that sort of opened me up a real lot that. That was like a big turning curve for me and that's when I started attending spiritualist churches.

Angie – Wow, that was pretty early on for you, so this has been a life long pursuit. I mean I knew it had been the majority of your adult life but I didn't know it started when you were so young. Most kids of that age are still, you know, playing with toys and trying to figure out who they are and you're already on this incredible path.

Dean – It wasn't something I bragged about in the playground believe me (laughing).

Cat – No, that would have got you beat up (laughing).

Dean – Yes, that would have definitely got me a few punches without a doubt (laughing). It is funny though, because of the beauty of the computer and the internet and things like Facebook and stuff like that. A lot of old school friends have got back in touch and they're amazed at what I do and they're just all like, you weren't like that at school, and I'm like, yes I was, I just wasn't going to tell you (laughing).

Angie – Oh man.

Dean – I've surprised a few.

Cat – My husband has told me about when he was a small child. He's always been very thoughtful, well advanced in thinking. He's extremely intelligent and he was in grammar school in the lower grade, maybe 3rd grade, and they were talking in the playground and they were talking about God and church and stuff, and he said they didn't go to church, and they said, well why not? He said because I don't believe in God, and it was like Lord of the Flies, they turned on him, and they as a mob, just started cornering him, throwing things at him and screaming things at him. It was extremely traumatising for him. So I can see why you wouldn't walk around saying here's my spirit guides.

Dean – It's definitely a strange one. I mean even through my adult life I kept it quite to myself because there's a lot of ridicule that comes with it. It comes with this religious sort of tagging that you're a Bible basher as they call it and all the rest of it. I don't do that and a lot of people in my work, healing or psychics, were not all preaching the gospel and all the rest of it, it's not about that it's just about helping people. Even the mediums just giving a message to somebody, that's healing, you're guiding them on their path, especially if they have lost a loved one, your helping them to understand that there is a life after death. That they are there to look after you, that you will see them again, and it's all helping you through. It's not about preaching about Jesus and God, you read about God's wrath and all the rest of it, I can't see a vengeful God personally? People spout so much gibberish about it and it just spoils the whole concept of the afterlife basically. I say to people, I don't know things about bio-chemistry but I know it exists, I don't know things about nuclear physics, but I know it exists, I just haven't took the time to study it, and if you don't take the time to study spiritualism then don't mock it, because it exists.

Cat – Well, people fear what they don't understand.

Dean – Definitely.

Cat – I think here in California at least that the climate is changing and it's not unusual to pick up the L.A. times and see ad's in the back for spiritual healing, for Reiki, for different modalities, where just 10 years ago that wouldn't have happened.

Dean – You seem very open out there. I've got a lot of friends in the USA, yourself included I'd like to add, but you seem very much open to the spiritual side of things in America than they do over here in the U.K. We are very pompous to be honest, we're very ignorant over here, we really, really are. I know there are a lot of us who do this work but as a population in general we are very tight lipped when it comes to talking about things like this. People don't seem to want to know about it over here which I find very unfortunate really.

Cat – You talk about the stigma attached and I didn't want to miss, wow what's the word I want? There's plenty of ignorance here too and there are pockets of enlightenment but even me 3 years ago, I would have laughed at the classes I've been taking and things I've been learning. Angie has been trying to teach me for 10 years and I just poo pooed her, and I knew it to be true I just didn't want to because of the stigma. So I'm new, I've finally come out of the spiritual closet (laughing).

Dean – That's one way of putting it (laughing).

Angie – Okay, so Dean you've studied a lot of different healing modalities, techniques, what have you, how do you choose what you work with, what's your basis and foundation of what you do. I mean there is a lot of different ways to approach this. What is your basic approach and how did you get to it?

Dean – To be fair I don't choose anymore, I completely leave it to (spirit) them now. I've studied many things, Reiki, in particular, to me that just kicked my whole world off. I really could feel the energy with that, it was fantastic stuff. Before people were telling me I was going to be a healer and all the rest of it, and I was putting my hands on their shoulders and they were saying all these marvellous things like, oh that's great and my pains gone and all the rest of it. I really wasn't feeling anything though I was just like, what's going on? But when I went and got attuned to Reiki I really did feel the energy, I could just feel it pouring out my palms, it was a very, very strange sensation and as I was being attuned I had the weirdest feeling running through my body. It was like been split in half. Half of me was really, really warm, really, really hot and the other half was absolutely freezing cold. It was just a mixture of energies, but the feeling was so immense, it was like electricity running through you. It was so cool and I thought wow, this is something that's got to be explored, that's got to be played with. Hence I went on and did my time, did my studying and moved up to being a Reiki Master and a teacher myself which is fantastic and I love attuning people too. But yes moving on to Kundalini that opened my eyes in another way, and it's a good thing to do to heal past lives and certain things like that, and you can get to the bottom with things like DNA healing and birth trauma, it's just amazing what you can do. I used to sort of assess the patient and see what was wrong with them, either finding it out myself through spirit or they would tell me, and I used to choose between various healing things that I thought they would need, and it all got a bit complicated to be honest. There was that much I needed to use from each individual modality. I was getting a bit confused myself and my spirit guides just were sort of laughing at me to be honest, and saying, why are you making it so hard for yourself? I was like, well I've got to do this and I've got to do that, and they just said, just stand there and let us do it you idiot (laughing). So I thought well, you don't usually fib, so I just will. So, I just let them do what they want now and the results are fantastic, so who am I to argue (laughing).

Angie – I was mentioning that earlier before you came on, you give all the credit to the Angel's and the guides, but don't you believe it takes a special person to facilitate this kind of work. I mean without having an open heart and an open mind and good, pure intentions would it not be kind of impossible for someone to be a conduit such as you are. I mean it takes a special person even still, even if they're (spirit) doing the work right Dean?

Dean – There's nothing special about me, dedicated I would say yes, dedicated, I can live with dedicated. I don't do ego, I certainly don't do hubris.

Angie – But it does take someone that has at least got an understanding, appreciation for it, a reverence such as you do I think? I mean I was going to ask initially can anybody do this and I imagine anybody can attune, because I know I've been in meditation and felt that total surge of energy, I imagine that's the same stuff your working with, but you see your working with it where as in meditation I'm just blissing out on it, your actually using it to help somebody else right?

Dean – Yes it is. I mean don't get me wrong you've got to have a compassion for whatever your healing, I mean for your fellow man for anything. You've got to have a heart. You've got to feel things. I am a big believer that anybody can do this, but if you've got hatred running through your veins then it's not going to happen is it, your not going to be that channel that you need to be, it's as simple as that because at the end of the day energy follows thought and if you're thinking bad things then you're not going to be healing anybody. It's not that anybody can do it should we say, you've got to have that heart and compassion. It's very hard to love a lot of things, I've had people put before me who I'm not a particular fan of, but I see it as a challenge and I won't turn anybody away whether I dislike them or not. I'm no Buddha (laughing), I don't love everybody (laughing), I wish I could but it's very, very hard, but when it comes down to healing then I'm talking to spirit all the way through my healing and I'm just begging for whoever's life is on my healing table before me, and that's what it is, I just want them so badly to be healed and to be well again. Don't get me wrong it doesn't always happen in one session, certain things like dealing with cancer, a lot of very, very bad viruses and diseases and stuff like that is going to take a lot of time. I always say to people who come to me that I guarantee you within four sessions there will be something different that you will see in your life. It may not be the major thing you're looking for but there will be a change somewhere. It's a building process it really is, but I've not had anybody yet who hasn't seen a difference.

Angie – Yes I know I did. Just saying we did it remotely but I was still quite impacted and I have to say when you worked with me, that month that we did the weekly sessions I was feeling so much better, more energised, it's a strange thing and it's a little hard to wrap your head around if you don't have much experience with this stuff to fully put your faith in a remote healing. It's one thing when someone's got their hands over you and you feel the energy kind of flowing into your body but when there's someone so far away, it's like well, I hope they find me over here (laughing), but the difference was profound for me, really incredible, I guess I went off on a tangent there.

Cat – Maybe an odd way of looking at it but spirits wouldn't be limited by distance I think, like walking through a door? Can I ask, I have a note here and it's in quotations and it says, bigger and colder each week as you worked, and you have mentioned the heat and the cold, so in your work is that what happens, the cold is the energy?

Dean – Yes it can build either way, depends what you are healing. One of the sort of things that is mentioned in many, many healing books and manuals is, if when healing there's heat from the hands to the problem it's usually pushing healing into whatever needs healing, your arm or your leg, or whatever. If it's cold then people sort of say its drawing stuff out of the body.

Angie – Ohh, that makes sense.

Dean – It's not a 100% written rule but that's how people sort of write it down and see it. With me when I first sort of started with Margaret who works (worked with me at the time) with me at Spiritualhart, I used to meditate at her house every Friday and we used to build our energies, go through the meditations to help each other, give each other guidance in (psychic/tarot) readings and things. I'd been healing for a fair while and we used to send out absent (distant) healing to the healing book together and this energy just started growing between my hands each week. It just started getting bigger and bigger and like you said, colder and colder and in the end my arms were fully outstretched. It was like holding an absolutely ginormous snowball, and it was so cold I was absolutely shaking and shivering with the coldness of it, it was such an immense feeling. I felt like I was outside in the North Pole or something it was so intense, but it wasn't a bad feeling it was just, what the heck is this? It was amazing and it took about 5 weeks, 6 weeks to grow this ball of energy to this size and that was when Ben Black Elk said to me, put it over Margaret, so I walked over to her and I put this ball of energy over her head and just took it all the way down her body. She felt it all, she felt the immenseness of it and the pure energy of it and straight away after we'd finished, she started building one of these energy balls herself and it started growing with her week after week and getting bigger and bigger and bigger. Margaret's been a really big help to me as a medium and a teacher and it's nice to pay her back because she put a lot of time and effort into me in the early days. She would only ever have ladies at her house, and I was the first guy she had ever invited to her house to teach and learn so I was quite honoured with that. It's so nice to pay her back and I've become her teacher too now as a healing teacher and I've attuned her to Reiki and things and to put that pure, direct attunement from spirit with a healing energy ball (into her), that was just an incredible day for both of us, it was fantastic.

Cat – I remember my first experience with Reiki was about 6 years ago. My friend Jerry, his nephew was in town. He was raised in Hawaii and his Mother is a Reiki Master and I had a very sick rabbit and we couldn't figure out why he was sick or where he was sick? The tests were inconclusive and this young boy he was 17 would put his hands above the rabbit, not even touching him, and running them back and forth, and I'm looking at him laughing inside, not to his face of course, and he told me that it's right here, it's in his (the rabbits) stomach. He was doing healing on the stomach and I just though well thank you that was very nice of you, but weeks later we find out that the rabbit's got severe intestinal stress, he got it spot on. Later that evening he also did it on me and so I closed my eyes. I'm the biggest sceptic in the

162

world so I was going to prove he was lying, and damned if I didn't feel something and I always knew where he was. I felt it as heat and tingling and so that was my first introduction to it. I probably shared that with Angie and said, I'm sure I imagined it, ha ha (laughing).

Angie – But there's no denying it really once you've experienced someone who knows what they are doing, there's really no denying it and that's pretty cool. I want to ask you if you think any and all ailments can be energetically healed or do you think that some people are basically stuck living out their karma like maybe they have a penance to pay or what not?

Dean – Mmmm, I wouldn't like to say really it's not my place I'm not God (laughing), however, I don't see why we can't try, if it's not to be done, then it's not to be done. I know there is a lot of illnesses and stuff we bring through karmicly, but then this is what I say about doing Kundalini, you can actually heal karma. So, it is a tough one, there's a lot of things you bring through with you, it's trying to find yourself as you go through life really, and if you can address the issues, and healing will help you do that if you're persistent, and if your dedicated then I don't see why not? But then you can go to the drastic end of the table with disabled people and, you know, you can't replace limbs so it's a very tough question. I used to work with disabled children and it was a fantastic job I loved it, a very heart breaking job on a daily basis but it was brilliant. To walk around pushing them around in their wheelchair and taking them from ward to ward or wherever it was great to be able to send them healing and nobody know (laughing), I was a bit sneaky (laughing).

Angie – That's great. Do you ever work with your team and you are sitting somebody out in front of you and you're ready to do your work and you're like, argh argh, no way, argh argh, we're not working with this one, has it ever happened where you feel blocked as a facilitator?

Dean – No, I've never felt blocked but you do get people like that. I have had people walk into the sanctuary, well I've had people actually not walk into the sanctuary, and this is because they are carrying negative energy. Negative energy can really take over the mind and the body of a person. The negative knows what's going to happen when it comes into my healing room and people have refused to come in, but it's not them refusing it's the negativity telling them, we don't want to go in there, because they know what's going to happen. It's going to get pulled out and it's going where it needs to go, so yes, I have had to talk people around and really try to get them to come into the room, and really tell them, you have to stay on the bed, don't get off the bed. It's not all love and light unfortunately there is a darker side, there is a negative side and it needs to be dealt with which is another big part of my job. Clearing houses, clearing people, you can't heal anybody when they've got negativity in them it's just not going to happen, it's just going to turn it around.

Cat – I was just going to ask that.

Dean – Yes, you have to deal with that first and it's become a really, really big part of my work dealing with the negative side of things.

Cat – You make it almost sound like an entity?

Dean – It can be, yes.

Cat – Wow.

Angie – Yes, that's actually my next question. In our personal talks you once in a while bring up neg's, and so that's the negative energy. It's really not negative energy right, it really is a force isn't it?

Dean – It can be, it's like if you've got an energy block within your system, it's going to cause you to feel ill. It doesn't have to be a massive negative block but if you're getting down or you're depressed then your body system gets down and depressed and causes blockages which causes illnesses, because it blocks all the meridians and chakra points, which is what we basically work on as healers, the seven main chakras. So there's simple things like that just picking up stuff in everyday life, but there are, unfortunately, bigger entities out there and negativities out there, and some people are carrying more than one and they don't realise. One of the big things I really want to do, I would love to do and I am in the process of trying to do is get into psychiatric wards and the mental health side of the medical profession. I am convinced that at least maybe 60/70 % of the patients that they have drugged up to the eyeballs can be cleared. They're just carrying negative energy and once you clear people of negative energy they can think for themselves again. All the drugs do is subdue them and turn them into zombies, which is not helping them at all.

Angie – Right, you have me on board there. You start that kind of research and I'm with you (laughing), I think it's fascinating and I have my own little thoughts on that as well. I absolutely agree and I can't wait to see where that goes for you.

Dean – Hopefully one day?

Angie – Yes. You know we're talking about the neg's, I've known several people throughout my life that have an aversion to church. They say, I can't stand going into churches or when I go in I feel like I'm going to freak out or explode or whatever. Do you think that's the same type of thing or whether there's clean energy in a church, maybe not all churches (laughing).

Dean – That's true (laughing).

Angie – A more pure loving energy and there's negativity within themselves that's giving them that aversion to being in that place do you think it's that simple?

Cat – No that's intelligence (laughing), I'm sorry (laughing).

Angie – Cue Dean (laughing).

Dean – There's too many answers to that one isn't there? (Laughing). I suppose it can be in a lot of peoples cases but I have to admit as well that my best friend who calls himself an atheist, hates what I do, but each to their own sort of thing. He's happy for me to do it he doesn't knock me, but he doesn't believe in it in any way, shape or form. You would not get him in a church for love or money but that's just because of his lack of interest of learning shall we say. It's not a bad thing, I know for a fact he's not carrying negative energy, it's just a bit of a negative attitude shall we say, but that's just because he's uneducated in the knowledge of all this. Unfortunately religion does come across quite boring, you're not taught the right things in school. You get the Bible rammed down your throat and these so called religious teacher's, theologians that I learnt with at school don't really know Jack. You're just reading from a book but you should be teaching about spirit you should be teaching about the afterlife, you should be teaching about love, you should be teaching about respecting one another. Then the world maybe wouldn't be such a messed up place but we don't teach that, we teach the politics of religion which is not a good thing really and it's not helping anybody.

Angie – And fear, like we know that there's love or fear and if they're teaching fear where's the love in their relationship. I guess that's my biggest issue with it.

Dean – I read the Bible and again I'm not going to knock it because it's got some great things in it but at the same time it just keeps harping on about this vengeful God, the wrath of God. Fear God at your peril and I just think, what have you got to fear him for, there's nothing to fear. He's not there to do anything nasty. It's because it's written, it's the rule, well I'm afraid that's not right in my eyes. I just can't float with a lot of it, but then again it's a book that's been written God knows how many times hasn't it?

Cat – I'm not against religion, I'm not against belief or anybody who wants to follow the basic principles in their heart, it's the organised money taking, that's what I'm against, the money grabbers and the people who collect it.

Dean – Absolutely.

Cat – That's how I was raised, you're going to pay for that, that's what you get, God has punished you.

Angie – They make it difficult.

Dean – They do. We've just had over in England, sorry actually in Scotland, at the top of the UK, the Pope's just been. There was big TV coverage of it all day about his visit's meeting all these politicians and all the rest. To me he's dressed in all these robes and all his gold and medallions and all the rest of it. It's cost the tax payer's millions and millions of pounds for him to come over and say a few words. You go on about the Vatican's millions and all the rest of it shouldn't this money be actually doing some good and helping people that need it?

Angie – Right.

Cat – Uhuh.

Dean – This is what I don't get my head around with religion and there's all these politicians there bowing to him and wanting to shake his hand. I'd like to know how many of them are actually Catholic or into religion? There's a lot of phoniness there for me.

Cat – Uhuh.

Dean – It's not something I could do. I'm very small, I work on my own as a healer and I set up little demonstrations to raise money for charity to do good. So I'm doing my bit in my eyes, but you hoarding all them millions for your religion, that's not doing good, that's not God's work and I'm not into that. Again I don't want to slate anybody's religion but if you're going to help people, well then please help them.

Angie – Makes perfect sense.

Cat – I really want to know, while I was researching and I wrote down temple of mar, and I really want to know what that mean's?

Dean – Temple of Mar is something I came across a few years ago and apparently it's in the spiritual realms and the Angelic realms. It is a big healing mansion and there is a fantastic book on it I read and I think it's by Angela McGerr? She takes you on her journey a spiritual journey, she shares it with you and it's just a place I would love to go. It just sounds an amazing place to see the Angels and have them work on your personal body and to actually open you up completely. It's quite a fascinating book, quite a fascinating read. I wanted to mention it on my website because I just fell in love with the place, and I just thought wow, that's a sanctuary (laughing), definitely a lot bigger than mine.

Angie – (laughing)

Cat – We need to do a second show.

Angie – Yes I know.

Cat – There's so much more to cover and he's got so much more to offer, and we're almost out of time and I feel like we just touched the tip of the ice-berg.

Angie – We still have over 5 minutes, we're good for now. I did want to ask in your mind what's the difference between an Angel and a guide and like psychic ability and healing? What delineates these differences that people might just glob them altogether in a big bunch?

Dean – Personally to me if you've got a spiritual guide then they have usually walked this Earth several times, hundreds of times, however many and they're just there to help you. When you pass over yourself you will learn the spiritual ways and you will become a spirit guide to somebody on the Earth plane yourself given time, and given your experience and your knowledge and all the rest of it which is great. Angels however are always Angels and will always be Angels. They are God's Angels they will always be there to work for God. They can take physical human form but they will always be Angels, they will not live a life as a physical form. As a physical form as we are when we turn to spirit we can never become an Angel, there is a complete difference there.

Angie – What advice would you give to our listeners who are looking to find a greater spiritual strength and maybe healing and physical well being, where would they even start if they're kind of new to this stuff?

Dean – If you're new to it and you want to seek a place out then I would do your homework definitely, because unfortunately there are a lot of people out there talking a good game but not playing a good game shall we say?

Angie – Okay right.

Dean – I've sat in a few circles and things myself and people are very disrespectful and try doing things like trance, and when you're new to this you've got to learn the absolute basics. You've got to learn from the very bottom, you've got to learn massive respect and you've got to learn massive protection, because when you're opening yourself up to the spirit world, you only want the good people coming through. You can't just open yourself up to anything. People who want to mess about with Ouija boards and stuff like that I just find you insane, I really do because you're opening up to another world and there is good and bad. When you are opening up fully like that you don't know what you are dragging through. So definitely do your homework and pick a reputable place. As for healing then I would just have to recommend Reiki as a fantastic place to start. It might not be for everybody but for me it changed my world, it really, really did. But again you would really need to check out your Reiki Master as well because if they're not doing the work and they're just in it for the money to attune you then you're not going to get the energies you want, it's as simple as that. You need a pure channel, somebody who's working well with it, has a lot of patients under their name. You've got to look after your body too, you've got to keep this channel pure and keep it working.

Cat – You might want to maybe find some spiritual groups, meet some people that have experienced these things with different people. That's what I did, I took different classes and through the classes I met different people who shared their experiences as healers. I just tried people until I found the proper fit and that's what worked for me.

Angie – Yes.

Cat – Like he said there's people out there that will blatantly exploit people who are already weak, just searching and they will take advantage.

Dean – Unfortunately yes, unfortunately.

Angie – So I guess the best ways are through referrals and what not or if somebody already knows, that's probably the best way then? So we have 3 minutes left is there anything we've left unsaid that you would like to share to our listeners Dean?

Dean – Not really, just if you're going to learn I would like to say find yourself a circle, but find yourself a closed circle, one that's run properly. You don't want to be in an open circle when you are beginning, a) because it's too advanced for you, b) anybody can sit in one and you don't know what's being brought to the table.

Angie – Okay.

Dean – Again, you really can't play with this stuff, it's got to be respect and protect.

Angie – It's power.

Dean – Yes it is power at the end of the day and it's got to be used well.

Cat – Well thank you very much for the way that you use it and the life that you bring to the universe with what you do, thank you.

Dean – Thank you for having me.

Angie – Yes, it's been a pleasure Dean. Maybe we'll do it again and cover a whole bunch of other questions, pick your brains some more.

Dean – Yes, let's put the world to right (laughing). It's been a pleasure, thanks very much for inviting me on.

Angie – Yes we'll talk to you soon.

Dean – Thanks a lot.

Angie – Bye. Wow, well, we've got like a minute left, maybe not because I've just lost my co-host (laughing). Well that was a total joy and what a cool person. If anybody's interested in contacting Dean I want to give his website again and that's www.spiritualhart.co.uk (this website was not the one used in the interview, but is the correct one to use if you wish to find out more about me and what I do?). He can be found on Facebook as well, I guess if you just search Dean Kingett, so you can find him one way or another or contact us, anything, anyway. I think anyone who's looking for a healer Dean is a fantastic choice, whether you're over in the UK or here in the US. So okay, that's that and I'm out, it was a great show, thank you all, bye.

APPENDIX 2

Many more of my free empowerments are on my website www.spiritualhart.co.uk and are easy to download. They cover many different life problems. The Angels, Archangels and Ascended Masters are amongst those guardians who can help you through taking the empowerments I have created through the years. You are welcome to give any or all of them a try. Listed here are the very first few empowerments I created and the reasons why I felt so compelled to do so can be found on the website

The calming spiritual waters empowerment

Archangel Gabriel's gift of joy empowerment

Archangel Michael's cutting the cord's empowerment

Archangel Raphael's healing empowerment

Archangel Uriel's peace and tranquillity empowerment

Archangel Zadkiel's forgiveness empowerment

Abundantia's abundance empowerment

Buddha's healing hands empowerment

Kuan Yin's compassion empowerment

Maitreya's education and inspiration empowerment

Merlin's divine magic empowerment

Moses braveness, trustfulness and leadership empowerment

Mother Mary's loving and caring touch empowerment

St Germain's violet flame empowerment

The hands of Jesus healing empowerment

The Holy Padre Pio's confessional empowerment

Aengus's love empowerment

Angel Akasha's hope empowerment

Ambriel's truth and clarity empowerment

Angel Astara's dreams and desires empowerment

Angel Francesca helps you decide empowerment

Angel Yvonne's animal connection empowerment

Avalokitesvara's open minded empowerment

El Moyra's shielding empowerment

Epona's crystal and nature healing empowerment

Isis' keep your balance empowerment

King Soloman's priorities empowerment

Lady Nada's female relationship repair empowerment

Lugh's persistence empowerment

Manjushri's listen empowerment

Melchizedek's law of attraction empowerment

Osiris's male relationship repair empowerment

Samson's strength empowerment

Serapis Bey's time to move forward empowerment

The Green Man's awakening empowerment

The Sphinx no fear empowerment

Thoth's manifestation empowerment

Vishnu's trust empowerment

All my channelled attunements are on my website www.spiritualhart.co.uk with a brief description of what they do.

Archangel Arielle's connection attunement

Archangel Cassiel's harmony and balance

Babaji's healing enlightenment attunement

Ben Black Elk's Shamanic healing system

Daniel and the Lions faith and prophecy attunement

Ganesh's obstacle moving and protection attunement

Horus protection and healing attunement

Krishna's power and protection attunement

The Ophiotaurus attunement

Paramahansa Yogananda's attunement

The Abaia magic attunement

The Acanthopholis attunement

The Acrocanthosaurus attunement

The Adar Llwch Gwin magic and protection attunement

The Albertosaurus attunement

The Allosaurus attunement

The Amargasaurus attunement

The Amphisbaena attunement

The Ankylosaurus attunement

The Anototitan attunement

The Apatosaurus attunement

The Apollo attunement

The Archaeopteryx attunement

The Archelon attunement

The Baryonyx attunement

The Brachiosaurus attunement

The Carcharodontosaurus attunement

The Ceratosaurus attunement

The Chasmosaurus attunement

The Coelophysis attunement

The Compsognathus attunement

The Corythosaurus attunement

The Dilophosaurus attunement

The Dimetrodon attunement

The Diplodocus attunement

The Dsungaripterus attunement

The Edmontosaurus attunement

The Elasmosaurus attunement

The Eoraptor attunement

The Gallimimus attunement

The Giganotosaurus attunement

The Heterodontosaurus attunement

The Homalocephale attunement

The Hylaeosarus attunement

The Iguanodon attunement

The Janenschia attunement

The Kentrosaurus attunement

The Kronosaurus attunement

The Lambeosaurus attunement

The Mammoth attunement

The Megaraptor attunement

The Monoclonius attunement

The Nothosaurus attunement

The Ouranosaurus attunement

The Pachycephalosaurus attunement

The Pan attunement

The Pegasus attunement

The Phoenix magic attunement

The Plateosaurus attunement

The Plesiosaurs attunement

The Psittacosaurus attunement

The Pterosaur attunement

The Saber Tooth Tiger attunement

The Scelidosaurus attunement

The Spinosaurus attunement

The Stegosaurus attunement

The Suchomimus attunement

The Triceratops attunement

The Trilobite attunement

The Tyrannosaurus Rex attunement

The Unenlagia attunement

The Velociraptor attunement

The Yangchuanosaurus attunement

White Buffalo Calf Woman attunement